COLLEGE AND UNIVERSITY APARTMENT HOUSING

DEBORAH CASEY-POWELL
EDITOR

PUBLISHED BY
THE ASSOCIATION OF COLLEGE AND UNIVERSITY
HOUSING OFFICERS — INTERNATIONAL

COPYRIGHT 1999
ISBN 0-945109-02-4

D1056947

TABLE OF CONTENTS

ABOUT THE EDITOR

Deborah Casey-Powell is Coordinator for Village Community Services at the University of Florida, Gainesville, Florida. She has worked in housing and residence life at the College of the Holy Cross, Holyoke Community College, and the University of Massachusetts. She also has worked in the private sector as a health educator for a health maintenance organization.

She has served as founding chair of the Publications Network, a committee for student affairs professionals interested in publishing and has served as the Florida state editor for the *SEAHO Report*. Deb also has been a member of the ACUHO-I Publications Committee for the past three years, and a member of the editorial board for the ACUHO-I Apartments newsletter. She has submitted a number of articles to the ACUHO-I *Talking Stick*.

Deb served as the Program Chair for the 1999 ACUHO-I Apartments Conference in Baton Rouge, Louisiana, and previously as a member of the ACUHO-I Program Committee. She also is a member of the ACUHO-I Apartments Committee and serves as the Celebrate Family Week chair. She has presented numerous programs at the ACUHO-I and Apartments conferences.

ACKNOWLEDGMENTS

In the process of writing and editing this book, I was able to educate myself about the benefits of writing for publication. I have learned from many of my colleagues that it takes time and dedication to produce a quality product. I have received tremendous support and positive affirmations from many of my colleagues, and I feel truly blessed to have had the opportunity to work on this educational piece.

I wish to thank a few of my colleagues for assisting in the completion of this book: Rena Buchan for her support and dedication to this time-consuming project, Joanna Jennie for copy editing and proofreading, George Peach and Monica Camardese for the cover design, the apartment housing professionals and faculty members who authored chapters, Jim Grimm for his commitment to my professional development, Vinnie Gore for editing the first family housing monograph, and ACUHO-I for supporting and funding this project.

I want to personally express my appreciation to Norbert Dunkel, ACUHO-I Publications Coordinator, for guiding me through the publication process and coordinating the production of this book. His guidance and patience motivated me to complete this project.

I would also like to thank my husband, Jeffrey Powell, Assistant Director of Housing at the University of Florida, for his support, encouragement, and commitment to my career goals and aspirations. He has influenced and challenged me personally and professionally to achieve my goals. This book is dedicated to Jeff for his continual support.

Deborah Casey-Powell
University of Florida
May, 1999

FOREWORD

It is with great honor and humility that I write this foreword for *College and University Apartment Housing*. This book contains chapters from many of the true leaders in the apartment profession today.

The ACUHO-I Apartments Conference began in 1978 at Colorado State University's mountain campus, Pingree Park. It began because many people, and Grant Sherwood in particular, perceived a need for professionals who work in apartment housing to gather together and discuss their successes and failures, to share their concerns and to discuss the unique communities for which they are responsible. The conference has grown from a small group of 17 to over 200 professionals who continue to gather and discuss many of the same issues.

Similar to the Apartments Conference, apartment housing on campuses began after the conclusion of World War II. Many married GIs returned home and were able to take advantage of the GI Bill that paid for their college education. As a result, married housing sprung up on many college campuses. Some of these barrack-housing modules are still being used to this day. Married housing has changed over the years, much like its clientele. Married couples have given way to single parent families, gay and lesbian couples, single graduate students, and even single undergraduates.

As Greg Roberts of the University of Saint Thomas said many years ago, "Apartment professionals are on the cutting edge of university life." As nontraditional students return to campuses, apartment housing is as popular as ever. In fact, on many campuses, apartment-style housing units are referred to as residence halls and are extremely popular for undergraduate students. These "residence halls" have private bedrooms and bathrooms, shared living room space and kitchen facilities. This sounds curiously like the definition of an apartment.

The ACUHO-I Apartments Committee continues to represent the needs of the apartment professionals. Benchmarking, quality of life and comparative department surveys, articles concerning apartments in the ACUHO-I *Apartments Newsletter* and the *Talking Stick*, and books similar to this one will continue to enhance the professional nature of our field.

Apartment professionals deal with many of the same concerns as residence hall professionals, but keep in mind those apartment communities never "close." Our units are open 365 days per year. Is it any wonder that we need a week each fall during our conference to get away, compare horror stories, and triumphs and failures with other people in similar situations. It is our hope that this book will serve in many of the same ways. By sharing the history, important information, tips for the professional, and hopes for the future, we are confident this book will be a handy resource and guide for you.

Joan M. Schmidt
ACUHO-I Central District Representative
Past ACUHO-I Apartments Committee Chair

PREFACE

What comes to mind when you hear the phrase "college and university apartment housing"? Do you think of undergraduate or graduate housing? Do you question if the phrase refers to single or married students? Are you wondering if traditional or nontraditional residents live in this environment? Does this phrase refer to host country students or does it include international students as well? If any of these thoughts come to mind, your interpretation of this phrase is accurate. College and university apartment housing consists of all these characteristics and more.

Purpose of this Book

Chances are that you are reading this book because you want to learn more about college and university apartment housing. You may be managing apartment housing as a chief housing officer, educating yourself as an apartment professional, researching other types of housing options, or just reading for your own development. Perhaps you have just accepted a new position in apartment housing and you are now the resource for the residents who live there. For whatever reason, your interest in campus apartment housing has directed you toward this publication.

The purpose of this book is to update housing professionals on the current issues and future trends facing college and university apartment operations in the 21st century. As you read and discuss the chapters, think about the history of campus apartment housing and its current development. Try to connect the information regarding the history, research, community, legal, and facilities issues that have plagued apartment professionals for years with the present issues.

Not all of the information will directly relate to your institution's apartment operations, but much of the information can be transferred to issues you may experience in apartment housing. Take the time to read the chapters that will directly impact on current issues you and your colleagues are facing on campus.

Historical Perspective

In 1991, the Association of College and University Housing Officers-International (ACUHO-I) sponsored the publication of the first family housing monograph, edited by Vinnie Gore. This publication focused on three functional areas: community services, facilities management, and administrative services. The 1999 book is a comprehensive reference which can be utilized as a resource for apartment operations entering the 21st century.

Since 1991, a drastic shift in resident satisfaction and needs has impacted apartment operations both in the United States and abroad. Residents are expecting college and university apartment organizations to offer more space, quality services, and added anemities. Housing administrators are expected to research and provide students with these options in order to compete with off-campus facilities and to fill college and university apartments.

The term "family housing" has been reevaluated by the ACUHO-I Apartments Committee and been redefined as college and university apartment housing. Throughout this publication, the term university apartments will refer to both undergraduate and graduate, single and family apartment housing operations.

Summary of Contents

The first chapter was written by Rena Buchan, the 1999 Apartments Committee chair. Buchan addresses the history of family housing and the development of the Apartments Committee and its annual conference. A chronological account of the Apartments Conference and the themes and topics discussed at those meetings is included in this chapter.

Donald Whalen presents the relevant research that has been conducted over the past thirteen years in apartment housing in chapter 2. The research cited by Whalen focuses on apartment resident satisfaction. He describes some of the collaborative research being conducted and the usefulness it will have for the housing practitioner of the future. Various methods of research that can be conducted in an apartment operation also are discussed.

In chapter 3, Deborah Casey-Powell and Patricia Griffin provide information regarding community services and programming. Casey-Powell and Griffin offer a unique perspective on definitions of community, program models, partnerships with the campus and local communities as well as resident involvement. Examples of each of these topics are found throughout the chapter.

Eric Luskin addresses the current legal, safety, and operational issues facing housing professionals in chapter 4. He covers the four primary factors: mission or institutional purpose, demographics of residents, facility and financial considerations, and legal precedents and risk management that impact on apartment complexes. Current laws and regulations are highlighted throughout this chapter.

Facilities management is the topic covered in chapter 5 by Todd Pignataro and John Ringle. They address the facilities and services required to provide quality maintenance and custodial services to residents. Establishing productive working relationships with campus maintenance and custodial services, meeting customer needs, and supervising facilities operations are discussed.

In chapter 6, Carey Roth from Stanford University addresses the comprehensive and long-range plans needed to develop an effective renovation and redevelopment strategy for apartment complexes. Specific topics that are covered include project scope, financial impact, project management options, contracts and policies, process control, tenant communications, project coordination and completion, renovation versus redevelopment, and capital improvements.

Silvia Echevarria Rafuls, Mary Howard-Hamilton, and Joanna Jennie describe the values and opportunities inherent in diverse residential environments, provide an overview of models and theories applicable to individuals and organizations engaged in intercultural experiences, and suggest strategies for enhancing residents' experiences in chapter 7.

Staff training and development are discussed in chapter 8 by Lori Patterson and Jana Severson. They address staffing patterns, interviewing strategies, orientation, and training, as well as performance appraisals.

Chapter 9 includes a model created at the University of Utah for student governments within college and university apartment housing. Katherine Carr shares the development and implementation of this student organization. She covers selection of elected officers, student government structure, funding, and the impact that student and resident governments have on apartment operations at Utah. Governance systems at four other institutions also are included in the chapter.

Nancy Lange and Joanna Jennie address mental health issues in chapter 10. They discuss apartment housing staff and resident needs as well as identifying current trends in staffing and interventions. Various issues such as developmental concerns, acculturation stress, interpersonal relationships, mental illness, and crisis situations also are covered.

The topic of child care is covered in chapter 11 by Su-Fen Lin. Four different institutions' child care programs are discussed. The areas addressed include history, licensed capacity, ages of children served, and funding. Lin concludes the chapter with a discussion of present and future challenges of child care on campus.

The final chapter focuses on future trends in apartment housing. Trends such as demographics, enrollment, international, programming, and facilities are examples used to show the future needs and issues in apartment housing. In closing the chapter, Martha Castleberry and Peter Rejto address the professional development trends needed to compete in a college or university setting. Examples such as Certified Property Management and the ACUHO-I professional standards are discussed.

The information provided in this book represents the current issues and future trends that college and university apartment professionals will face in the 21st century. I am confident that this publication will help everyone interested or invested in college and university apartment housing to address those challenges in positive and productive ways.

Deborah Casey-Powell
University of Florida
Gainesville, Florida

The History of Apartment Housing

Rena Buchan
Assistant Director of Village Housing
University of Florida

History of Apartment Housing

Introduction

Before embarking on an analysis of the numerous components which contribute to the success of apartment housing, it is important to review the evolution of this type of housing on campuses. This chapter includes a brief history of why apartment style housing emerged, the 21-year history of the Apartments Conference of the Association of College and University Housing Officers-International (ACUHO-I), a summary of all 20 conferences, and a brief look into the future of apartment housing.

The Development of Apartment Housing

In the United States, the concept of a residential college was founded by Harvard College in 1636. Its foundation came from Oxford and Cambridge Universities in England where the residence was a basis of formal and informal education. Many students came from long distances, needing a place to live, and the availability of rooming houses in the small towns was limited. Therefore, most colleges provided residence units to accommodate this housing challenge (Winston, Anchors, & Associates, 1993).

From the Civil War to the turn of the century, higher education in the United States became more popular. As territories achieved statehood, more land-grant institutions were developed and used the residential college model (Overall, 1976). In addition, women began to enroll during this time. The states tried their best to keep up with the demand for housing by passing laws to use state funds to build residences. Soon the federal government had to become involved to assist the financially strapped states.

As World War II raged on, enrollment dropped significantly. Once the war ended, there were two dramatic changes in the nation's universities. At the conclusion of World War II, there was a huge increase in students on college and university campuses. On some campuses, the student population almost doubled as veterans entered the educational system. Facilities were overcrowded. Campuses lacked facilities for both sleeping and eating.

Due to this overcrowding, the objectives and methods of higher education had to be reviewed. From 1946 to 1947, the greatest influx of students came from married couples and families with a military background. Because of the urgency and national scope of these housing needs, Dr. S. Earl Thompson, the Director of Housing at the University of Illinois, proposed that directors of housing from around the United States meet to discuss their housing problems. This special meeting began the formation of ACUHO-I (Association of College and University Housing Officers, 1998).

In the United States, many students would not have been able to attend a college or university without the passage of the Servicemen's Readjustment Act of 1944, commonly known as the GI Bill of Rights. This bill provided financial aid to allow any veteran to attend the institution of his or her choice. More than 2,250,000 American veterans after World War II benefited from this legislation (Haydock, 1996). The bill was designed both to serve as a reward and to lessen the economic impact of returning military veterans on the economy. The bill also had an equalizing effect for the majority of veterans Olsen, 1968). Individuals who might never have had the opportunity to attend school could now afford to attend. Institutions began to receive federal aid to build housing and dining facilities as well as academic buildings. However, institutions feared that high standards of education would decline due to the presence of the veterans. To the surprise of many, just the opposite effect occurred. The bill was successful and far exceeded expectations. The bill helped develop communities of middle class citizens that were the basis of much of the postwar prosperity in the United States (Breedin, 1972).

The numbers of married students in the United States grew steadily after World War II, and continued to increase after the Korean War as well. In the 1970 census, about 23.7% of students identified themselves as married. To date, about 15 million veterans have received a chance to live their part of the American dream by attending a college or university (Clinton, 1994).

Due to the increase in students, facilities were stretched to their limits. Temporary housing was created to offer students and their families a place to live. In many cases old army barracks were relocated to college campuses. Trailer courts were hastily designed and placed on campuses. Surplus government buildings were utilized for dining areas, recreational facilities, convenience stores, laundry rooms and child care facilities (nursery schools).

Once it was determined that married students were not just a temporary phenomenon but rather a permanent addition to the campus, federal monies were sought to build apartments on campus. The fact that facilities were cramped, had little storage space, lacked privacy and were noisy did not deter families from seeking housing on campus (Olsen, 1968). Students sought well-maintained areas, reasonable policies and procedures, and economical costs.

More than 60% of married students had children when they arrived on campus (Green, 1965). The fact that couples had children to occupy their free time had a significant impact on their level of involvement in student activities on campus. Not only did children take up students' time, they also depleted their finances, and in some cases, affected their marital happiness.

There were very few two-student families. The male was usually the student. The typical role of the female was to assist her husband in earning his degree. In most cases, this arrangement was for financial reasons. If someone in the family did not continue to bring in an income, the possibility of attending school was a lost dream (Moen, 1992). The other challenge was related to the caretaker role with the children. Since the husband was in school, the burden was placed on the wife to take care of the children.

Married students made little use of on-campus support services. Lattore (1972) researched personnel services offered to married students and reported that although there was a need for services, the programs were inadequate when serving the married student population. The findings by Lattore supported previous research completed by Dressel (1963), King (1970), and Oppelt (1965).

With the postwar influx of married students, student services departments were challenged to publicize their services to the married population and to be sensitive to their needs. The student services profession believed that a specific position in student services, such as a trained professional in marital counseling, should be devoted to dealing with married students. Intentional programming in the areas of social development, recreational activities and educational events was included (Moen, 1992). The possibility of offering child care at these events was also explored. Information on financial problems was introduced to discuss sources of income, low-cost services, family budgeting, and so forth. Special welcome programs were offered to new married students. The notion of campus-wide day care was introduced. This service was proposed not only for the married students, but also for faculty and staff. The service was often subsidized by the institution, with a smaller user fee for each family. The expansion of health care benefits (insurance) for the spouse and in some cases for the children was considered. There were limited services to the student's dependents but low-cost initial primary care was offered for those who needed it.

Housing was challenged by institutional leadership to offer on-site child care programs. The beginnings of child care cooperatives were formed within housing complexes. Finally, housing operations developed common areas for recreational and educational purposes, often a building or a vacant apartment to hold a limited number and type of events.

The greatest challenge emerged regarding mental health issues. With the pressures of academic requirements, marital issues, raising children, and, in many cases, being far from family and a close support network, married students displayed numerous mental health issues. It was noted in many instances that married students preferred to use services offered on campus rather than in the surrounding community. This was also evident when services were offered to the spouse. Areas of concern were far reaching, from child rearing and skill building to role conflicts between the student and his or her spouse (Moen, 1992).

The Development of the ACUHO-I Apartments Conference

As mentioned earlier, the formation of ACUHO-I was due primarily to the presence of married students on campus. Once the influx of GIs stabilized and theorists began to promote their student development theories based on traditional-aged students (18- to 21-year-old undergraduates), the focus at the national level of ACUHO-I shifted to the residence halls. The issues of married students on campus were still prevalent but not of primary concern.

In 1978, Grant Sherwood, then the Associate Director of Housing at Colorado State University, initiated the first conference by inviting family housing administrators to meet at Pingree Park, Colorado. The first seminar, entitled "Student Family Housing: Community or Conglomerate?" brought together family housing professionals to discuss programming for children, spouses, and international residents.

Twenty-three participants (including the organizers) attended the first conference, representing a range of job responsibilities from directors to program assistants. This conference created a special opportunity for family housing administrators to meet and discuss issues pertinent to the population with whom they worked on a daily basis. These participants, considered the experts in their professional areas, presented all of the programs at this first meeting.

The participants concluded that the initial 1978 seminar was a success and that another seminar would be planned in the future, with Grant Sherwood's continued leadership.

The content of the first seminar is worthwhile to note. The focus was on services and programming. The void of services offered to married students was ever present.

The responsibility and sometimes burden fell to the housing administrators. Community building was the focus, providing opportunities for residents to give feedback on their needs. The following questions raised were taken directly from the seminar proceedings (Smith, 1978, p. 1).

1.   Why should housing administrators be concerned with programming for the families it houses?

2.   Is there a theoretical basis for programming for families in college and university housing facilities?

3.   How do we train people to do family housing programming, to help build a sense of community?

4.   How do we deal with the attitudes of residents who expect services such as baby-sitting at a minimal cost (or free) to them through fees or rent increases?

In addition to these questions, special interest sessions included: community or conglomerate, developing and maintain a sense of community in family housing, counseling services in family housing, activity or community centers, child care centers, family housing governance, children's programs, single parent programs, funding and grants for family housing, student spouses, and international students.

The conference was convened again in 1979 with a break in 1980. In 1981, the apartments housing administrators met once more. The group discussed the promoters and inhibitors of community development, student governance and the distribution of responsibility, orientation of new residents, newsletters and the formation of a distribution list, student input in program development, international student concerns, staffing patterns, training and job descriptions, and the importance of assessment. The group maintained its small attendance of approximately 40 participants.

In 1982, the group gathered at the University of Illinois. A definition of families was created during this seminar. The theme for the conference was "In Search for a Model." Family housing now encompassed more descriptors, including married housing, nontraditional housing, family housing, and apartment living. Resident demographics were now not only U.S. students but also students from over 80 different countries at some institutions. The discussion of limited research in the family area was a focus. Additionally, ACUHO-I President Gary B. North gave the keynote address. The connection with ACUHO-I was strengthened. Rather than group discussions, 16 different interest sessions were offered. The seminar recruited planners and implementers from all over the country. Through conversation with ACUHO-I, it was suggested that the seminar become a part of the Special Purpose Housing Committee (currently the Apartments Committee). A plan was suggested for host sites for future meetings. The staff at Colorado State University made a commitment to hosting the seminar every third year and the annual apartments meeting became a permanent component of apartment housing administration.

In 1983, the seminar took place in Houghton, Michigan, hosted by Michigan Technological University. The format was described as unique in that it encouraged maximum interaction among those attending. Twelve interest sessions were offered and five general sessions. The seminar addressed issues involving international students and families, cross-cultural training, and acculturation. Attendance was at an all-time high of 41 participants.

The seminar returned to Pingree Park in 1984 and became an official ACUHO-I-sponsored conference. Attendance was at 60 participants, keeping an "Open Door" was the theme, directed toward international students and families, a continued focus from past conferences. This conference also attracted a number of colleagues from Canada. There were a number of newcomers and their presence was noted throughout the conference literature. Interest sessions included computer usage, Canadian programs, and cooperative programs with academic departments. The direction of the conference became more purposeful with the planning of future sites.

In 1985 and 1986, the conference was held in Vermont and Georgia respectively. Attendance by delegates reached a plateau during those two years. In 1987, the University of Utah hosted the conference, with 91 delegates in attendance. The development of a program committee to solicit programs and assist the host committee in the planning of the conference was instituted in Utah. This was also the first year that exhibitors attended, and an awards banquet was offered to the participants. The conference was taking on many new aspects. The buddy system (now referred to as the new member program) was created to match seasoned delegates with new delegates. A newsletter was designed to better communicate to the participants throughout the year the research, programs, and issues that were important to apartment professionals. Round-table sessions were offered with discussion of staff training, facilitating community pride, and renovations for the 1990s. The format of the conference at Utah was a turning point in the history of the conference and for the group of apartment professionals.

In 1988, the conference went to the West Coast and the Arrowhead Conference Center, hosted by UCLA. A record attendance of 140 participants utilized the conference center's facilities. A core group of delegates, many from the very first conference, wrote a position paper, entitled the "Report of the Family Housing Conference Governance Committee," focusing on the future role of the conference and the future relationship the group would hope to have with ACUHO-I (Barber, Campbell, Francisco, Hutchins, Moen, & Stoddart, 1988). The committee's recommendation was to develop a more structured relationship between the family housing conference and the Apartments Committee within ACUHO-I. As stated in the report:

> It is our hope that the structure we are recommending will overcome inconsistencies that have occurred in the past. That it will provide a sound organizational structure for the future regardless of the players. The recommendations provide a structure that will hopefully provide direction and leadership while maintaining our openness, receptiveness, and spontaneity. (Barber et al., 1988. p. 1)

Following this opening paragraph were 20 proposed resolutions. The report was accepted by the delegates and passed for review to ACUHO-I.

This document has served the apartments group well and remains as the foundation for the current Apartments Committee. In order to continue to attract more new delegates (especially the emerging professionals from higher education administration graduate programs), the graduate student scholarship (currently the New Professional award) was developed. As for interest sessions offered, areas covered were digital phones, apartment renovations, organizational restructure, marketing, and research in family housing.

In 1989, Gull Lake, Minnesota, was the conference site hosted by the University of Minnesota. The theme was "Coming of Age" and it was descriptive of how the group had grown. There was an exhibition room complete with exhibitors and a swap shop for information exchange. Again, the topics presented were far reaching, from programming and focusing on our international students and families to a new topic regarding external relations with the private housing sector.

In 1990, tradition was broken by the University of Oregon, Eugene. This was the first conference held in a downtown hotel. The long history of going to a resort-style complex was changed. The conference attendance continued to increase by 40 more delegates, now totaling 180.

Finally, in the 1990s, apartment professionals began coming to terms with a broad definition of family. Several programs focused on this specific topic. Included in the program booklet was the first comprehensive listing of participants with their home institutions and addresses.

In 1991, the University of Tennessee in Nashville hosted the conference with the theme of "Vision Possible." Topics for discussion centered on residents' behaviors, adolescents, mediation between neighbors, campus crime, and understanding the changes in apartment professionals.

The University of Florida hosted the 1992 conference in Orlando, using a local theme of "Going for the Magic." Since change had been the focus of the apartments group, one of the keynote speakers addressed surviving change. Session topics included developing vision, single parents, customer service, and cable television in student apartments.

During the early 1990s, attendance remained steady at about 140 delegates. The University of Washington hosted the conference in Seattle in 1993 with a continuance of many of the topics already highlighted. The following year, the conference was in Austin at the University of Texas, with attendance at 160 delegates. The focus of this conference was on professional development. Also discussed were topics related to compliance with the Americans with Disabilities Act (ADA), computerized work-order systems, domestic violence, and other resident behavior issues.

In 1995, a consortium of seven Michigan schools hosted the conference on Mackinac Island by taking a "Step Back In Time." Themes at this conference centered on redevelopment of facilities, behavior of residents (especially in dealing with difficult people), child care on campus, and long range planning. In spite of the challenges of getting to the site, attendance was very high, with 163 participants.

The program committee with the host schools also held a pre-conference workshop on staffing and decision making. The format and information was well received by those attending. This resulted in the inauguration of the Apartments Institute in San Diego in 1996, held prior to the regularly scheduled conference. With over 40 participants, the institute addressed resident area governance, staffing, and decision making. In the tradition of the apartments professional meetings in the past, colleagues were considered the experts in certain areas and served as the instructors.

During the regular conference, the topic of retirement was introduced because some of the founding members of the apartments group were beginning to make plans for their future. Also addressed were ongoing discussions of legal issues, especially in eligibility requirements, smoke-free apartments, and lead-based paint.

The beautiful Colorado Rockies at Estes Park was the 1997 destination and "Achieving Great Heights" was the theme. Safety and health issues, recycling, and peer mediators were the highlighted presentations at that conference.

In celebration of the 20th year, the 1998 conference was held in Vermont. The theme was to experience "A Season for Change." With over 170 participants and over 20 exhibitors, the Apartments conference had emerged into a well-planned professional development meeting. What had not changed were many of the topics discussed at previous conferences. Issues such as the definition of family, understanding international residents, conflict resolution, and building and maximizing programming on a very limited budget were addressed again, similar to presentations at Pingree Park in 1978.

The question then remains: Have the issues confronting apartment professionals changed? The concluding evidence from past conferences confirms that the issues are not different but the methods to deal with them are. What has dramatically changed are the numbers of housing professionals working with issues of single parents, unsupervised children, and integration of single graduate and undergraduate students into apartments facilities.

Throughout its 20-year history, the Apartments Conference has been sensitive to the concerns and issues brought forward by the population living in the apartments. As long as apartments professionals continue to share the wealth of knowledge brought in by the many experiences and programs, the Apartments Conference will remain a viable component within the ACUHO-I committee structure.

Future Changes in Apartment Housing

The population in the apartment area is changing once again. Trends in the student population have shown some change. No longer are apartments for the exclusive use of married couples with and without children. Now housing areas are a conglomeration of many representatives from all over the world. Issues of acculturation are ever present for these international residents. Attempts to make the transitions into living areas have been successful through welcome videos, on-campus-living brochures in multiple languages, and offering English classes as a second language.

Family demographics have changed significantly as well. Some institutions permit domestic partnerships in their living complexes. Many students can have a roommate reside with or without a contractual agreement with the university. Parents of students reside in the apartments and in many cases are accepted and welcomed as part of the community culture.

More students are arriving on our campuses requiring special needs in their housing facilities. More apartment units are being renovated to be compliant with ADA standards, making it much easier for students with a disability to attain their education. More students dealing with mental health issues have the opportunity to meet with counselors on site rather than go to some other campus or off-campus agency (see also Chapter 10).

Staff are trained in crisis protocol, basic counseling skills, and methods to deal with neighbor-to-neighbor disputes. Some institutions provide safe houses on campus for domestic violence cases. Policies and procedures and those who administer them are more sensitive to the wide variety of needs of the apartment population.

Not only are apartment professionals dealing with issues related to the well-being of their residents, but also of intense concern for many institutions are issues related to aging facilities, many of which are over thirty years old. Some facilities are practically crumbling around tenants. In the 1980s, facilities issues centered on radon, asbestos removal, and the upgrade of kitchens. In the 1990s, facilities are in need of fire code corrections, lead paint removal, playground safety, carbon monoxide protocols, and halogen lamps. Domestic water lines are in need of repair and replacement. Sewage lines are old and constantly in need of maintenance.

With the constant use of computers by residents, the upgrade of telephone lines and easier access to the Internet are current resident expectations. Many administrators are prepared to discuss the reality that in some cases the patchwork care needed in these old facilities is not a wise use of revenue. The decisions either to tear down and rebuild or to simply tear down and not replace aging buildings are serious options to consider. The short history of on-campus families at some institutions may come to an end due to these facilities challenges.

The ultimate goal of many apartment professionals is to offer safe, clean, and economical housing to university students. It is with the daily challenges faced that housing professionals continue to strive to meet these primary needs. As history has demonstrated, apartment professionals have had to adjust to changes in the resident population and the need to upgrade facilities. Many challenges are ahead for institutions in the new millennium.

In the following chapters, readers will have the opportunity to review numerous issues facing apartments professionals today. For those working in apartment housing, the Apartments Conference has been a constant support group, a group of people rich in resources and talents. The quality of many apartment programs is due in part to this strong professional network. Apartments professionals continue to be an integral part of many campus housing operations and within ACUHO-I itself.

References

Association of College and University Housing Officers-International. (1998). *History of the Association of College and University Housing Officers-International.* Columbus, OH: ACUHO-I.

Barber, N., Campbell, J., Francisco, B., Hutchins, B., Moen, C., & Stoddart, D. (1988, October). *Report of the family housing conference governance committee.* Presented at the Family Housing Conference, Arrowhead Conference Center, Lake Arrowhead, California.

Breedin, B. (1972, March). Veterans in college. *American Association for Higher Education, 4.*

Clinton, W. (1994, June). *White House briefing.* Remarks of President William Clinton in a ceremony to commemorate the 50th anniversary of the GI Bill.

History of Apartment Housing ──────────────

Dressel, F. B. (1963). *An evaluation of selected personnel services offered to married students at Indiana University.* Unpublished doctoral dissertation, Indiana University, City.

Green, M. A. (1965). *The married undergraduate student and the student personnel program.* Unpublished doctoral dissertation, Teachers College, Columbia University, New York, NY.

Haydock, M. D. (1996). The G.I. Bill. *American History, 31*(4), 52.

King, D. N. (1970). *A comparative and descriptive study of married students at Oklahoma State University.* Unpublished doctoral dissertation, Oklahoma State University, Stillwater.

Lattore, P. A. (1972). *Evaluation of selected personnel services offered to and proposed for married students at the University of Northern Colorado.* Unpublished doctoral dissertation, University of Northern Colorado, Greeley.

Moen, C. (1992). Development of family housing. In V. Gore (Ed.), *ACUHO-I Family Housing Monograph* (pp. 2-8). Columbus, OH: ACUHO-I.

Olsen, K. W. (1968). *A historical analysis of the G.I. Bill and its relationship to higher education, 23.* Syracuse University, New York Research Institute.

Oppelt, N. T. (1965). Characteristics and activities of married students. *Journal of College Student Personnel, 6*(6), 228-231.

Overall, J. U., IV. (1976). *Higher education and the servicemen's readjustment act of 1944.* Paper presented at the Conference on the Federal Presence in Higher Education.

Smith, M. M. (Ed.). (1978). *Student family housing: Community or conglomerate?* Proceedings of a seminar on student family housing programs held at Colorado State University, Fort Collins.

Winston, R. B., Jr., Anchors, S., & Associates. (1993). *Student housing and residential life.* San Francisco: Jossey-Bass.

Research in Apartment Housing

Donald F. Whalen
Coordinator of Departmental Research
Iowa State University

Introduction

Research is a necessary part of college and university apartment housing administration. It is important not only that administrators understand how to meet the needs of their residents, but also that we demonstrate how the housing program complements the educational mission of the institution. The former helps us with the financial bottom line; the latter helps us remain a necessary component of the university. This chapter includes a review of published research related to apartment housing, followed by a discussion of why it is important for apartment housing staff to conduct research, and some examples of how this can be accomplished. In addition, the extensive collaborative research conducted by the Apartments Committee will be described, and its usefulness to the housing practitioner examined. Because the topic of research is a broad one, only a cursory discussion of some of the issues is included here.

Reasons for Conducting Research

Conducting research takes resources that could well be used on other things. Yet it is important, as Schuh and Upcraft (1996) pointed out, citing survival, quality, affordability, strategic planning, policy development, decision making, and politics as reasons for conducting research. Even if only a limited amount of research is possible, it is important to conduct a balanced research program to address a variety of issues.

There are several other general reasons for conducting research:

1.   To describe to others the quality of the program provided. This is important information for the institution's president, Board of Trustees, faculty, students, and prospective residents.

2.   To improve the quality of the program, including the facilities and services provided. Information is regularly needed regarding what residents need and want from their apartment housing.

3.   To remain financially solvent. It is important to know why residents live in the apartments and what they like about living there. If residents as customers are satisfied, they will more than likely continue living where they do and will tell others why they like living there. Satisfied residents will help keep occupancy high and revenues flowing.

4.   To validate the expenditure of funds. Residents are often critical of rental increases. Good research can help explain to residents the need for expenditures.

5.   To help in planning. Information is needed regarding the apartment population and how that population might be changing in the next year, the next five years, and longer. Information is needed about what the competition is providing and how the overall market may change.

6.   To answer a specific question. Often administrators need quick information to help them make a decision.

7.   To document how the apartment housing program complements the academic environment. Housing operations often include an educational component for students, spouses, and families about a variety of topics. It is important to document how these extracurricular activities provide learning outcomes that are congruent with the institutional mission statement.

Previous Research in Apartment Housing

To assist in research efforts, it is often helpful to be knowledgeable about research to apartment housing. Previous research, even when done at other institutions, can provide insight into current issues for student apartment housing.

Research for college and university apartment housing has not been extensive. Moen (1986) compiled an extensive bibliography for family and apartment housing. The bibliography has not been updated, but still serves as a good summary of early research on apartment housing. This early research gave us a better understanding of the needs of what were then referred to as married students. Apartment housing in the United States was a new phenomenon, heralded in with the return of veterans to colleges and universities following World War II, thanks to the GI Bill (Frierman, 1980; Moen, 1976).

Lattore (1972) discussed services offered to family housing and students. He also talked about which services should be made available to students with families (Lattore, 1975). Gore (1991) promoted a focus on individual student growth as part of student development. Financial distress was well documented as a primary concern for family students by Augustin and Mishler (1986), Frierman (1980), Greenberg and DeCoster (1976), Lattore (1975), and Paul, Rei, Ostrow, and Shigetomi (1984). Danes and Hira (1987) discussed money management knowledge. Whalen and Winter (1991) examined finances and expenditures of family housing students to determine the role of inexpensive housing.

Whalen and Winter (1987) found that students who knew more neighbors experienced less stress. Community development was studied by Beyerlein, Brandel, Hamilton, Nededog, and Thoman (1982). Gottlieb (1981) studied social support and participation in family housing. Moore, Hinkle, and Forrest (1978) examined the psychosocial needs of married students and proposed a social center and outreach program for married students. Whalen and Morris (1989) found residents expressing greater social distance from object groups reported less satisfaction with the community environment and with the opportunity to interact with residents from other cultures.

Moen (1976) proposed a needs assessment inventory for students and spouses. Schuh (1985) focused on three types of programming for family housing: remedial, preventive, and developmental. Brechtel and Cherwak (1978) discussed recreation needs in family housing. Earnest (1985) recommended programs for international students. Smith and Erickson (1985) prepared a compendium of successful programs.

Shere (1987) studied student satisfaction with apartment housing and found that satisfaction with physical services, but not social services has a significant impact on overall housing satisfaction. Phillips (1989) examined physical dimensions of the environment and residential satisfaction. Paul et al. (1984) assessed needs of residents in family housing and how planned changes can make a difference in residents' satisfaction with the community. Twale and Damron (1992) studied resident satisfaction with the environment.

Gilbert (1982) studied the impact of graduate school on the family. Morris and Whalen (1988) examined preferences for place of study in student apartment housing. Simono, Wachowiak, and Furr (1984) studied the effect of a variety of living environments on student attitudes regarding living conditions, location, social and leisure activities, finances, and academics.

Frierman (1980) surveyed university apartment directors regarding policies and procedures in family housing. Selby and Weston (1978) compared the attitudes of freshmen living in residence halls with freshmen living in apartment housing regarding residential policies and physical environments.

Whalen (1989) provided summary information regarding part-time, live-in staff positions for apartment housing. Geier (1991) conducted a study of time spent by live-in staff members in residence halls, graduate housing, and apartments.

This research can help the housing professional to better understand the nature of apartment housing. While the list is by no means comprehensive, it does provide a cross-section of apartment housing literature. It also is important for this research base to be increased, so new research should be shared through publications of the Association of College and University Housing Officers-International (ACUHO-I), such as the *Talking Stick* and the *Journal of College and University Student Housing*, in the adult education literature, and other research publications.

Recent Research Conducted by the ACUHO-I Apartments Committee

Two research initiatives have been promulgated by the ACUHO-I Apartments Committee to provide useful information for apartments professionals. In the first initiative, practical information was collected for apartment housing staff. Beginning with a pilot survey (Amaro & Whalen, 1989), and followed by three additional studies (Whalen, 1990, 1993, 1996), information about administrative, assignments, residence life, maintenance, and facilities was collected and compiled in a publication that was disseminated to participants and then made available through ACUHO-I. These reports shared practical information about community assistant positions, the number of maintenance staff in the various trades, and the rental rate structure for each participating institution.

The second initiative was the development of an apartment resident satisfaction survey for administration to college and university apartment housing students. Participating institutions administered the surveys, and the results of the aggregate data analyses from all institutions were presented in one report (Crull, Whalen, Liao, Pate, & Rochford, 1997). Thus, participating institutions could benchmark responses to the questions on a state, regional, or international level. There are currently no plans by the Apartments Committee to continue this survey; however, the Apartments Committee will attempt to co-sponsor with Engineering Benchmark, Incorporated, a benchmarking survey for apartment housing professionals.

Methods of Research

Many methods are available for conducting research. Written surveys, telephone surveys, focus groups, individual interviews, and feedback forms are common research methods.

Surveys

Surveys can provide both quantitative and qualitative data. Quantitative data can be used for statistical analyses. Qualitative data are more subjective. A written response to an open-ended question is one example of qualitative data. Quantitative data are less open to interpretation. Using a variety of accepted methodologies, qualitative data are summarized and interpreted. Although quantitative methodologies have dominated social science and educational research, qualitative research is becoming increasingly popular. Software is now available for analyzing qualitative data. One popular piece of software, Non-Numerical Unstructured Data Indexing, Searching and Theory-Building (NUDIST) software, is highly accepted within the academic community, and resources to help use it can be found at most institutions (Lavalli & Walsh, 1996).

Written surveys can take many forms. It is important to choose the option which best fits the objective and the apartments environment. Some basic methods are described in this section.

Broad surveys. A survey is a good research tool because it can be any length, it can be administered in whatever time frame is convenient, it allows respondents some time in responding, and results can be compiled fairly quickly.

Broad surveys which are done periodically provide good information on how residents feel about apartment living. Information is collected from residents about their satisfaction with all aspects of the apartments—residence life, office services, lease arrangements, maintenance, custodial services, and general facilities. Such surveys are frequently called "quality of life" surveys. Regularly conducting the survey can allow results to be benchmarked against results from previous years. Or results can be benchmarked against other institutions' results if the same questions are used. The 1996 Apartments Survey provided the opportunity for benchmarking against a number of other institutions.

One problem inherent in a comprehensive survey is the length. Residents may choose not to complete a lengthy survey. To address this problem, some institutions have chosen to break the traditional "quality of life" survey into smaller components. Separate components can be administered to separate populations. The components also can be administered in subsequent years, so residence life issues may be the topic of the survey one year, custodial and maintenance issues the next year, and administrative and office services the following year. Then the cycle can be repeated. Results can still be benchmarked. A disadvantage to the yearly rotation method is the necessity of administering a survey every year.

The use of optical scanning sheets, often called "bubble sheets" can greatly reduce research time by eliminating the need for entering data by hand. Responses for each survey are electronically scanned and placed in a data file. Most residents are familiar with these bubble sheets. For most scanners to read the data, responses must be made using a Number 2 pencil. Therefore, it is a good idea either to emphasize the need for responses to be made using that writing instrument, or to provide one to each respondent.

Research sampling can provide apartment housing professionals with reliable information. Administrators often feel they have to survey the entire resident population to get reliable results. Sampling, if done appropriately, can provide reliable data, and with less expense.

Topical surveys. Smaller surveys, usually on a single topic, can be conducted to provide quick feedback. The advantage of being small increases the probability of a good response rate. Small surveys can be conducted to answer a specific question. Will students support a specific change that is being considered? Which of several options are residents more likely to support? These kinds of brief surveys can help an administrator with a decision.

Program evaluation surveys can be administered following any community program or service. These quick surveys can provide immediate feedback about the success of the program in meetings its objectives.

Like program evaluation surveys, brief surveys administered following completion of requested maintenance can provide immediate feedback about resident satisfaction with the repair. With certain information coded onto the survey before distribution, such as a code for the shop or the worker, information can be accumulated regarding resident satisfaction with the services provided for each shop and work crew. Care must be taken not to rely too heavily on such surveys in evaluating personnel, but this type of survey can be helpful in providing current and prompt feedback about how employees perform their work.

Needs assessment surveys. A survey at move-in time, often called a "needs assessment," can provide information about residents' perceived needs, including their desire to participate in various community activities, and their willingness to help in planning activities. In addition to providing a current and steady flow of resident information, this survey method has the additional advantage of identifying new residents who are willing to participate and help in the community.

Vacate surveys. Similarly, a survey at the time of move-out, often called a "vacate survey" can provide insight into resident satisfaction at a time when the resident is most likely to be honest. One disadvantage of this survey might be to bring returns only from those who are most and least satisfied. However, by offering incentives for return of the survey, such as pizza coupons or movie passes, a higher return rate and more reliable picture of resident attitudes can be obtained. This information can provide an ongoing assessment to promote improvements in services, especially those that receive the worst ratings.

Telephone surveys. Telephone surveys are popular because they can be used to collect information very quickly, and can be conducted anywhere. A disadvantage is that telephone solicitation is becoming increasingly overused, and residents may not be willing to participate. As with other kinds of surveys, certain procedures must be followed. For example, care must be taken to ask questions objectively and in the same way to each telephone respondent. An excellent reference for conducting telephone surveys, as well as written surveys, is *Mail and Telephone Surveys* (Dillman, 1978).

Internet surveys. Surveys conducted over the Internet are becoming increasingly popular. Respondents who are technologically proficient like them because the survey can be completed quickly and returned with a few keystrokes. Researchers like them because the respondent enters the data, thus eliminating the possibility of data entry errors by the researcher. Thus, data collection occurs more quickly. But as much promise as this method may hold, it involves technical expertise and software that many researchers do not have or cannot afford. Internet surveys also require that those being surveyed be technologically proficient.

Interviews

Interviewing is a very reliable research method. Interviews can provide detailed information about a topic, small or large. A person provides information not only about *how* they feel about a certain issue, but also *why* they feel that way. However, although this research method is very reliable, care must be taken not to taint the interview with the interviewer's views or attitudes. One disadvantage is the time involved in conducting interviews. Not only must the interviews be conducted, but information must then be transcribed and compiled into meaningful summaries. The previously mentioned NUDIST software program is one such program that can help summarize the data (Lavalli & Walsh, 1996).

Focus Groups

Focus groups are very helpful in providing qualitative data. While surveys can provide insight into *how* residents feel about particular issues, focus groups can provide information about *why* they feel the way they do. Focus groups usually consist of 6 to 10 participants (Krueger, 1994). These group interviews have the advantage over individual interviews in collecting the opinions of more people at one time. They should not be used with emotionally charged issues where strong conflicting opinions are likely, or where confidentiality is an issue. Proper facilitation is important to assure that responses will truly reflect the feelings of the participants. A very good resource for conducting focus groups is *Focus Groups* (Krueger, 1994).

It is important to use multiple methods of collecting information whenever possible to obtain the most reliable data. Each of the methods described above has strengths and weaknesses that can be overcome by combining research methods.

Learning Outcomes

The primary reason housing professionals have conducted research in the past has been for program improvement. Most apartment housing operations have developed a mission statement that clearly states their goals. Objectives have then been decided based on the stated goals specific to apartment housing. Most research, then, has focused on measuring the success of each objective. Research provides ongoing feedback (formative research) for staff and residents as to the success of meeting the objectives. This feedback allows for alterations in the apartments operation to better meet the objectives. In addition, summative research is conducted periodically (e.g., quarterly, semi-annually, annually) to help substantiate progress to institutional administrators and to help respond to external interests.

A more recent focus has been on measuring learning outcomes. The idea is that if apartments are considered to be part of the university, then the relationship should strive to be more than that of an "auxiliary enterprise" that houses students. Most apartments professionals support the educational mission by providing safe and comfortable housing. However, to be more actively involved with the academic mission of the institution, apartments staff must further strive to enhance the student learning experience. Housing professionals must make evident that student learning continues outside of the classroom as a result of living in apartment housing. They also must demonstrate that the objectives expressed by the institutional mission statement are being addressed in apartment housing as well as in the classroom. Many institutions already deliver planned programs and written information, and counsel students individually to help them (and often their families) to learn. When these things are done intentionally to support the educational mission of the institution, it is to the advantage of staff to document this student learning through planned research.

Although learning outcomes, like departmental objectives, can be developed at any time, they work best when they are developed or reaffirmed at the beginning of each academic year. A good model for conducting research on learning outcomes might include the following questions:

1. What is the educational outcome being sought by the housing staff?
2. What specific learning component will be achieved by the student?
3. What relevant experience will be provided to help students learn the component?
4. How will the learning of the desired component be measured?
5. What are the assessment findings?
6. What improvements might be made based on assessment findings?

There can be many relevant experiences, some of which may already be in place for accomplishing the objective. The relevant experiences can include things such as planned programs or activities, or publications that provide information, but the experiences must be measurable.

For example, one objective of the institutional mission statement might be to increase students' understanding of technology. One educational outcome to help students understand technology might be to better understand how to communicate using a computer. To achieve this outcome the apartments staff might provide a program aimed at gaining a basic understanding of how to use the computer to access electronic mail and the World Wide Web. One might count the number of attendees to determine to what extent the program is used. To measure whether students have learned from the program, one might ask attendees to take a brief test before the program to determine their level of knowledge, and then to repeat the same test at the end to determine how much they learned as a result of the program.

The same research methods of surveys, interviews, and focus groups can be used in measuring learning outcomes. Instead of focusing on whether or not resident satisfaction is increased, the focus is on whether or not learning has occurred as a result of the program or experience provided. It is difficult to isolate when and where learning occurs. Care must be taken when possible to isolate where the learning occurs. As with measures of program effectiveness, multiple measures should be used whenever possible.

The Challenge

Conducting research is necessary today, and will become increasingly important in the future. Housing professionals must demonstrate, among other things, the effectiveness of their programs, the learning outcomes of their programs, and the need for continued operation and funding. It is no longer enough to provide an effective apartments program; housing professionals also must know how well its resident students are doing academically and how many are retained within the institution.

Good research will allow housing professionals to demonstrate the effectiveness of our programs and the contribution of apartment housing to the institution. It also can help to improve apartments programs to increase the bottom line. Satisfied customers will stay in the apartments to improve occupancy and increase revenue. Research can help determine where inefficiencies may be present, or where increased awareness of residents may better preserve facilities and prevent repairs. To be successful, however, staff time must be dedicated to conducting research, student researchers must be utilized, and collaboration with faculty and staff must be sought.

References

Amaro, M., & Whalen, D. (1989). *The 1989 apartment survey*. Columbus, OH: Association of College and University Housing Officers-International.

Augustin, J., & Mishler, C. (1986). Coping with the costs: How adults pay their college expense. *Journal of Student Financial Aid, 16*(3), 4-12.

Beyerlein, M., Brandel, R., Hamilton, M. Nededog, A., & Thoman, S. (1982). Community development in family housing: Identifying promoters and inhibitors. *Journal of College and University Student Housing, 12*(2), 8-13.

Brechtel, J. B., & Cherwak, D. (1978). Recreation needs in married students' housing. *Journal of College and University Student Housing, 8*(2), 16-17.

Crull, S., Whalen, D., Liao, T.-M., Pate, R., & Rochford, H. (1997). *Resident satisfaction in apartments*. Columbus, OH: Association of College and University Housing Officers-International.

Danes, S., & Hira, T. (1987). Money management knowledge of college students. *Journal of Student Financial Aid, 17*(1), 4-16.

Dillman, D. A. (1978). *Mail and telephone surveys: The total design method*. New York: Wiley.

Earnest, D. (1985). Programming for international students in a family housing setting. *Talking Stick, 2*(6), 20-21.

Frierman, H. (1980). *Untitled* (survey results). Unpublished manuscript, Rutgers University, New Brunswick, NJ.

Geier, L. (1991). *A work sampling study to determine the relative work content of resident assistant, community assistant and resident manager positions at Iowa State University.* Unpublished manuscript, Iowa State University, Ames.

Gilbert, M. (1982). The impact of graduate school on the family: A systems view. *Journal of College Student Personnel, 61*(3), 128-135.

Gore, V. (1991). Family housing: Challenging the residence hall paradigm. *Talking Stick, 8*(6),7-10.

Gottlieb, B. (1981). Social support and social participation among residents of a married student housing complex. *Journal of College Student Personnel, 22*(1), 46-51.

Greenberg, R., & DeCoster, D. (1976). Assessing the needs of married students and their families. *NASPA Journal, 13*(3), 25-34.

Krueger, R. A. (1994). *Focus groups: A practical guide for applied research* (2nd ed.). Thousand Oaks, CA: Sage.

Lattore, P. (1972). *Evaluation of selected personnel services offered to the services proposed for married students at the University of Northern Colorado.* Unpublished doctoral dissertation. University of Northern Colorado, Greeley.

Lattore, P. (1975). Married students: Needs research and programs. *Journal of College and University Student Housing, 5*(1), 24-27.

Lavalli, T., & Walsh, B. (1996). Beyond beancounting. *Microtimes* [On-line], *162.* Available Internet: http://www.microtimes.com/162/research.html

Moen, C. T. (1976). *The development of an education needs assessment inventory for married students and spouses at Iowa State University.* Unpublished doctoral dissertation, Iowa State University, Ames.

Moen, C. (1986). *Residents of family and single student apartments in higher education: A selected bibliography.* Columbus, OH: Association of College and University Housing Officers-International.

Moore, M., Hinkle, J., & Forrest, D. (1978). An experimental social center in married student housing. *Journal of College and University Student Housing, 13*(2), 145-150.

Morris, E. W., & Whalen, D. (1988). Preferred place of study for college students living in university apartments. *Housing and Society, 15*(1), 30-40.

Phillips, S. (1989). Factors related to residential satisfaction in family housing. *Journal of College and University Student Housing, 1*(1), 306.

Paul, S., Rei, J., Ostrow, E., & Shigetomi, C. (1984). A demonstration of organizational change in family housing. *Journal of College and University Student Housing, 14*(2), 8-14.

Selby, T., & Weston, D. (1978). Dormitory versus apartment housing for freshmen. *Journal of College and University Student Housing, 19*(2), 153-157.

Schuh, J. (1985). Developing programs in family student housing. *Journal of College and University Student Housing, 15*(2), 26-30.

Schuh, J., & Upcraft, L. (1996). *Assessment in student affairs: A guide for practitioners.* San Francisco: Jossey-Bass.

Shere, L. (1987). *The relationship between area, services, and satisfaction with housing for family and single students in the University Student Apartment Community.* Unpublished thesis, Iowa State University, Ames.

Simono, R., Wachowiak, D., & Furr, S. (1984). Student living environments and their perceived impact on academic performance: A brief follow-up. *Journal of College and University Student Housing, 14*(1), 22-24.

Smith, K., & Erickson, M. (1985). *Successful programs in an apartment setting.* Columbus, OH: Association of College and University Housing Officers-International.

Twale, D., & Damron, J. (1992). The quality of residence life at Auburn University: An environmental assessment study. *Journal of College and University Student Housing, 22*(2), 14-18.

Whalen, D. (1989). Live-in staff for apartment housing. J*ournal of College and University Student Housing, 19*(2), 12-15.

Whalen, D. (Ed.). (1990). *1990 Apartments survey report.* Columbus, OH: Association of College and University Housing Officers-International.

Whalen, D. (Ed.) (1993). *1993 Apartments survey report.* Columbus, OH: Association of College and University Housing Officers-International.

Whalen, D. (Ed.). (1996). *1996 Apartments survey report.* Columbus, OH: Association of College and University Housing Officers-International.

Whalen, D., & Morris, E. W. (1989). The impact of social distance on community in university apartments. *Journal of College and University Student Housing, 19*(1), 22-27.

Whalen, D., & Winter, M. (1987). Neighbor interaction and stress in family housing. *Journal of College and University Student Housing, 17*(1), 28-34.

Whalen, D., & Winter, M. (1991, May). *The role of inexpensive housing units in a student apartment community: An expenditure analysis.* Paper presented at the Sixth Annual Conference on the Sociology of Housing, Minneapolis, MN.

Community Services and Programming:
A Search for Balance

Deborah Casey-Powell
Coordinator for Village Community Services
University of Florida

Patricia Griffin
Program Coordinator
University of Michigan

Community Services and Programming —————————————

Introduction

Apartment housing operations offer the most dynamic yet challenging issues involving community development. Administrators and staff are confronted daily with questions and concerns regarding the community in which their residents live. The student and family populations found in these communities are not only diverse in nature but also unique when compared to traditional college students. Therefore, it is important to find ways to develop community to meet apartment residents' diverse needs.

The term community development has become a buzzword in the housing field. At many institutions, it has been used as an assessment tool to determine whether a housing operation is meeting its residents' needs. Conneely (1992) reported that many apartment administrators acknowledge the presence or absence of community in their apartment complexes as a factor in the assessment of the success of their operation. As the issue of community development increases on college and university campuses, apartment staffs are being asked to evaluate their programs and services to determine if they provide an open environment for community development to exist. At the same time, apartment housing professionals are fully aware of the challenges involved in creating community for this population.

The goals of this chapter are to define community development and services; evaluate staff, resident, and program models; address resources and funding; discuss facilities; assess instruments used for determining community; consider the multicultural population; examine at ways in which residents can contribute to and invest in communities; determine partnerships and advocates needed to bridge housing with the academic and city communities, and suggest ways to build community through resident involvement.

Defining Community Development and Services

Community development has been defined in a variety of ways. Some authors have referred to community as a territory or geographical location while others have defined it as an interdependence, a form of membership, or a shared emotional connection with others (Conneely, 1992).

Most apartment operations encourage residents to make their new living environment their home and develop neighborhood definitions of community based on their needs and shared values. This can be a positive approach to defining community development of a specific neighborhood since the members of that community take an active role in its creation. A definition for community in apartment housing should consist of residents and housing professionals combining their goals, values, and beliefs.

Since members of apartment communities are from various parts of the world, their ideas and values regarding community may differ from those of housing staff. For example, residents may all be living within the same physical location that they call home, yet the shared values and activities in that environment may be markedly different from their home of origin. How then do these residents participate in their new community and not jeopardize their cultural values? For example, do all residents discipline their children the same way? A family from the Middle East may discipline children differently than a family from the United States. Although each family has a set of standards from its own cultural background, they may be very different from each other. Each family may respect the other's method of discipline, but neither may agree on that form of discipline. Since these residents now live in an environment where community standards have been determined for discipline, how will they adapt to those standards? The idea of educating residents and including them in the process of defining community standards for discipline is a perfect example of residents working together to develop community.

Traditionally, the concept of community embraced the notion of commonality. However, new definitions include the idea that community also involves the sharing of differences. Tierney (1993) suggested that in the 21st century, student affairs professionals will build communities based on their abilities to create and sustain environments which encourage the crossing of cultural zones, and engage in dialogues which honor differences while searching for commonalties.

In the past, apartment housing programs have defined community as a group of individuals who live in close proximity and share common interests and goals. Residents were interdependent for the fulfillment of certain needs. They shared expectations in their community and assumed responsibility for meeting expectations while maintaining respect and consideration for each individual (Conneely, 1992). These communities also valued the diversity of its members and encouraged standards that celebrate both similarities and differences.

However, this traditional definition of community is changing in apartment housing. Many definitions have focused on a homogeneous concept of community rather than diversity. Now, administrators are looking at the diversity of ideas, skills, and experiences of their residents to bring a community together. Making the environment more inclusive and empowering can increase community development in any setting.

Komives, Lucas, and McMahon (1998) discussed community not just as a place where interaction occurs, but as a spirit of connection and commitment that sustains relationships and purpose. For example, an apartment community may have a student governing board that acts as a liaison between residents and housing administration. This board must work as a team to accomplish its goals. This team of residents must have a process to make decisions, a means to communicate, and a commitment to some level of participation by community members. The spirit of connection and commitment to one another and the community must be present or the student board will be ineffective.

Gardner (1990) referred to eight elements that must be present in order to have an effective community:

1. Wholeness incorporating diversity.
2. A shared culture.
3. Good internal communication.
4. Caring, trust, and teamwork.
5. Group maintenance and governance.
6. Participation and shared leadership tasks.
7. Development of new members.
8. Links to the outside world.

Community Services and Programming ——————————

Each of these elements should be considered by both residents and apartment administrators in the creation of a definition of community. Finding the elements that best fit that specific community can connect people to one another and provide that spirit of community.

Staff and Resident Models to Build Community

Housing administrators in the United States and in other countries are providing more services to residents based on the complexity of family needs, the international population, the academic pressures, and the financial stresses. Due to these complexities, housing professionals have created community development models and services as a means to decrease student and family isolation and pressure.

Originally, apartment communities on campus were based on a landlord-tenant relationship. Today, many apartment complexes in the private sector still function in this way. However, housing administrators have moved beyond the landlord-tenant relationship toward a more community-oriented model. This model is based on the assessment of the needs and values of diverse resident, staff, and student populations.

Since resident needs have been the focal point of community development models, many colleges and university housing programs have developed a community services program. Some organizations have hired professional staff to implement programs such as mental health clinics, child care, social services and academic support for residents. Others have taken a simpler approach to community services by having their residents implement the programs and services themselves.

In addition, the diversity of residents—whether they are single students or families—has warranted the need to continually reassess the services offered to residents. Whalen (1996b) suggested that resident satisfaction regarding housing comes from both physical and community services. Issues of physical environment, child care, recreation facilities, social space, programs, and activities were identified as important factors in determining housing satisfaction. Other resources provided to residents within their communities may include social work and counseling, health education, mediation and outreach services.

Residents learn to depend on each other in these communities because they are there for a common purpose and goal. They share common interests and goals because it helps them maintain a sense of belonging to a community. However, the problem with this type of community is that members become so focused on their own goals that they forget about the goals of the community around them. For example, many residents have additional pressures of not only their studies but also obligations to family, work, and financial matters.

Peck (1987) identified four stages that he felt created a true community. The four stages are pseudocommunity; chaos; emptiness; and true, authentic community. Within each stage a group moves toward community while constantly changing values, beliefs, and ideals.

For example, when residents move into an apartment complex, housing administrators call the complex a community. In reality, the residents are living in a pseudocommunity. The relationships that initially form are superficial and underdeveloped.

Residents might walk by and greet or acknowledge one another in a courteous manner but they do not know each other.

As residents become more involved in the community setting, resident cliques may form based on where people live, their cultural backgrounds, or whether or not they have children. This stage is the chaos stage where residents find themselves siding with their peer group on issues. This can be an extremely difficult stage for residents who find themselves unable to communicate because of language barriers or a lack of confrontation skills.

The third stage is emptiness, when residents may feel that listening and understanding one another are more important for everyone than functioning on assumptions and stereotypes. People hear other point of view and are willing to look at both sides of a situation. Lastly, the true, authentic community is one that still has conflict, but consensus is mutual among everyone for the good of the overall community.

Much of the discourse about community chronicles its absence or the search for community (Boyer, 1990). For many residents in apartment complexes, the issue of whether or not community exists is secondary to their personal goals. Residents not only are pressured to find resources to pay for their education but also are concerned with finding ways to support their families financially. Consequently, the challenges of developing a community in apartment housing is exacerbated by shrinking resources and complex family issues.

Whether students are in a specific college or professional school, the goal is to graduate with a degree from an accredited institution of higher learning. Although apartment communities also may be made up of spouses and children, one cannot overlook the main reason these additional residents are on campus. The purpose of each role—whether student, spouse or child—is to work toward and support the completion of an academic degree.

Initiatives which demonstrate that residents are valued members of a particular community take a variety of forms. This resident-centered focus was reinforced by Palmer (1997), who addressed the vital need of students to be introduced to a world larger than their own experience, which also enlarges their sense of community. A few factors administrators should consider important in residents feeling valued include recognizing that residents are dealing with the "routine" stresses of college or university life, adjusting to a new environment, needing to create support systems to replace those they left behind, acculturating to a new society, and coping with family stresses (Palmer, 1997).

Today's campuses are focused on student issues, but often do not address the issues of dependent family members. Since housing professionals identify these dependents as valued members of the community, it is imperative to be advocates on campus for this nontraditional resident population. The basic needs of these family members can be met by illustrating to colleagues in other Student Affairs divisions how services can be extended to this population.

Another factor that has had a direct impact on resident satisfaction is involvement within the community. Selby and Weston (1978) supported the notion that the opportunity to participate in policy formation and implementation of programs has a direct, positive impact on residents' outlook toward their living situation. Upon arrival on campus, many residents evaluate their living conditions as adequate and inexpensive for their short-term residency. Castleberry and Rejto (1996) addressed the idea that many resident and family problems were a result of inadequate information which created unrealistic expectations about the housing environment. "Residents arriving with these unrealistic expectations suddenly discover that they must quickly either realign their needs to what is available or attempt to meet their needs through alternate means" (Castleberry & Rejto, 1996, p. 8). Residents who decide to realign their needs often become involved with neighbors and the community. This enhances the residents' experience and the living environment becomes a secondary concern to the relationships they develop with others.

Engaging Staff and Residents as Community Facilitators

With growing support for community development and customer-service-based operations, most campus apartment housing programs engage residents as community facilitators. Since the early 1980s, the involvement of resident peers to support apartment community life has made a significant impact on resident satisfaction. Many institutions hire part-time, live-in resident staff who perform a variety of tasks designed to be responsive to resident needs. Live-in staffing models are as varied as the institutions of higher education around the globe. However, common themes tend to relate to staff helping residents feel welcome and respected, balancing the needs of individual lifestyles with the needs of the larger apartment housing community, and being responsive to resident concerns.

Often staff responsibilities include welcoming new residents, providing area resources, conducting apartment orientations, programming, facilitating conflict mediation, and, in some cases, even completing minor appliance repairs. Whether the staff title is "Resident Assistant," "Community Aide," "Community Development Advisor," or "Apartment Manager," the mission of the resident staff position generally relates to peers providing service and support in a diverse community.

According to the 1996 ACUHO-I Apartments Survey, 95% of the institutions surveyed hired live-in staff who work 10 to 20 hours per week, and most receive either a cash stipend or in-kind remuneration such as a rent credit (Whalen, 1996). Hiring staff who represent the cultural diversity of the population demonstrates a commitment to the multiculturalism of that community and provides active role models.

As apartment communities become richer in cultural diversity, hiring multilingual student staff supports residents in developing relationships across cultural boundaries. For those who speak English as a second (or even third) language, being able to communicate in a native language during the transition period can ease the access to housing services.

Apartment staff are usually the first line of communication with residents. They are viewed as the community builders and developers. However, residents should also share the responsibility for building community. Again, resident involvement evolves not only out of the actions and opportunities that staff can create, but also based on the presence or absence of a number of conditions that affect residents' interactions and perceptions of their environment. Beyerlein, Brandel, Hamilton, Nededog, and Thoman (1982) suggested that residents consider the elements of proximity, common facilities, guidelines, and social environment as factors that must be provided in order for community to develop.

Beyerlein et al. (1982) identified these conditions as "promoters" and "inhibitors." Promoters include effective members of the community, such as staff who actively participate in the development of programs and activities. These events empower staff and residents to become actively involved. Inhibitors can be such things as a poorly maintained environment or inadequate facilities for group activities or family events. For example, program opportunities may be abundant and staff may have maximum contact with residents, but if resident apartments and the external living areas are in poor condition or they have no place to gather, the sense of community can be negatively affected.

Who sets the expectations for developing community? Do residents evaluate and develop ways to meet those needs or does the staff assess and meet residents' needs? Kretzmann and McKnight (1993) suggested that both groups have untapped resources that can contribute to mutual community development. Their concept is based on an asset-based orientation, an internal focus on the community's own agenda, its problem-solving capacity and a relationship-driven action plan. Accessing residents' skills, interests, and experiences via a "capacity inventory" or other instruments subsequently allows the community to mobilize residents and their assets to achieve community goals and objectives (Jennie, Buchan, & Casey-Powell, 1997). Kretzmann and McKnight (1993) suggested that residents may become more invested in their apartment community as their potential contributions are solicited and thus implicitly valued.

Staff and Resident Leadership Opportunities

Leaders can motivate themselves and others to participate in their communities through relationships. One of the greatest untapped resources in apartment communities are people with leadership skills. Many residents have or had professional jobs and careers that have exposed them to various leadership skills and styles. Most residents are interested in participating in activities if their peers are participating, and the issues addressed will enhance their quality of life. Successful apartment complexes are those that create an environment where residents have an active role in the development of their communities. Residents who feel they are a part of their community will participate more and share common resources. For example, residents are often willing to volunteer and donate time or equipment to enhance their living environment if they feel connected to the community. Staff must recognize the tremendous potential in resident communication and volunteerism. They must be willing to establish and maintain a climate where residents may develop and maximize their contributions.

Involvement in programs and activities is also associated with a number of factors including a commitment to (a) participating in community action, (b) helping others clean up the environment, (c) promoting racial and ethnic understanding, and (d) valuing a meaningful philosophy of life.

Community Services and Programming ――――――――――

Volunteerism

Some housing programs receive limited or no funds to support the live-in residence staff, leaving program coordinators to address the need for community support services in other ways. One common practice is to involve residents as volunteers who have an opportunity to make a positive contribution to the community in which they live. Astin (1996) stated that one of the most impactful aspects of individual development is that of peer group interaction. Recruiting residents to volunteer as a way for them to connect with other residents can be personally rewarding while providing a needed service to the community. Most residents sacrificed a support network when they moved to a campus apartment complex, whether their former home was 100 miles away or 3,000 miles away. Volunteering can offer a way to create a new support system and to build confidence in those wishing to practice new language skills. For those who may be taking a career hiatus while supporting a spouse or partner who has returned to school, volunteering can be a way to continue personal or professional skill development while contributing to the community.

Volunteerism offers some resident control in the surrounding environment, and all who participate do so willingly. Volunteers tend to be motivated by a reliance on generosity, friendly persuasion, and a desire for a better environment. Providing volunteer opportunities demonstrates an investment in building relationships with residents. While these reasons can be useful in recruiting volunteers, in order to retain them, the experience must be meaningful to each individual. Knowing each person's motivation for volunteering will help staff create a dynamic situation in which that person's needs can be met, and a positive challenge may prompt him or her to continue. Recognition for one's contributions is critical, especially if it is expressed in ways that are valued by each volunteer. Learning when public recognition is valued and when a private expression of appreciation will be more heartfelt is a life lesson that can well serve all.

There are a number of ways to recruit residents not only for programming events but also for leadership positions. As stated earlier, Kretzmann and McKnight (1993) recommended surveying residents and evaluating their expertise and skills to identify potential volunteers who could present free educational sessions, career-oriented classes, physical activities, and so forth. The topics and activities from residents who volunteer are unlimited. One of the most common ways to recruit resident volunteers is through door-to-door flyers, newsletters, or personal invitations. These publications can be generated weekly or monthly depending on the staff and the mode of distribution. Personal contact either by telephone or in person is another way that residents can be informed of events, activities, or volunteer opportunities.

Volunteers are an important component of a resident-centered program. Volunteerism is an inexpensive and effective way to increase resident awareness of programs and activities. It is also a means for residents to contribute and invest in their community. Student involvement is enhanced when students experience community (Kuh, Schuh, Whitt, & Associates, 1991), and student learning and development are honored by involvement (Astin, 1996). It is not always possible for a professional with an administrative job to make the most effective decisions without input from the residents who experience the impact of those decisions. Whether residents are involved as volunteers or paid staff, given their day-to-day experience in apartment housing, they can validate the effectiveness of administrative decisions. This can be another way to assess the effectiveness of community development.

Technology

Technology is another means of communication and recruitment of volunteers. With the development of electronic mail and subsequent institutional requirements for students to utilize current technological advances, staff and residents can remind others of programs and events as well as solicit people to volunteer. This new form of communication is quick and environmentally safe for everyone.

Computers can also be utilized as a tool for community development and interaction. The computer is a connecting device. It connects people all over the world. Electronic mail systems, home pages, web pages, listservs, and chat groups are just a few examples, not to mention the possibilities that may emerge with virtual communities that allow students and housing professionals the opportunity to learn from one another. Some visionaries suggest that communities in the future will be based not on finding the common bonds among members, but on a bond achieved when members open themselves to the full potential that exists within the environment.

Computers can enhance residents' access to local and worldwide sources of interest. Banning (1996) referred to computers as "safe gathering places" where an individual may experiment without taking great risks. When seen as a connecting device—as opposed to a barrier to interaction—the possibilities are endless. Listservs, distribution lists, databases, and chat rooms are ways to initiate contact and ultimately foster a very new form of community development. This mode of communication potentially can reduce isolation and increase networking.

Current computer technology can be used as a communication link to residents in order to complement the social and educational interaction opportunities that housing professionals work to provide residents through programs and activities. In a recent ACUHO-I resource paper (Hicks, DuBois, Pyatt, & Ventola, 1995), housing professionals were challenged to become educated and competitive about electronic competence since the future will include this evolving technology. Computers can assist professionals in keeping the student affairs focus on students, their learning, and their development.

One challenge within apartment communities is to draw people out of their apartments and into the community. Interactions between residents and staff, both formally and informally, are a means to developing open and trusting communities. Unfortunately, technology has had both a positive and a negative impact on neighbor-to-neighbor relationships. Technology has allowed people to communicate while in isolation. Residents do not need to know their neighbors because they do not need to leave their apartments. Residents' desire for more privacy, higher levels of technology, and enhanced security may counter efforts to build a sense of community or to program for diversity. It is often too easy for residents in neighbor-to-neighbor disputes to ask for apartment or complex changes without ever talking with their neighbors. Consequently, residents become comfortable retreating to their apartments and not becoming involved in their communities. This may be due to a lack of understanding of diverse populations, or may result from avoiding those who are different or retreating from any uncomfortable confrontation. One way to combat these issues is to assess the desired outcomes with the residents and staff. Administrators can play an active role in creating dialogue and connectedness with the community by evaluating how to bring people out and make them feel more comfortable.

Computers also are used in the creation of newsletters, which are one of the most effective means to communicate with residents. A newsletter can be distributed door to door and can offer suggestions on campus and community resources, updates on policies and procedures, and information about programs and activities.

Safety and Security

Another means to get members active in their community is to involve them in safety and security issues. Residents and staff can create and monitor their own living environments. Since residents in apartment complexes are responsible for their living environment, each must take an active role as a protector and reporter. They participate in protecting their environment and that of their neighbors. Serving on judicial boards; reporting neighbor disputes, domestic violence, or unsupervised children; assisting with grounds inspections and upkeep; and participating in "take back the night" programs are four examples of ways to get residents involved in safety issues.

Staff and residents must communicate what is acceptable in their environment and their roles and responsibilities in contributing to safety standards. Witnessing and reporting safety and security concerns can be difficult for neighbors and staff but is a civic duty in any community.

Recognition Programs

Incorporating incentive programs and recognition for volunteers are important components of the continual success of programs and activities. Most residents volunteer because they want to make a contribution to their community or fellow residents. However, getting residents to continue to volunteer can be a challenge. Recognition of some type can be one means to motivate them to continue serving their community. There are a number of tangible and intangible rewards for volunteers. Intangible rewards consist of opportunities to meet new people, learn from new experiences, and become socially involved in a community. Many international residents appreciate the opportunity to volunteer because it assists them in improving their language skills. Volunteering also reduces isolation, especially in a large campus community where an international student or spouse may be the only representative of his or her country. In addition, spouses who cannot work in the host country because of visa restrictions may also appreciate the opportunity to contribute since volunteer service can be added to their résumés.

Tangible rewards such as the International Honorary for Leaders in University Apartment Communities, an organization started at the University of North Dakota to recognize student and spouse volunteers, would be a more distinguished recognition. One program developed at the University of Florida called WELLBUCKS has been a successful incentive program. Each time a resident volunteers to participate, points are awarded and then redeemed at the end of each semester for prizes. Certificates, thank-you notes, newsletter articles, and pictures are all ways to recognize residents and reward them for extended service.

Program Models to Build Community

The principles that guide current programming models blend concepts from models of student development, wellness, family development, and community development. As outlined in the Council for the Advancement of Standards for Student Services/Development Programs, particular attention is paid to programs being purposeful, coherent, based on human development theory and learning characteristics, and reflective of the demographic profiles (Miller, 1997). These general standards speak to the need for programming to teach ways of developing global awareness and leadership skills. In addition, the standards prompt a recognition of life transitions and pressures of a cultural, academic, financial, and family nature. Whalen and Winter (1987) observed that programming resulting in structured social interaction among residents was successful in minimizing the likelihood of neighbors being a source of stress for each other. Ten years later, Whalen, Crull, Liao, Pate, and Rochford (1997) found this to be a continuing pattern. Of 50 schools surveyed in Australia, Canada, and the United States, 67% responded that stress is not produced by neighbors' actions. This reinforces the importance of intentional community development efforts as a way to reduce the alienation of a densely populated living environment. The diversity that results from individuals coming together in such a special living environment brings challenges and support to most communities.

Traditional wellness program models continue to excel in addressing the social, physical, intellectual, cultural, emotional, and spiritual development of students and their dependents. Providing opportunities for individuals at many different developmental levels to examine how wellness operates in their lives challenges all to consider alternative methods and lifestyles. This may manifest itself in events focused on child care, exercise and nutrition, or relaxation workshops in which residents assist each other in identifying dynamics in their lives. When peers assist each other in this way, a sense of empowerment is reinforced, while recognizing the community of which they are a part. Programming that supports healthy family development while validating individual needs is critical. The most common programs address social interaction needs, skill building, and cultural affirmation. A critical concept of a healthy community will be the messages that are heard, especially that people are valued over things, which can be reinforced through these types of people-centered programming.

Current programming models being are also learning centered, supportive of relationship building, and challenging within a larger academic community. This direction parallels the learning community philosophies in residence halls. Learning centers and other academically focused housing options have been given renewed attention in recent years. This learning community model utilizes "learning focused" campus resources to challenge and support residents as they seek to better understand the world. Supporting the concept of lifelong learning, a learning community model appreciates new and common interests, while providing leadership and group development opportunities.

Community Services and Programming

Resources and Funding for Community Development

A learning-focused community services program impacts organizational foundations and requires institutional support and funding. This concept should be part of ongoing discussions with staff, colleagues, and residents to continue to build support. Some institutions have had success in creating this vision and advocating for financial support from institutional sources, resulting in a solid budget that prioritizes community services. Regardless, gaining access to external funding sources is a reality in the life of any venture. Partnering efforts with other units within the academic community and external to the university have seen remarkable success. Zeller (1997) described the need for creative budgeting strategies to allow college and university leaders to achieve institutional goals, including community development.

Depending on state legislation or private philanthropy, limitations and access issues do vary, but funding is also available through federal government agencies and corporate foundations. Grant guidelines specify eligibility requirements for types of projects and geographic locations that specific monies can support. This information has become more accessible as technologies expand and staff make better use of available resources. Making use of resources available from the Internet, listservs, and professional associations can support the creative funding process.

Facilities for Creating Community Development

The building boom of the 1960s resulted in many facilities that no longer meet the needs of current residential communities. Some institutions are fortunate to have community centers to serve as common gathering spaces for residents. Still, depending on the size of the housing program, such facilities may not be in close proximity to the residents being targeted. Consideration needs to be paid not only to public gathering spaces, but to the overall physical design of the apartment community.

Some apartment housing operations have created programming space and community centers within their apartment complexes by remodeling laundry rooms and renovating vacant apartments or storage spaces. Other housing operations may use off-site space such as schools, churches, parks and day care facilities (Paul, Rei, Ostrow, & Shigetomi, 1984). One example of an institution that offers a variety of facilities is the University of Arizona, where apartment residents have access to a weight room, a swimming pool, a preschool, and six study rooms.

Banning (1996) noted that the high density facilities that exist on most campuses hinder student preferences for both privacy and staff dedication to fostering community. A balance of support for both privacy and community development may be a better fit for residents of future generations. Banning suggested that the notion of privacy within community is a realistic philosophy which can have a powerful impact on future construction or remodeling for future community-centered buildings.

Creating gathering and common spaces for the residents of the 21st century must address different issues than those that drove construction during the 1960s. Spontaneous interactions through informal but intentional small group gathering spaces was noted by Kuh et al. (1991), as an important component of community development.

Strategically placed bulletin boards and chalk boards for residents to communicate with each other are also important in commons areas.

In the event of new construction, proximity to academic campus buildings as well as access to schools for children is a priority. Banning (1996) suggested a design to protect resident privacy while moving toward extending social relationships in an environment where residents feel more in control. Another proximity issue was noted by Whalen's (1996) survey for ACUHO-I, in which 39% of the respondents cited proximity to campus as a main reason for living in a particular apartment community, which can be a strong marketing tool.

Assessment Tools for Determining Community

As the campus community constantly changes, so must the assessments of the current community and of the effectiveness of community development interventions. Many institutions implement entrance surveys to evaluate the initial customer service performance and exit surveys prior to a member leaving the community, as well as an annual survey of all residents. Event-specific evaluations by residents have proven helpful in developing an ongoing dialogue about programming and activities. To target more specific topics of discussion or to understand issues and concerns of residents, focus groups also have been utilized as a form of direct feedback to administrators. Whatever assessment tools are chosen, continual assessment is part of a vibrantly evolving community services program.

Assessment of on-campus apartment housing programs will be invaluable as studies continue in the public and private market to determine factors that impact occupancy. Given the competition with the private sector to serve the same student population, it is important to know what makes a college or university apartment program different. What is it that will draw students and families to live in one apartment housing community or another? For many, the role of the resident staff will have the greatest appeal. For others it may be the amenities that are provided as part of the physical apartment setting or it may be the intentional support programs and community development opportunities that are viewed as investments in residents.

Multicultural Population

Most student apartment communities are diverse not only in age but in culture. Many residents come from all over the world with different ethnic traditions and values. This can enhance yet challenge the apartment community. Fostering a multicultural understanding can promote education and growth at any point in a person's academic or personal life. One way to enhance this cultural diversity is through dialogue and discussion. Steps to build multicultural relationships must include a commitment from administration and a willingness to assess what exists and what is needed to help people come together in these diverse communities. Examples of programs for diverse populations include discussion groups, international socials or potluck meals, People Awareness Week, English or other language classes, play groups, cooking classes, international holiday celebrations, and family traditions. As these programs are developed to build community, it is important to remember that not all communities are alike. Residents can often become challenged by the idea that if no one offends them they will not offend anyone else. This is another example of Peck's (1987) pseudocommunity. He suggested that when a community says that everyone interacts superficially through the use of social skills it defeats the true concept of community. His idea of true community is one in which members make another's condition their own.

Banning (1996) defined community not by forming groups around sameness, but by opening oneself to the full diversity that exists within the apartments community. It is accepting and evaluating the richness and diversity of these communities that makes the apartment housing experience such a success.

In developing diverse apartment communities, staff and residents must have mutual trust of, respect for, and commitment to one another. Administrators, staff, and residents must work together to develop common goals for their communities. All must share their vision, as well as communicate and involve each other in the development of their community.

Ways in Which Residents Can Contribute to and Invest in Communities

Since it is the responsibility of housing staff to assess the needs of their communities, it is important that a positive relationship exists between housing administration and its residents. Housing personnel need to develop a relationship with staff and residents that is based on trust. Empowering residents to have an active role in the decision-making process—whether it is approving rental increases or planning renovations—will assist housing administrators in building trust and positive relationships with the residents. For example, if residents understand why policies and procedures are being changed, they can trust that the decision was made after careful consideration.

In addition, residents' frustration levels decrease when communications through their resident government or housing publications are utilized. These forms of communication allow residents the opportunity to be a part of the decision-making process which may have a direct impact on their participation.

Banning (1996) addressed the idea that a community is a system that has interdependent components which function to maintain themselves. He identified two distinct approaches to community. One is the macro level, which is an attempt to make an impact on the larger community. The other is the micro level where community is developed in smaller groups.

Campus-wide events such as homecoming, athletic events, and theme-week programs are all examples of macro community building activities. For national theme weeks, the entire college or university community is involved with the program. Theme weeks include faculty, staff, and students in the planning and implementation of events. A sense of campus pride and spirit can be shown through these activities to all members of the community. These events inspire community spirit but may be less successful in building build lasting community relationships.

One type of micro-level community development involves small groups of volunteers that plan programs and activities that are of interest to a specific apartment complex or building. Examples of these activities include potluck dinners, arts and crafts activities, English classes, clean-up days, and babysitting cooperatives. These events build relationships between neighbors, and a commitment to their living community.

Small-group sharing of similarities and differences enhances the experience for all those involved and fosters a sense of ownership toward others.

Partnerships and Advocates in the Local Community

Recognizing that no single program can be all things to all people paves the way to create coalitions as one way to utilize area resources to benefit residents. Partnerships with campus departments as well as local agencies support their need to contribute to the community, make efficient use of resources, and create innovative supports. Requesting a collaborative venture of other professionals can often serve as a validation of the unique contributions that those professionals offer to the broader community. The keys to developing effective campus and community relationships include honesty, competence, listening and sensitivity, and commitment to follow up (Sandeen, 1993). Potential outcomes include increased funding for initiatives that are deemed important for the population or the program, opportunity for further collaboration, networking with peripheral or less-familiar agencies, more effective problem solving, an improved sense of community, and better service for residents.

Campus Coalitions

Many academic programs have curricula that are community-based, prevention-oriented, and multiculturally sensitive with an empowerment-based model of service delivery. These departments may welcome an invitation to build a coalition. Examples of potential campus and community partners for housing programs include student government and leadership groups, public safety departments, legal services, health care professionals, colleges of nursing or dentistry, counseling centers, sexual assault prevention offices, international centers, schools of education, social work faculty or agencies, psychology faculty or professionals, public health departments, and public school systems. In a partnership, all members are beneficiaries. Students within those agencies or departments may gain a unique form of internship; others may experience a coalition as an opportunity to support and extend programs to minimize stress levels and enhance coping skills. This bridging of academic and student life is important for all.

At the University of Michigan, a coalition was created by the partnership between the International Center, Counseling Services, the School of Nursing, the University Center for the Child and Family, and the family housing staff to provide comprehensive free services and support for family residents. While receiving support, family members are engaged in building a stronger sense of community. If these staff groups were working independently, many of the services provided would not be possible.

Community Coalitions

By developing a relationship and partnering with the local community, residents have the opportunity to interact with agencies and organizations that they may not otherwise have known. This encourages residents to become more invested both in their education on campus and in the community in which they potentially may live after completion of their academic goals. Organizations such as the Safe Kids' Coalition, the Children's Miracle Network, day care facilities, school systems, and hospitals are all examples of places that residents can become involved and, in some cases, can access resources from these agencies. For example, at the University of Florida, a grant was written in conjunction with the Safe Kids' Coalition for free car seats for residents who met certain financial requirements.

Residents interact with their campus and local communities to understand and learn skills to develop solutions to social, civic, and ethical situations. Community members benefit from this interaction by having additional help and resources, being exposed to new ideas, and building personal as well as professional skills. The local community also benefits from this interaction because residents become of services offered and may utilize a company or organization due to its involvement with residents. These companies also are aware that residents and students gain valuable experience and are potential employees through this support network.

Conclusion

Developing community services and programming in apartment housing can be challenging yet rewarding. By taking a deliberate approach to meeting the needs of this diverse population apartment professionals can offer residents a dynamic living environment. Since apartment professionals are confronted daily with community development issues, careful consideration should be taken to identify and define community. Staff should evaluate various types of community and programming models, determine resources needed to fund community and build partnerships with the local and campus community, and identify ways in which residents and staff from diverse backgrounds can contribute to their communities.

Community requires that residents not remain in isolation. Rather, residents must be in relationship with each other and their community to be an effective community. As discussed, one way to foster resident interactions is to include them in program planning and implementation, policy and procedure development and implementation, and facilities issues. While many campuses struggle to form communities, few would argue about the essential importance of community and its significance in providing quality experiences for students and their families.

Apartment housing is one of the many diverse communities found on college and university campuses. Community clusters based on culture, age, children, academic majors, professional colleges, athletic programs, school zones, and personal interests may exist in any apartment complex. These clusters are examples of smaller communities within the campus community bound by the common goals of being a community of people committed to learning and to advancing their own education and that of others (Komives et al., 1998).

As housing professionals address the future community service needs of apartment residents, more research must be done to determine the effectiveness of community relationships. Professional literature on educational programming and community development is limited. Schuh (1985) reported that no feature articles and only one abstract discussing family housing were found in *The Journal of College and University Student Housing* between 1979 and 1983. He also reviewed the 1985 index for the first

14 volumes of this publication and found only six articles on family housing among the 365 published during the period. The ACUHO-I *Talking Stick* has dedicated a few issues to family and apartment housing over the past few years, but again the research is limited. More research needs to be conducted by apartment housing professionals to better understand the impact that community services have on residents.

Komives et al. (1998) asserted that knowing about community, philosophically believing in the worth of community, and being skilled at developing and sustaining community are essential aspects of administrators in developing community. The diversity of apartment housing populations requires an approach to community development that is deliberate and well executed. Combining professional staff, students, and other residents in the community development philosophy can assist in the creation of a community that is based on mutual respect and understanding.

References

Astin, A. W. (1996). The role of service in higher education. *About Campus, 1*(1), 14-19.

Banning, J. P. (1996). Designing for community: Thinking "out of the box" with porches. *Journal of College and University Student Housing. 26*(2), 3-6.

Beyerlein, M., Brandel, R., Hamilton, M., Nededog, A., & Thoman, S. (1982). Community development in family housing: Identity promoters and inhibitors. *Journal of College and University Student Housing, 12*(2), 8-13.

Boyer, E. L. (1990). *College: The undergraduate experience in America.* New York: Harper & Row.

Castleberry, M., & Rejto, P. (1996). Using communication as an intervention strategy in family housing. *Talking Stick, 13*(6), 8-9.

Conneely, R. (1992). The development of community. In V. Gore (Ed.), *ACUHO-I family housing monograph* (pp. 29-35). Columbus, OH: ACUHO-I.

Gardner, J. W. (1990). *On leadership.* New York: The Free Press.

Hicks, L. M., DuBois, L., Pyatt, K., & Ventola, J. A. (1995). *Technology trends in college and university housing.* Columbus, OH: Association of College and University Housing Officers-International.

Jennie, J., Buchan, R., & Casey-Powell, D. (1997). *It takes a village to raise expectations: Mapping and mobilizing residents' assets.* Paper presented at the meeting of the ACUHO-I Apartments Conference, Estes Park, CO.

Kretzmann, J. P., & McKnight, J. L. (1993). *Building communities from the inside out: A path toward finding and mobilizing a community's assets.* Evanston, IL: Center for Urban Affairs and Policy Research, Northwestern University.

Komives, S., Lucas, N., & McMahon, T. (1998). *Exploring leadership for college students who want to make a difference.* San Francisco: Jossey-Bass.

Kuh, G. D., Schuh, J. H., Whitt, E. J., & Associates. (1991). *Involving colleges: Successful approaches to fostering student learning and development outside the classroom* (pp. 305-321). San Francisco: Jossey-Bass.

Miller, T. K. (Ed.). (1997). *CAS: The book of professional standards for higher education.* Washington, DC: Council for the Advancement of Standards in Higher Education.

Palmer, P. J. (1997). Teaching and learning in the community. *About Campus, 2*(5), 4-13.

Paul, S. C., Rei, P. S., Ostrow, J., & Shigetomi, C. (1984). A demonstration of organizational change in family housing. *Journal of College and University Student Housing, 14*(2), 8-14.

Peck, M. S. (1987). *The different drum: Community making and peace.* New York: Simon & Schuster.

Sandeen, A. (1993). Developing effective campus and community relations. In M. Barr and Associates (Eds.), *Student affairs administration* (pp. 300-312). San Francisco: Jossey-Bass.

Selby, T., & Weston, D. (1978). Dormitory versus apartment housing for freshmen. *Journal of College Student Development, 19*(2), 153-157.

Schuh, J. (1985). Developing programs in family housing. *Journal of College and University Student Housing. 15*(2), 26-30.

Tierney, W. G. (1993) *Building communities of difference: Higher education in the twenty-first century.* Westport, CT: Bergin & Garvey.

Whalen, D. F., & Winter, M. (1987). Neighbor interaction and stress in family housing. *Journal of College and University Student Housing, 17*(1), 28-34.

Whalen, D. (1996). *1996 Apartments survey report.* Columbus, OH: Association of College and University Housing Officers-International.

Whalen, D., Crull., S., Liao, T.-M., Pate, R., & Rochford, H. (1997). *Resident satisfaction in apartments.* Columbus, OH: Association of College and University Housing Officers-International.

Zeller, W. J. (1997). Two cultures united: Residential programs of the twenty-first century. *Journal of College and University Student Housing, 26*(2), 7-13.

Legal, Safety, and Operational Issues

Eric Luskin
Director of Residence Life
DePaul University

Legal, Safety, and Operational Issues ———————————————

Introduction

For campus apartment managers, legal and operational issues are influenced primarily by the following factors: mission or institutional purpose, demographics of resident populations, facility and financial considerations, and legal precedents and risk management. A synopsis of each concept follows.

Mission or Institutional Purpose

When managing any real estate on behalf of others, one begins with a thorough understanding of the owner's goals and objectives. Therefore, when managing on-campus apartments, the educational role of the institution often becomes the centerpiece for operations. The creation of habitats on campus typically is undertaken for the very purpose of furthering the educational role of the institution. Everything else is incidental. As such, the management of residential communities is based on helping residents achieve their academic goals. Practices that interfere with this objective should be reviewed. Consequently, rules and operational decisions have long been made with deference to the educational mission, distinguishing on-campus property management from most off-campus, for-profit management companies.

Demographics

Operational decisions can be expected to vary based on the resident population. Single-student housing, for example, generally accommodates young adults at least 17 years of age. On the other hand, in housing for families of students, faculty, and/or staff, residents ranging in age from infants through senior citizens are not uncommon. Laws or regulations often are established to protect families and children (e.g., the Fair Housing Act, lead-based paint notification, etc.) for which campus housing management must ensure compliance.

The dependents of campus community members typically have little political clout as nonmatriculated individuals. However, the quality of life for dependents has a huge impact on the academic achievements of nontraditional students. Therefore, housing managers often will become advocates for this special group of residents and will promulgate policies that help protect their interests, when possible. Determining and then understanding resident demographics, therefore, is important in developing appropriate management practices and acknowledging special needs.

Facility and Financial Issues

While this may be more obvious than the others on surface, to those outside the profession the relationship between facility design and policies may seem more apparent than real. For example, facilities that include food preparation areas must devote increased attention to cleanliness, pest control, and fire safety. Even the impact of collective bargaining agreements may be significant for quality control issues and cost containment measures. In recent years there has been increasing financial pressure on housing departments, as more institutions expect housing to operate as an auxiliary service without other financial support. Differences between budgeted and actual occupancy figures increasingly impacts cancellation policies, occupancy time limits, eligibility factors, and other, perhaps previously protected, policies.

Legal Precedents and Risk Management

Legal requirements and reducing exposure to risk should be considered in virtually every policy. Housing management has a duty to protect institutional assets and minimize significant interruptions to residence life and property operations. While legal guidelines vary according to federal, state, provincial, local, and institutional expectations, they generally direct attention to safety, clear communication, and/or due process.

These factors provide a framework for the discussion that follows on marketing issues, leasing and assignment issues, and recent health and safety issues. While this is clearly written from the perspective of institutions in the United States, the guiding principles are relevant to international colleagues working in on-campus apartment housing communities. Obviously, all practitioners are encouraged to consult with legal counsel regarding local ordinances and legislation.

Marketing Issues

"Residence Halls" or "Apartments"—Legal Implications

There has been increasing discussion, even confusion, in recent years about whether U. S. and Canadian landlord-tenant laws apply to college- or university-owned and -managed residential property. On the surface, there appear to be good reasons why institutions may want to circumvent landlord-tenant protocol, which include the ability to more easily change assignments or terminate occupancy without prior approval of the student, to change entrance door locks when deemed appropriate, and to provide easier access for university officials. In the United States, additional concerns about landlord-tenant law may include Fair Housing Act regulations governing marketing and assignment processes.

As a result, some institutions have gone to great lengths to avoid landlord-tenant nomenclature in their marketing and contractual documents in an effort to distance themselves from this notion. In such cases, the contract between the resident and the institution may be referred to as an "agreement" instead of a lease. Additionally, all facilities may be referred to as "residence halls," including those offering private kitchens and bathrooms.

At other institutions, the pendulum swings the other way, and a lease serves as the binding contractual document even in more traditional residence hall settings with community bathrooms. Among the advantages for using a lease and operating within full compliance of prevailing landlord-tenant laws are the increased options in responding to lease violations by occupants. If a student resident has violated the terms of the lease and the institution's student conduct code, processing may occur by following prescribed procedures through either or both documents.

Legal, Safety, and Operational Issues

While practices vary widely, some patterns are emerging. Residence hall accommodations most often avoid lease terminology, while apartment operations, especially for family housing or where a "joint and several" clause is used (see the section below on leasing and assignment issues), increasingly are likely to depend upon a lease arrangement. However, it is not uncommon in single student apartments, where students are obligated only for their own bed space within the unit, to call the contractual tool an "agreement," a "license," or simply a "contract."

Perhaps the most important question in this debate is "Why shouldn't landlord-tenant law apply?" "What makes us different?" Certainly, there is the obvious educational relationship to the institution discussed in the Introduction, which creates a special-purpose housing arrangement. However, this position cannot be assumed without some risk. If it looks like, smells like and feels like an apartment—and a challenge occurs—the court may well ask "Why not?" Regardless of doctrines, guiding principles of fairness, clarity, and due process are the best mechanisms to keep such discussions out of the courtroom.

Fair Housing Considerations

The 1968 Civil Rights Act (Title VIII) provided for fair housing opportunities throughout the United States. In 1988, the Fair Housing Amendments Act was enacted. This Act added handicapped and familial status to protected classes and significantly strengthened enforcement provisions. Today, these two protected classes alone account for more than 60% of all Fair Housing Act claims.

College and university housing operations generally have sought fair and equitable assignment practices in a manner which has probably outpaced the off-campus market, at least regarding such protected classes as race, national origin, and religion. However, higher education has for most of its history discriminated by gender and familial status in housing. For example, many family housing operations discriminate on the basis of marital status. Virtually all single student operations discriminate on the basis of gender, since typically only same-sex students are assigned to the same room or apartment. Familial status discrimination is the entire basis for family housing operations, albeit in favor of families. (Protection against familial status discrimination is primarily designed to prohibit favoritism towards single individuals or families without children.) No known challenges to these practices have been successful.

The Fair Housing Act defines handicap as (a) a physical or mental impairment which substantially limits one or more of a person's major life activities such as walking, seeing, working, hearing, or caring for one's self; OR (b) has a record of such impairment; OR (c) is regarded as having such impairment (Goss & Johnson, 1994).

Familial status is defined as (a) one or more individuals who have not attained the age of 18 years being domiciled with a parent or other person having legal custody or the designee of such parent, OR (b) anyone who is pregnant or persons who are *in the process* of securing legal custody of any individual who has not attained the age of 18 years (emphasis added; Goss & Johnson, 1994).

The Fair Housing Act (or more likely the Americans with Disabilities Act for residence hall applications) applies to campus housing operations and is a tool for any person meeting the definition who feels that he or she has been discriminated against.

Most college and university administrators are aware of these obligations and as a minimum direct continual good faith efforts toward bringing practices and facilities into full compliance.

When campus housing operations are exclusively for single students, higher education has historically and successfully prohibited students with dependents from occupancy. Ironically, campus housing operations are probably more susceptible to violations of the Fair Housing Act regarding familial status discrimination when students with dependents are provided accommodations. Once the decision is made to make housing accessible to students with dependents, like off-campus properties, it becomes ill-advised (a) to refuse to rent an apartment within the community on the basis of children; (b) to limit the use of privileges, services, or facilities based on family status (although reasonable policies may be established for safety purposes); (c) to restrict families to particular areas of a property; or (d) to charge different rents or security deposits to families.

Campus housing staff should exercise caution when discussing housing options with applicants. Guiding applicants from federally protected classes toward properties where *management* thinks they will fit best is called "steering." Steering is inherently illegal. Even if it is done innocently or with the intent of providing the best possible product and match for the applicant.

For example, there may be a temptation to assign an applicant who has a mobility impairment to a first-floor apartment, which already is modified for wheelchair use. However, if the applicant wants a third-floor apartment because of the view, and such an option would be open to an able-bodied applicant, discouraging the disabled applicant is an example of steering. (The student must be willing to pay for the necessary modifications to the upper floor apartment.) Statements to avoid in this situation include: "Don't you think you would be better off in another apartment?" "I think you would be more comfortable somewhere else."

A more appropriate response might be: "We have apartments available that already have been converted to accommodate wheelchairs. Would you be interested in seeing any of them?"

The same holds true for a student parent of a youngster, who may be steered to an area where playground equipment is nearby. Instead, it is safer to say, "Here is a map of our community with available apartments marked. The map also shows community amenities such as parks, bus stops, playgrounds, etc. Let me know your preferences."

The law is intended for adults to be able to make their own decisions, and to protect parents' rights to freely decide what is best for their children.

Application, Security, and Prepayment Fees

As long as there are no state, provincial, or local codes to the contrary, housing management may collect fees, security deposits, and other prepayment assessments. Specifications as to what the fees cover and under what conditions they might be returned must be spelled out clearly to applicants in advance. State, provincial, and/or local codes may limit maximum amounts and may identify the conditions under which they are received and how they must be applied and/or returned. The different mechanisms are generally defined as follows:

Application fee. This covers administrative processing costs. It is usually nonrefundable.

Security deposit. This deposit is collected to offset possible charges for cleaning and/or damages after vacating, as well as for any other contractual nonperformance. Security deposits seem to have become less popular on campuses in recent years for three reasons: (a) an increase in regulatory requirements on how the money may be used and resulting accounting processes; (b) existing institutional encumbrance already on students' records for unfulfilled obligations; and (c) an improvement in the competitive position for on-campus operations, since off-campus properties usually require a deposit.

Prepayment. Used as a reservation fee to secure a space for a future term, this fee usually is applied in full toward housing costs if the applicant assumes occupancy as agreed. A prepayment (or reservation) charge appears to be used with increasing regularity because of the positive effect of reducing the number of "no-shows," which are caused by new applicants who make reservations on more than one campus, and also by returning students who are considering moving off campus. Unfortunately, this occurs at the expense of others who may be declined or wait-listed for housing, or placed in temporary overflow accommodations, if all beds in the system appear to be reserved. Vacancies that do not surface until after fall classes begin can, on many campuses, create an empty bed for the year that negatively impacts financial operations.

This is not considered a deposit, since the money is applied in full toward housing charges. There is usually a date during the summer (for fall term occupancy) which, once passed, makes the prepayment nonrefundable. The date selected should still provide adequate time for housing staff to fill the vacancy.

Pricing and Promotions

In a competitive market, housing managers and returning students alike often are acutely aware of differences in facilities, amenities, and pricing between the off-campus market and campus housing. In on-campus operations, there is a propensity for all apartments with the same number of bedrooms to be priced the same. Perhaps this is the result of equity concerns, or the desire merely to keep things simple. If demand is high and vacancy low for all apartments, this pricing policy may make sense. However, if this is not the case, campus managers should learn some of the marketing strategies that work at off-campus complexes.

In marketing any product, when inventory is high and not moving fast enough, the price is probably too high for the perceived value. The apartment business is by no means immune to the laws of supply and demand. The answer to this problem is to offer cutting-edge programs, services, and facilities that the market wants, at competitive prices. While swimming pools and carports may not be possible, amenities such as microwaves and ceiling fans often are.

Rental rates. Off-campus rental rates often are adjusted according to two main factors in addition to apartment size: special features (amenities) and market conditions. Apartment rates may be adjusted for the condition of appliances, view, floor, proximity to parking or laundry, and new carpeting, to name a few. Additionally, off-campus managers are quite knowledgeable about which apartments rent first and which sit the longest when vacant, and they initiate promotions accordingly. These often consist of a lower initial rental rate, more flexible terms such as month-to-month rentals, no security deposit, or even one month of free rent. Vacant apartments help no one.

Too frequently, on-campus managers do not take such marketing ploys seriously. With increasing financial expectations placed on college and university auxiliaries, perhaps it is time for a paradigm shift. It may be necessary to look a current resident in the eye and share the reason a new resident has a different rental rate. It will not always be easy. Clearly, this becomes easier with the support of high level officers at the institution. However, it is done all the time off campus and makes sense. In some "rent control" environments, different rates for the same or similar apartments is not only commonplace but a financial necessity. The purpose is to keep the overall cost competitive for all.

Cancellation and Withdrawal Policies and Practices

Institutional responses to residents who cancel their contract and vacate the premises before the end of the term vary widely. Institutions which allow residents to vacate with little or no penalty justify this as a supportive environment to accommodate the changing schedules of a diverse student body. Others find justification because of long waiting lists, and no apartment remains vacant for long. Still others have a "joint and several" clause in their contracts, requiring full payment for the remaining occupants of the apartment, so there is no effect on income if some leave so long as at least one paying resident remains!

If, however, there is not a long waiting list and no joint and several clause, allowing residents to walk away from their contractual arrangements for campus apartment housing is anything but user friendly for the vast majority of students. Convenient, no-doubt, for the minority of residents who will take advantage of such freedom, but for future generations of residents who must pick up the cost of a higher vacancy allowance than would otherwise be the case, it may be a tough pill to swallow.

There is also a wide variety of approaches among institutions that do hold residents to their contracts. Some will hold residents to the full term of the contract once classes have started, without exception. Others allow residents to cancel with some sort of penalty, such as a month's rent and/or half of the remaining rental charges on the full term of the contract. For some, cancellation charges apply only during the first few months of the contract. Still others hold residents only to prior written notice in lieu of a specific cancellation charge, which is usually one to two months.

Each institution must ask: "Once a resident contractually agrees to the length of the rental term, under what circumstances (if any) are we comfortable with other residents absorbing the cost of vacancies incurred by allowing some to cancel and vacate?" This is the question at hand, with which each operation must come to grips.

Leasing and Assignment Issues

Contracts

Whether a formal lease or a less formal agreement type of instrument is used, a contractual relationship clearly exists between the institution and resident. Some contractual elements have emerged as important issues for campus apartment administrators, specifically as they relate to the assignment process.

In most circumstances, the contractual relationship should at least spell out the type of accommodation assigned, the cost for the housing and other services, the length of the contract, and the obligations of both parties to maintain the space. The contract itself should be straightforward and concise, whether a complete informal agreement or part of a very detailed lease. It should not contain marketing information about the facilities or programs. It should not list every rule for which residents will be held accountable. It should, however, refer to those documents containing such conduct information and clearly state that those documents (and which editions, if this is something changed regularly) are incorporated within the housing contract. Some reference to reasonable changes in policies and how they will be announced also should be included.

Only the most serious behavior or policy violations which would likely warrant lease termination should be included in the text of the contract. For some institutions, that will include violation of nondiscrimination policies and acts of violence, for example. Others might include failure to comply with the institution's pest control program. For all, it should include nonpayment of rent!

Section 8 and HUD Arrangements

Under the guidelines of the U. S. Department of Housing and Urban Development (HUD), regulations have been promulgated to serve families with limited financial resources. The main purpose is to provide rent support to families until they are better able to provide for themselves. As a consequence, the rent subsidy provided through Section 8 is based on a regionally determined financial need, regardless of institutional financial aid. Student families with limited incomes often qualify for the HUD rent subsidy program. As a result, there are advantages for institutions in working with Section 8 funded programs.

On the other hand, there are often several concessions required on the part of the institution. These include holding rent at the same level for 12 months; compliance with all Fair Housing Act guidelines; upper limits on rental rates and apartment sizes, depending on the size of the family; inspections by HUD officials; and compliance with applicable building codes. Usually, these are all within reason and not difficult for most campuses to comply with. However, the one concession that will sometimes throw a wrench into the process is that HUD requires use of its lease agreement. While most institutions also will require the resident to sign the usual contractual document at the institution, the HUD agreement specifies that in case of conflict, its document shall prevail. Its document does not allow the landlord to terminate tenancy based on institutional affiliation (or lack thereof). Many schools have developed arrangements with local HUD offices which clarify that continued occupancy is contingent upon institutional eligibility standards. This is encouraging. It is time for some national advocacy in this regard so that student families eligible for Section 8 funding can have the same access to campus housing as other student families on all campuses.

Joint and Several versus Individual Contracts

Contracts for space in typical residence halls are issued to each individual. On the other hand, in many apartment operations, especially in off-campus apartments, units are often rented as a whole unit, with all adult occupants responsible for the entire rent in the event one or more of the occupants default. The legal term for this is "joint and several" liability. Renting by the entire apartment reduces rent loss risk to the institution and sometimes permits residents to exercise control over who may share the space, usually within qualifying parameters spelled out by the institution.

Single residents who are new to the area may desire individual space rental because it reduces their dependence on a particular roommate. Some institutions are now considering renting apartments either by the unit or by the space. There is an understandable temptation to vary rates depending upon institutional financial risk. However, if families are accommodated anywhere within the complex, care should be taken not to violate the Fair Housing Act by creating different rates for the same or similar facilities based on familial status.

Early Move-In and "As-Is" Acceptance

On some campuses apartment managers are faced with high demand and insufficient resources to prepare all apartments when needed. Incoming student families sometimes arrive early. All of this sometimes results in students requesting to move in prior to the completion of routine maintenance and/or cleaning. The concept of early move-in can be an attractive one, assuming outstanding issues are cosmetic and not life or safety related. Advantages include improved occupancy statistics, cost avoidance by not having to pay cleaners to prepare an apartment, and more seamless transitions between residents. There are also the perceived advantages of not having to worry about poor paint and flooring conditions, since these situations usually call for accepting the apartment in an "as-is" condition.

Potential problems arise because of several issues. First, the excellent opportunity to perform preventive maintenance at turnover may be lost, which can avoid a tremendous amount of follow-up maintenance calls during tenancy. Also, if a preventive maintenance checklist is followed, cost savings can be realized through energy- and utility-saving measures such as stopping water leaks, checking appliances, and adjusting heating controls.

Second, residents are inclined to believe that accepting an apartment "as is" means that they are relieved from the obligation of keeping conditions clean and sanitary during occupancy. Preexisting conditions from the previous residents, such as pest infestations, pet odors or damage, or recurring mold or mildew problems, are much harder to solve in an occupied apartment.

Third, the chance to observe, inspect, and repair major deficiencies—which could lead to a loss of a valid "certificate of occupancy"—is decreased by missing the opportunity to make proper modifications at turnover. This can result in residents with-holding rent, lawsuits, and increased landlord/tenant disputes.

If events dictate that "as-is" leasing is unavoidable, property managers are strongly urged to protect themselves with a simple cleaning waiver, to be signed by the new resident. For example:

> In consideration for providing me early possession of my assigned apartment, I accept the apartment in its current "as-is" condition. I understand that I may sub-mit maintenance requests for any broken or nonfunctioning item. However, I ac-cept full responsibility for cleaning. Additionally, upon vacating, I will leave the apartment in a clean and orderly condition as outlined in (*pamphlet or brochure*), which I have received. I also understand that university personnel may perform a routine inspection of the apartment during the next two weeks to identify needed repairs.

Lead-Based Paint Requirements

Because of increasing awareness of the dangers of lead-based paint (LBP), espe-cially to children, new U. S. requirements have been established in recent years by the Environmental Protection Agency (EPA) and HUD which impact the sale, rental, or renovation of residential property. Since September 6, 1996, residential property man-agers have been required to provide renters with information regarding the existence of LBP in all residential construction built before 1978. All rental applicants and renewing residents must receive (a) a government pamphlet on lead paint hazards (*Protect Your Family from Lead in Your Home,* EPA747-K-94-001, May 1995; U. S. Environmental Protection Agency, 1996), (b) a disclosure form detailing any lead paint hazards in the apartment community, and (c) easy access to reports that describe lead paint hazards within the community (Walsh, 1996a). Property managers are required to have each adult renter acknowledge receipt of the LBP disclosure form by signature, and to have available a summary of all testing which has been done on the unit or complex prior to occupancy. Complete test results must be provided if requested.

There are tough penalties for noncompliance, including civil fines up to $10,000 per violation, criminal fines up to $10,000 per violation, and triple damages for appli-cants or residents who successfully sue for a lead-based paint injury. There are four ex-ceptions for noncompliance (Walsh, 1996a):

1. No lead exists in the apartment community, as verified by a state-certified lead paint inspector. Call (800) 424-LEAD for a list of certified inspectors.

2. The apartment community is for the elderly or disabled.

3. Accommodations are efficiencies or rooms (since children are unlikely to be present), which exempts most residence hall operations.

4. When nonrenewable leases of 100 days or less are used.

College and university housing managers should take the initiative to determine conclusively the presence of LBP in the communities they manage, especially if there is any chance that children might be present. Should LBP be encountered, approaches toward removal or encapsulation may vary widely, and different measures may be cho-sen to deal with chewable surfaces (below five feet) as opposed to other surfaces. However, only EPA-certified and -trained contractors and personnel may perform any remediation techniques.

Additionally, for all buildings built before 1978, the EPA issued new rules on June 1, 1998, that govern renovation projects. These new rules went into effect as of June 1, 1999. Compliance requires communication and paperwork, and is intended to put residents on notice whenever the dangers of LBP are increased.

All residents must receive the same pamphlet provided during the reservation or leasing process, and either they must sign an acknowledgment that they received the pamphlet or staff must certify that they were delivered. Fines for violating these rules can run as high as $25,000 per violation per day and include the possibility of imprisonment.

Renovation is described as "the modification of any existing structure, or portion thereof, that results in disturbance of painted surfaces" (Walsh, 1998b, p. 2). Simple painting when there is no scraping or sanding probably does not fall under the definition of renovation. However, scraping or sanding is common practice when painting, which obviously disturbs painted surfaces and should be considered covered by the new rules. The EPA was expected to provide guidance on this and other issues early in 1999.

The required information must be distributed prior to commencing any renovation project after June 1, 1999, but no more than 60 days in advance. The LBP pamphlet must be given to at least one adult resident of each apartment, either by mail or by hand delivery. Presumably, most will also want to include an explanatory letter describing the project and the possibility that the work may disturb lead-based paint, and that as required, a copy of the EPA pamphlet is enclosed.

If mailed, U. S. Postal Service certificates verifying the mailing at least seven days in advance are required and should be filed for safekeeping. Hand delivery involves more paperwork, as each resident must sign an acknowledgment form stating that it was received before the renovation work began. If the resident is not home, or signature is refused, the staff member must sign the form indicating the pamphlet was left. When renovating a common area, delivering the pamphlet is not required, but every resident in the community must receive a letter informing them of the renovations and telling them that the pamphlet is available. Again, documentation of efforts is important, but it is not necessary to get signatures from each resident for common area renovations.

Those responsible for complying with these rules are the "renovators" of the apartments and/or common areas. If employees of the institution handle the work, then, of course, the institution becomes the actual renovator required to comply with the procedures. However, if an outside firm is contracted to do the work, it is actually up to the contractor to distribute the required information to the housing office and to the appropriate residents. There are six exceptions for noncompliance (Walsh, 1996a, 1998a):

1. No lead exists in the apartment community, as verified by a state-certified lead paint inspector. Call (800) 424-LEAD for a list of certified inspectors.

2. The apartment community is for the elderly or disabled.

3. Accommodations are efficiencies or rooms (since children are unlikely to be present), which exempts most residence hall operations.

4.   Needed repairs are minor, including minor electrical work and plumbing that disrupt two square feet or less of painted surface per component.

5.   Needed repairs are in response to an emergency, where work must occur as the result of a sudden, unexpected event posing a health or safety issue.

6.   Renovations are performed as part of a lead abatement project.

Occupancy Restrictions and Limits

It makes sense to identify in advance all occupants of the apartment and their affiliation with each other and with the institution, since placement of families not only depends on their preferences and apartment availability, but also is influenced by the apartment and family size. Most campuses require full-time institutional affiliation (student or staff). In a family housing operation, other occupants must be a spouse, partner, or legal dependent of the student. It is not uncommon for some restrictions to be placed on the maximum duration for occupancy. Many institutions also require all adults in the household to sign the contractual agreement as additional leverage to help ensure full compliance with all terms and conditions. For example, the University of Michigan Family Housing lease agreement (1997a) stipulates the following:

> Lessee shall maintain eligible status throughout the term of the Lease. If the eligible Lessee is married, or in an eligible domestic partnership, his or her spouse/ partner residing in University Housing shall cosign this Lease and thereby assume joint and several liability for the obligations therein. Should Lessee's position be altered to the extent that Lessee fails to maintain eligibility, Lessee immediately must notify the University in writing. At any time following the termination of Lessee's eligible status, the University may terminate this Lease upon thirty days' written notice.

Note that in the event the student withdraws from school, (or an employee is no longer on staff), the obligation is on the resident to notify the housing office, but only the institution may terminate the contract (or "lease" in this case) because of this change. This is simply a way to maximize management options. If rent payments are up to date and there are no other applicants waiting, it may be desirable to allow the current resident to continue occupancy through the end of the contract. This applies equally to both single student and family apartment operations.

By allowing occupancy for those who fall outside institutional eligibility definitions, expense is added for normal wear and tear as well as for any extra utility consumption which may be included in base rent. Regardless of the legitimate size of the household, however, it is still advisable to place an upper limit on the number of occupants for any particular apartment. Beside the facility-related issues just mentioned, this is necessary in order to maintain an acceptable degree of safety.

However, the Fair Housing Act requires maximum occupancy levels to be "reasonable," and not applied in such a way to limit occupancy by families. Occupancy limits must be applied evenly without regard to age of occupants. For example, if a three-person limit is established for a one-bedroom apartment, then a couple with an infant, or a couple with a teenager, or a single parent with two children, all qualify equally based on family size. HUD has recently reaffirmed its own interpretation of "reasonable," which is maximum occupancy limits of no less than two per bedroom (Oetjen,

1998). Substantial documentation to support a lower maximum is strongly suggested, such as exceptionally small bedrooms, local ordinance, and so forth.

Subleasing and Guests

In order to make best use of on-campus apartments for their intended purpose, contractual agreements with residents usually prohibit a sublet. In some cases, it is permitted but only with the approval of the housing office, which ensures that eligibility requirements are met, new occupants receive pertinent information, and records are updated.

Policies regarding visitors within single student operations are usually straightforward. With the possible exception of occasional overnight guests, no others may occupy the apartment. In family housing operations, however, the matter can become more convoluted. Since the purpose of many family housing operations is to help maintain institutional access to nontraditional students, issues of exchanging housing for child care (where apartment size would allow) or accommodating extended family sometimes visiting from other countries, often surface.

Each year at the conference of the Apartments Committee of the Association of College and University Housing Officers-International, there seems to be discussion on how to enforce policies which prohibit residents from taking in "boarders," whether friends or family. The University of Michigan, working with the Residents' Council, developed a policy that actually allows students to register guests for extended stays beyond a month for an extra fee. While this by no means eliminates violations, it permits residents to comply with policy and still have others in their apartment, provides additional leverage when violators are identified, and provides relief to the community in terms of extra revenue for the extra resources consumed by long-term guests (University of Michigan Family Housing, 1997b; see Appendix A).

Damage and Cleaning Assessments

Excessive cleaning or repairs (beyond normal wear) should be built into the base rent for all residents. Since the majority of residents provide reasonable care for the premises during occupancy, the extra costs for damages and repairs should be passed on only to those responsible. The guiding principal is to spell out in advance the expectations and general basis for cost assessment. Let residents know what they are responsible to maintain, what inspectors will look for when vacating, and how much they will be charged. Encourage residents to be present for the final inspection and explain up front the appeal process, in the event they feel they have been treated unfairly. If a high dollar figure is expected for cleaning or damage charges, make sure photographs or a videotape is taken, so there is little doubt about the actual conditions in the apartment.

If charges are withheld from a security deposit, it is particularly important to make sure legal counsel reviews the process. Local, state, or provincial legislation may include a prescribed protocol to follow, exclusions on using deposit money for cleaning expenses, definitions of "damage," and so forth.

A major key in defining damage and cleaning charges, which must always reflect actual average costs and never include any punitive amounts, is the condition of the apartment upon check-in. This forms the baseline from which changes in the condition may be measured. The best system is for a staff member to actually accompany the new resident to the apartment and inspect the facilities together for missing items, needed repairs, or cleaning. Signatures from both residents and staff at the time on a report help provide a high level of clarity and the assurance that the report is completed and returned in a timely fashion. Unfortunately, many operations do not have the resources for this process, especially during summer turn-around when 100 apartments a month or more may be assigned to new residents in larger operations.

Alternatively, the report should be explained to the resident at check-in. Have the resident acknowledge, along with the receipt of keys, that they are also in receipt of the condition report and that they understand that failure to return the report by a specified date shall indicate all furnishings are present and the apartment is fully functional and clean. When the report is returned to the housing office, validate one copy and return it to the resident, explaining that it should be kept for their records for their proof of delivery.

Fairness, consistency, and due process, along with protection of institutional assets, are important elements in establishing a process with integrity. Compromise will often come into play when considering appeals. If, in the judgment of management, there is no justifiable basis for the appeal, it is nevertheless more cost effective at times to settle for a reduced amount. This goodwill gesture often improves the last impression for the vacating residents, generates quick payment, and reduces effort associated with possible further appeals.

Abandonment

Within landlord-tenant law, "abandonment" is a legal term referring to the condition when residents vacate the premises without notice, usually prior to the end of the term. It may be helpful to define the rights and responsibilities of both parties in such cases within the contract. The main issue from the management perspective is whether or not to repossess the apartment and prepare it for a new resident. However, changing the locks too soon can be costly if the resident later returns and files suit for an illegal "lockout."

The key is to do some investigative work and collect hard evidence before changing the locks. A checklist, developed in advance, reviewed by legal counsel, and supported by the institution, should be used to help determine if it is reasonable to reclaim the apartment. This checklist should include such items as: (a) past due rent, (b) unsuccessful efforts to contact resident, (c) comments from friends or neighbors about the residents moving, (d) vehicles missing from the parking lot, (e) disconnected utilities, (f) uncollected mail, (g) removal of personal items (especially items with high value), (h) children no longer enrolled in school, (i) spoiled food.

How many of these items are necessary to warrant reclaiming possession of the apartment? Unfortunately, there is no clear answer, as this will depend on the strength of the evidence and the laws of your state or province. However, relying upon only one or two of these is risky. Relying on any number of them, as long as rent is up to date, can also involve a fair amount of risk. (See Appendix B for sample court cases relating to illegal lockouts; Walsh, 1997).

Explaining institutional policy on this subject in the contract can only help if problems later develop. Again, from the University of Michigan Family Housing lease agreement (1997a):

> If the Lessee is physically absent from the apartment and owes unpaid rent, and if the University has reason to believe in good faith that Lessee has vacated the apartment with no intent to continue Lessee's residence, then the apartment will be deemed conclusively to have been abandoned by Lessee. In addition to any other of its remedies, the University may enter into abandoned premises to perform decorating and repairs and to relet the apartment . . . A determination that the premises have been abandoned shall also constitute a conclusive determination that all personal property of Lessee remaining on the premises has been abandoned. Lessee shall pay to the University any costs associated with removing such personal property from the premises.

Community Rules and Enforcement

Whenever people live in close proximity to one another, especially for residents enduring the rigors of academia, conflicts are apt to occur. The issues of noise (and what constitutes "noise"), use of space, dependent play and conflicts, living habits, and/or cooking habits often come to the forefront for campus apartment managers to resolve. The special academic nature of the community requires that residents maintain their ability to study and sleep according to a variety of schedules. While there must be respect for individual differences in lifestyles, when these conflict with community values, the scales generally are tipped in favor of the community.

The silver lining in responding to conflicts that arise is the opportunity inherent in a "teachable moment." This "moment" usually involves encouraging patience and trying to sense another's perspective. Differences among residents of a campus apartment community often are exactly what make the experience so positive and memorable.

For campuses using a lease and following landlord-tenant laws, some behavior may be a violation of the campus student conduct code as well as the lease, which technically provides options for housing managers. Depending on institutional remedies delineated in the lease, this may be a more prudent and helpful way to respond. Regardless, to the extent possible, community rules, as well as consequences for not abiding by standards, should be clear and incorporated into the contract.

Access and Privacy Issues

Most apartment managers have an interest in balancing a resident's right to privacy with needs to access the apartment when necessary in the operation and/or protection of the premises or occupants. Typically, management reserves the right to enter the premises upon invitation, with reasonable notice, or immediately in matters deemed an "emergency." Let residents know that service requests are interpreted as an invitation by the resident to enter the apartment to effect repairs as soon as possible.

Legal, Safety, and Operational Issues

A good practice is to intrude as little as possible and always leave a notice after entering. Work closely with residents who have special concerns. Be clear when maintenance or pest control procedures are required. Work within the schedules of residents whenever possible. Consider providing a student-staff escort to unfamiliar contractors or those working on a one-time basis before allowing access to occupied apartments.

Use of Premises for Personal Business

The use of state property on public campuses for private gain often is prohibited. When this is the case, limitation on apartment use needs to be clearly stated, since many student families may plan on a child care program or other business out of the home in order to make ends meet. In recent years, with the development of the World Wide Web, a home business is easier than ever for almost anyone, so mention of the policy in the contract is warranted.

If there are no specific regulatory provisions imposed, why not allow residents to pursue business opportunities in their apartments? Prohibiting interference with apartment operations and any disturbance to others makes sense. Requiring residents to use the premises in a quiet, peaceable, and lawful manner, primarily for residential purposes, also has merit. Within these stipulations, however, there is plenty of room for students to earn money at their home.

Recent Health and Safety Issues

Radon Testing

Radon is a naturally occurring radioactive gas that can be present in soil and rocks. It results from radioactive decay of uranium in rocks and soil. Radon concentrates below building foundations and within basements due to differences in air pressure between the soil and the complex. It cannot be seen, smelled or tasted.

Awareness and concern has steadily increased since the U.S. Surgeon General warned that radon is the second leading cause of lung cancer in the United States: "Indoor radon gas is a national health problem. . . . Millions of homes have elevated radon levels. . . . When elevated levels are confirmed, the problem should be corrected" (Benson & Moore, 1997, p. 46). The true magnitude of the health risks associated with radon, however, is controversial. Long-term exposure to elevated levels of radon has been conclusively shown to cause cancer, especially among smokers. Health risks without long-term exposure is not clear (Benson & Moore, 1997).

Regulation of radon in U. S. residential properties exists mainly at the state and local levels. The EPA, the Centers for Disease Control and Prevention, and the Surgeon General all have issued recommendations, and local agencies generally refer to EPA guidelines for testing and remediation. The EPA (U. S. Environmental Protection Agency, 1992) recommends the following testing steps:

Step 1. Take a short-term test with a test kit which displays the phrase "Meets EPA Requirements," or hire an EPA-qualified or state-certified radon testing company to conduct tests for you. If results exceed 4 pCi/L (picocuries per liter), the EPA recommended action level, take a follow-up test (Step 2) to validate accuracy.

Step 2. Follow up with either a long-term test or a second short-term test. If validated results are needed quickly, take a second short-term test. High initial short-term results of more than twice the recommended action level warrant another short-term test for quick validation. For a better understanding of the year-round average radon level, a long-term test is best.

Step 3. Repair or remediation is recommended if the average of the first and second tests is 4 pCi/L or higher.

Apartment repairs in response to high radon levels may involve either passive or active remediation. Passive remediation includes caulking or repairing cracks in basement or ground-level floors, openings around drains or sump pumps, basement wall cracks, gaps around service pipes, and areas where the water supply enters the building. In most instances, these measures will solve most radon levels between 4 and 10 pCi/L.

Active remediation may be required to solve radon levels greater than 10 pCi/L. Active remediation usually involves "sub-slab depressurization," which is a system of pipes and fans which will remove radon gas from below a concrete floor and foundation before it can enter the residence. It is recommended that an EPA or state-certified radon contractor install such a system.

Carbon Monoxide Protocols

Carbon monoxide (CO) is a colorless, odorless, poisonous gas that is a by-product of incomplete combustion of burning fossil fuels such as gas, oil, wood, or coal. In apartments, malfunctioning appliances such as furnaces, ovens, clothes dryers and water heaters usually are the cause of high CO levels. When malfunctioning appliances are not adequately ventilated, the amount of CO in the air may rise to a level that can cause illness or even death. Other CO sources include vehicle exhaust, cigarette smoke, blocked chimney flues, fuel-burning cooking appliances used for heating purposes, and charcoal grills used in unventilated areas.

CO poisoning victims may initially suffer flu-like symptoms including nausea, fatigue, headaches, dizziness, confusion, and breathing difficulties. Elevated blood pressure, cardiac trauma, brain damage, coma, and even death may result from CO poisoning.

At present, there are no federal laws in the United States that require testing for CO. However, Underwriters Laboratories, Inc. (UL), recommends annual inspection of fuel-burning appliances, as well as installation of UL-listed CO detectors outside of sleeping areas and near all fuel-burning appliances (Underwriters Laboratories, Inc., 1994). Additionally, residents should be reminded with some regularity: (a) never to use the oven or stovetop burners for home heating; (b) for apartments with individual furnaces, to be sure to keep the furnace-blower door closed; (c) to use and store all fuel-powered equipment outdoors in well-ventilated areas; and (d) never to use charcoal grills indoors.

When responding to CO poisoning symptoms or an audible alert from a CO detector, service personnel should have immediate access to a CMX-271 confined space meter or equivalent device to measure levels of CO near all possible sources. Staff should receive prior training in the calibration and use of this device. Normal readings should be 0-2 PPM (parts per million). If sustained meter readings are greater than 5

PPM, appliances (or other sources) should be turned off and ventilation provided immediately, and qualified service personnel contacted for emergency repairs.

Asbestos

Asbestos is the common name for a group of naturally occurring minerals that are heat resistant, strong, and flexible, and which last almost forever. These favorable properties resulted in the widespread use of asbestos for many products until the 1970s, including pipe insulation, floor and ceiling tiles, and roof shingles. The mere presence of asbestos does not necessarily represent a health hazard. Hazards arise from damaged and exposed asbestos that is easily powdered and can become airborne.

Asbestos fibers are found almost universally in outdoor air in both urban and suburban areas. Autopsies performed by the Department of Pathology of the University of Michigan have found asbestos in the lung tissue of 100% of the samples taken (University of Michigan Housing Facilities, 1991). Statistics released by the National Safety Council and the EPA indicate that asbestos disease is responsible for only 0.092 deaths per 100,000 per year (University of Michigan Housing Facilities, 1991). The vast majority of people who contract an asbestos-related disease are smokers, as cigarette smoking has a synergistic effect with asbestos. Recent EPA tests determined that asbestos levels in the air in buildings with asbestos-containing materials—regardless of whether those material are in "good" or in "bad" condition—are at or near asbestos levels in outside air (University of Michigan Housing Facilities, 1991).

The EPA recommends that a four-step process be used for asbestos-containing buildings: surveying, ongoing inspections, labeling, and treatment. All four steps should be performed by EPA-certified environmental consulting and remediation contractors, or trained and certified in-house personnel. Labeling provides clear warning to present and future occupants and service staff of the asbestos location.

When an asbestos hazard is found, there are three methods of treating asbestos-containing materials. These are removal, encapsulation (covering the asbestos with a material designed to bond to the exposed asbestos, thereby preventing fiber release), and enclosure (constructing a barrier between the asbestos material and the environment). The method used depends on a number of considerations, including the nature of the particular hazard and the estimated costs for the different approaches.

Since asbestos is probably located in most campus apartment communities, barring complete removal, occasions will continue to arise that require an immediate response. Therefore, it is strongly recommended that arrangements be made in advance for an emergency response plan to address asbestos as a high priority hazard.

Playground Equipment

Recent accidental deaths of children on playgrounds have heightened the awareness of many family housing apartment managers and risk management offices alike. In 1991, the U. S. Consumer Product Safety Commission (CPSC) dramatically revised standards previously published in 1981. Most playground equipment manufactured before 1991 no longer meets CPSC guidelines. Removal, repair, or replacement is recommended (U. S. Consumer Products Safety Commission, 1991a).

The standards were established to improve safety for children and, therefore, risk exposure can be significant if children are injured on equipment that does not meet CPSC guidelines. The new guidelines also set standards for surfacing below and around play equipment, as well as the design of the playground environment. The Playground Audit Guide (U. S. Consumer Product Safety Commission, 1991b) is a useful tool for apartment managers to evaluate all aspects of a playground. It uses a priority system to identify actions needed for upgrading.

The *Guide* recommends that an audit sheet be completed for every piece of equipment and every playground. These reports should be kept on file for the life of the equipment and play area. After the audit is completed and playgrounds upgraded, regular inspections are recommended so that deficiencies can be identified and addressed in a timely fashion.

Also since 1991, Federal guidelines stemming from the Americans with Disabilities Act (ADA) have mandated that new and renovated facilities open to the public must be accessible to individuals with disabilities (Christoph, 1997). New guidelines currently under consideration contain further strict recommendations regarding playground surfacing and play equipment access. If adopted, this will clearly impact anyone planning, building, or renovating playgrounds. Surfacing, ramps, and transfer points are all to be addressed to help ensure a safe and accessible environment for all. Further information on proposed guidelines can be obtained by contacting the Office of Technical and Information Services, Architectural and Transportation Barriers Compliance Board, 1331 F Street, N.W., Suite 1000, Washington, DC 20004-1111; (202) 272-5434, extension 34.

Windows and Screens

Many local communities have ordinances regarding windows and/or screens. These may include:

1. Window openings must be of a specific size.
2. A specific number of locks is required.
3. Windows must be lockable in an open position.
4. Windows must not be able to be lifted out of place from the outside.
5. Screens must be easily removed for evacuation purposes.

Some of these requirements may be applicable only to first-floor windows, or windows in the sleeping areas of basements. Apartment managers should be familiar with applicable codes and regulations for compliance.

An all-too-common problem experienced by those renting to families with small children is the occurrence of a child leaning against a screen and tumbling out when the screen does not hold the child's weight. This can be catastrophic when it occurs from a second-floor window or higher. Some manufacturers have begun placing warning stickers on screens to alert parents to the potential danger. Apartment managers also should issue frequent warnings about such possibilities to parents of small children, emphasizing the following points:

1. Do not leave small children unattended in rooms with open windows.
2. Avoid placing pieces of furniture directly under windows.

3. Utilize locks that secure a window in a partially open position, preventing it from opening wide enough for a child to slip through.

4. Do not underestimate a child's ability.

5. Remember that window screens are intended to keep insects and other pests out; they are not designed to keep children in.

Halogen Lamps

Halogen lamps, by design, generate a tremendous amount of heat. As a result, campus housing has had its share of fires ignited by torchiere-style (floor-standing) halogen lamps, which have either fallen or have been too close to combustible materials.

The U.S. CPSC (1997) has issued a warning to consumers that halogen tubular light bulbs in most torchiere-style lamps can reach temperatures of 976 to 1200 degrees F. In 1996, the CPSC received reports of 189 fires and 11 deaths related to these lamps. In contrast, incandescent bulbs can reach from 260 to 340 degrees F (U. S. Consumer Product Safety Commission, 1997).

A recent survey of 120 large colleges and universities indicates that 63% already ban torchiere-style halogen lamps, and another 19% intend to do so. Some institutions ban only 500-watt halogen bulbs. Underwriters Laboratories, Inc., issued a bulletin on April 2, 1996, urging consumers to replace 500-watt bulbs in torchiere lamps with 300-watt halogen bulbs. Underwriters Laboratories, Inc., now restricts manufacturers to a maximum 300-watt bulb and several new safety features in lamps made since May, 1996. However, lots of older-style lamps are still in use (Underwriters Laboratories, Inc., 1996). For a sample of the University of Maryland's World Wide Web posting regarding halogen lamps, see http://www.inform.umd.edu/DES/fire/halogen2/htm.

Child Abuse and Neglect

When a young child who cannot adequately care for him- or herself is left unattended and the situation is brought to the attention of staff, it sometimes poses a dilemma. Intervening may be interpreted negatively by the parent or guardian, perhaps alleging overreaction, insensitivity to cultural differences, or maybe even a Fair Housing Act violation. Doing nothing, however, could result in injury to the child with possible institutional liability.

For apartment housing operations, clear language describing acceptable norms for child supervision should be articulated. From the University of Michigan publication, *Your Guide to Family Housing* (1997b):

> The care and safety of residents' children is of the utmost importance to the Family Housing community. Children may not be left for any period of time without adult supervision. Parents are held responsible at all times for the behavior of their children. The University retains the right to use all available Lease provisions and to cooperate with any local or state agency when cases of child neglect or abuse are made known.

Walsh (1998b) suggested four steps in responding to such situations:

Step 1. Take the child home and make contact with the parents. An unsupervised child should be approached carefully and asked where he or she lives. Explain to the parents the concern for the safety of children and the community behavior standards that may apply. If the child is not able to communicate where he or she lives, or the parents are not home, proceed to Step 3 and follow up with the parents later.

Step 2. Contact the parents in writing. Serious first occurrences, or less serious repeated occurrences should result in written follow-up. The letter should stress the circumstances of the incident, the concerns with safety, the seriousness with which the incident is viewed by management, and the possible consequences should this behavior continue.

Step 3. Contact Social Services, Child Protection Services and/or the local police authority. If the letter is not sufficient to prevent child neglect from reoccurring, and/or supervision is needed and the parent or guardian is not available, make this call! The child's safety is the primary concern, and safety oversight should be provided by those most equipped to respond, not property managers. In some locations, managers with knowledge of child abuse may be *required* to notify appropriate authorities.

Step 4. Terminate the residents' contract for the apartment. On what grounds? This is where a policy directly listing child neglect is particularly useful. Without this, consider the "quiet enjoyment" clause if the child was causing a disturbance. Additionally, parents who neglect their children are probably breaking the law, so if there is a provision barring illegal activity, that could also be applicable. Check with legal counsel for guidance. Doing nothing further when incidents continue puts the child at risk and increases institutional liability.

The primary goal in responding to unsupervised children is to place their safety in the hands of their parents. Additionally, if necessary, it is important to demonstrate that management has responded reasonably to all known potentially hazardous situations.

Domestic Violence

This is another sad crime that managers of family housing operations sometimes face. It seems that residents who are victims of domestic violence are turning more and more to the apartment managers of the communities where they live for assistance, which may become particularly challenging if the alleged perpetrator is the student and the victim is the spouse or partner.

There are two general proactive measures campus apartment managers should establish. First, confirm that existing language in the campus student conduct document and/or contract provisions are crystal clear about zero tolerance for violence, and that it applies to all residents, not just student residents. Violence should be defined as broadly as possible, to include not only physical and sexual assault, but also dating violence, domestic violence, stalking, threats, intimidation, and indecent exposure, whether against family members, visitors, or other residents, and whether conducted in person, or via telephone, facsimile, or computer transmissions.

Secondly, work with local reporting and support agencies to determine the known frequency of reports, existing protocol and support services, and advice on difficult situations. Consider tapping these resources for staff training and educating residents about what to do if they suspect violence within the community.

There is one situation where appropriate response by apartment managers is fairly clear. This is when a resident presents a "restraining order." This is a written order issued by a court mandating one person to stay away from another. This often provides the main shield a person has for protection against a violent spouse, and staff should go out of their way to honor and help enforce the order. Specifically:

1. Get a copy. Ask the resident to show it to you. Copy it and keep it on file.

2. Verify the order is genuine. It should be signed and dated by a judge, and the phone number of the court should be listed.

3. Ask the resident for a photograph and description of who is identified on the order. Make copies and keep them on file.

4. Alert staff. If a resident shows the property manager a restraining order, and it is verified as authentic, merely placing the information in the resident's file is not a reasonable response. Send a memo, with photo and description, to the security team, office and maintenance staff, resident managers, and others working on site who may have occasion to see this individual. Provide them with the expiration date of the restraining order, the apartment address, and instructions to call the police and warn the resident if they see the person in the community.

5. When the current restraining order expires, contact the resident to verify if a new one has been obtained.

6. Change locks promptly if requested by the resident. This may be a difficult situation if the person named on the restraining order is a resident also listed on a lease document. However, in most situations, there is more to worry about providing reasonable protection to the resident, especially after being placed on notice, than about an allegation of an illegal lockout or unlawful eviction. Consult with legal counsel on this one.

Conclusion

Campus apartment managers can afford to ignore the impact of health, safety and legal issues on their operations about as much as a truck driver can ignore the center dividing line on the highway. While there may be more safety cushions for the apartment manager than for the truck driver, including more resources for assistance, the manager is nonetheless also at the wheel. The manager guides the direction for campus operations, dealing with the potholes, hills, and curves every day. Detours and delays have to be artfully negotiated with both the shippers and the investors. Delivering the precious cargo on time, on budget, and in one piece, is not as easy as it sounds to anyone who is not doing the actual driving.

The rewards, however, are significant. When the destination is finally reached and the manager can say good-bye to the residents who came along for the ride, it creates a certain sense of satisfaction. To know that someone's academic pursuits were within reach because of the "transportation" provided, and that what they learned along the way is likely to be as lasting as what was gained in the classroom, is a special feeling indeed.

Acknowledgments

The author would like to thank Daniel Halloran, University of Michigan, and David Stoddard, Oklahoma State University, for their assistance and advice in writing this chapter.

References

Benson, D. J., & Moore, G. K. (1997, August). Assessing radon concerns in residential properties. *Multifamily executive.* Yardley, PA: MGI Publications.

Christoph, N. J. (1997, April). Planning accessible play facilities. *American school and university.* Overland Park, KS: Primedia Intertec.

Goss, R. C., & Johnson, M. K. (1994). *Legal issues and fair housing for property managers.* Paper presented at the Multi-Housing World Convention of the National Council of the Multifamily Housing Industry of the National Association of Home Builders, Atlanta, GA.

Oetjen, S. (1998, June). *UNITS.* Alexandria, VA: National Apartment Association.

Underwriters Laboratories, Inc. (1994). *Questions and answers about carbon monoxide and CO detectors.* Northbrook, IL: Author.

Underwriters Laboratories, Inc. (1996, April 2). *News release.* [On-line]. Available: http://www.ul/com/about/newsrel/nr-halo.htm

U. S. Consumer Product Safety Commission. (1991a). *Handbook for public playground safety.* Washington, DC: U. S. Government Printing Office.

U. S. Consumer Product Safety Commission. (1991b). *Playground audit guide.* Washington, DC: U. S. Government Printing Office.

U. S. Consumer Product Safety Commission. (1997). *Shedding the light on halogen lamps.* Washington, DC: U. S. Government Printing Office.

U. S. Environmental Protection Agency. (1992). *A citizen's guide to radon.* Washington, DC: U. S. Government Printing Office.

U. S. Environmental Protection Agency. (1996). *Compliance assistance approach to lead-based paint disclosure requirements* (Section 1018). Washington, DC: U. S. Government Printing Office.

University of Michigan Family Housing. (1997a). *Lease agreement.* Ann Arbor, MI: University of Michigan.

University of Michigan Family Housing. (1997b). *Your guide to family housing.* Ann Arbor, MI: University of Michigan.

Legal, Safety, and Operational Issues ———————

University of Michigan Housing Facilities. (1991). *Q & A: Asbestos* (revised) Ann Arbor, MI: University of Michigan.

University of Michigan Housing Facilities. (1995). *Response procedures: Carbon monoxide issues.* Ann Arbor, MI: University of Michigan.

Walsh, M. M. (1996a, May). Follow new lead paint disclosure rules, avoid tough penalties. *Professional apartment management.* New York: Brownstone.

Walsh, M. M. (1996b, December). How to deal with residents threatened with domestic violence. *Professional apartment management.* New York: Brownstone.

Walsh, M. M. (1997, August). Use "abandonment checklist" to decide whether to change locks of absent residents. *Professional apartment management.* New York: Brownstone.

Walsh, M. M. (1998a, December). How to comply with new lead paint rules when renovating. *Professional apartment management.* New York: Brownstone.

Walsh, M. M. (1998b, December). Take four steps in dealing with unsupervised children. *Professional apartment management.* New York: Brownstone.

Appendix A

University of Michigan Family Housing (1997b)
Friend and Family Visitation Policy

This Policy was established primarily in the interest of child care, and is different from the Sublet Policy because it allows residents to have additional occupants reside with them while the Lessee resides in the apartment as well. However, since increased occupancy increases operating expenses, residents with occupants other than dependents identified on the Housing application are expected to pay an additional fee. In this way, additional residents will have minimum impact on future rent increases.

There is no charge for visitors staying less than four weeks per year. By the end of the four weeks, however, residents are expected to register their visitor(s) at the Family Housing Office and pay the fee of $30 per additional visitor, per month. There is no time limit for how long visitors may reside with eligible residents. However, visitors beyond four weeks will not be approved if maximum occupancy for the apartment is exceeded or if there is no child residing in the apartment. Residents may request a variance to this policy by submitting in writing specific circumstances to the Director of Family Housing.

Failure to register a visitor by the end of four weeks will result in a service charge of $75 to the resident, plus prorated visitation charges. Once registered, guests are entitled to most of the same access to Family Housing programs, services and facilities as other residents.

Division of Student Affairs — University Housing
The University of Michigan

Appendix B

Sample Cases Relating to Illegal Lockouts (Walsh, 1997b)

Example One: A Connecticut owner thought that a resident had abandoned the apartment. So, in the last week of July, the owner changed the locks and let painters paint the apartment. But the resident had paid the July rent. The resident returned and sued the owner for illegally locking her out.

The owner claimed he reasonably believed the resident had abandoned the apartment. But, since rent had been paid to the end of the month, the court said the owner couldn't treat the apartment as abandoned and thus was guilty of a lockout. It ordered the owner to pay a penalty of twice the monthly rent (Denino v. Valenti).

Example Two: After repeated attempts to phone and visit a missing resident without success, a New York City owner changed the locks. The resident returned and sued the owner for locking her out. The court ruled that the owner had acted illegally and the resident should be allowed back into her apartment. The owner didn't have enough evidence to conclude that the resident had abandoned the apartment, the court said (Mitchell v. City of New York).

Example Three: Two Delaware residents left their apartment with rent unpaid. About three weeks later, a manager entered and noticed broken and badly soiled furniture. Also, the refrigerator and cupboards were full of moldy, rotten food. The owner thought the residents had left for good, so he changed the locks and cleaned out the apartment.

The residents returned and claimed that they'd just gone to visit relatives in Pennsylvania. They sued the owner for locking them out. The owner claimed they'd abandoned the apartment so he couldn't be liable. A court ruled that even though the condition of the apartment and the furniture created an 'inference' that the apartment had been abandoned, the owner should have formally evicted the residents (Drylie v. Woods).

Facilities Management

Todd Pignataro
Assistant Director of Housing

John Ringle
Assistant Director of Housing
Utah State University

Facilities Management

Facilities management of campus housing has become more complex as operations are faced with the dilemma of aging buildings and increased competition with off-campus providers. If housing administrators fail to innovate and provide quality service to the resident, they will be outpaced by competition and eventually outsourced by their own operations. Mandatory residency requirements are short-term solutions that ignore the core problems within operations and facilities. Professionals must be willing and able to compete with both the private sector and other institutions for student residents.

By developing facilities management programs that focus on service and quality, administrators can provide a major advantage to the housing department. This requires both new thinking and cooperation with administration and residence life. This chapter will examine some of the keys to change within the facilities management area.

Human Resources

Employee interactions and high levels of cooperation become key components of an effective service delivery strategy between the physical facilities staff and residence life personnel. Providing as many opportunities as possible for understanding each staff's respective responsibilities, worldviews/perspectives, and expectations from supervisors is a primary management goal. Some institutions have elected to designate staff liaisons to meet on a biweekly basis (or as needed, should particular circumstances dictate) to discuss issues that arise, situations that occur, vandalism that must be addressed, and so forth, and often simply to share a beverage and donut together. Information from these meetings is disseminated to respective staff in order to ensure an informed view for all concerned. Staff (one resident assistant, one housing representative, one maintenance worker, one quality control person) also are cross-associated every semester to perform quality inspections and safety checks, assess cleanliness standards, conduct required testing and minor or routine maintenance adjustments, and issue relevant citations for policy or safety violations as needed. The process is cooperative, mutually supportive, and effective. These are only a few examples of ongoing opportunities to build bridges of cooperation, ownership, and understanding between cross-departmental work teams that have the interests of the residents and their facilities uppermost in their work-related assignments.

Employee selection in facilities management departments presents several challenges. Due to the wide range of responsibility within the department, a variety of skills and skill levels are required. Identifying these skills and objectively evaluating potential candidates helps assure the success of the department and reduce employee turnover. A variety of selection techniques exist for evaluating potential candidates. One of the most effective of these tools is the comprehensive structured interview (Harris, 1989). The comprehensive structured interview combines job simulation, job knowledge, and situational questions into one tool for selection.

Employee Selection

Regardless of the technique used in the selection process, a few concepts are universal. The first step in designing an employee-screening device is job analysis. This analysis identifies the key requirements of each position in the organization (Conway,

Goodman & Jako, 1995). The next step involves deciding how much structure to build into the process and formulating relevant questions. Research has shown that by introducing high levels of structure the interview process can be significantly improved (McDaniel, Whetzel, Schmidt, & Maurer, 1994). It is also important to determine how applicants will be evaluated, and by whom. Consensus should be reached with regard to a method of rating. The final step is to train evaluators on use of the interview tool and on proper interviewing techniques. This assures that evaluators follow the necessary procedures so that bias or misunderstanding is minimized.

In order to analyze positions within the physical facilities department, both supervisors and front-line workers are asked to identify all tasks associated with their daily job responsibilities. These tasks are then grouped into several key categories, then ranked in order of importance by the staff, and verified by the work order database. After this process is complete, appropriate interview questions can be developed that are associated with the job description. The process provides insight as to whether job descriptions of the operation accurately reflect the work being performed by each category of worker.

After each position has been analyzed, the comprehensive structured interview tool can be created. The format includes questions pertaining to job knowledge, job-related situational questions, and job simulation. High levels of structure eliminate bias and assure that the most qualified candidate is selected. Anchored scales should be used to help standardize the selection process.

The comprehensive structured interview is developed to automatically weight the job categories relative to importance for job performance. For example, the job analysis process at Utah State University indicated that a maintenance job consisted of tasks that involved plumbing (an average of 26% of tasks), HVAC (26%), electric (22%), appliance repair (17%), and carpentry related (9%). Therefore, 26% of the questions are plumbing related, 26% are HVAC, 22% are electric, and so forth. This weights the interview toward the most important job tasks. Two types of scales are used for rating responses by the evaluators. Questions in the first section are either right or wrong. The next sections are rated on a scale of one to seven due to the fact that the questions can be partially right, and some answers can be more complete than others, depending on the experience level of the candidate. One question is included that allows the evaluator the opportunity to rate a situational response relating to customer service. Finally, space is provided for the evaluator's comments and total score. All selections are made based on the highest acceptable total score.

The next step in the development process is to establish an answer key to all questions. This is accomplished by involving a panel of supervisors and workers. Lists of answers are developed and minimum acceptable scores established. For complex questions, checklists are developed and points are given for the number of items discussed by the applicant from those lists. Examples of good and poor answers are provided on the key. This eliminates the necessity for evaluators to have extensive knowledge of all positions and job responsibilities.

The final step in implementation of the interview process is evaluator training. The objective of this training is to acquaint all evaluators with the selection technique being used. Also, training in general interviewing skills is provided. Interviewers serve on the selection committee for a full calendar year. Training consists of an eight-hour training seminar focusing on institutional and departmental hiring requirements, use of the comprehensive structured interview, and general interviewing techniques.

The comprehensive structured interview presents an objective format for evaluating candidates. The high levels of structure improve the validity of the process. By having interviewers serve for one year, the process is professionalized and consistent, and most bias is eliminated. Any time that service is the primary responsibility of an operation, it becomes imperative that the best employees are selected. This helps improve the quality of the service provided and reduces expenses associated with turnover and training.

Employee Evaluation and Training

In any operation, it is important to provide ongoing feedback to employees. The evaluation is one formal method to provide feedback and to establish expectations associated with job performance. Although standardized evaluations are often difficult to use and may not achieve the desired results, they may still be useful as a starting point. At Utah State University, the facilities department has developed an evaluation tool that makes the process of evaluation more useful and relevant. This tool is a comprehensive list of job tasks that are related to each position within the department. The evaluations are subdivided into three primary categories for nonsupervisory personnel. These categories are performance of duties (80%), safety and chemicals (5%), and customer service (15%). For supervisors, the categories are performance of duties (60%), safety and chemicals (5%), customer service (15%), and supervision of staff (20%).

The first step in the development of the evaluation tool is the same as in the development of the interview, that is, job analysis. During this step, supervisors and frontline workers list in detail the tasks for each job in the physical facilities department. These lists include everything from mopping floors to work attendance. Daily tasks vary from position to position. However, the safety, customer service, and supervisory expectations are the same for all employees regardless of department. These detailed lists become the basis for evaluation.

The next step in forming the evaluation tool is to apply an anchored scale to each task and expectation. After each main responsibility grouping, space remains for supervisor and employee comments. During an evaluation, the supervisor rates the performance of the employee for each job task. This provides structure to the evaluation and allows managers to comment on individual job tasks instead of making generalizations.

The final step is to average the scores in each of the main groupings of tasks. These averages are then weighted to reflect their importance to the overall job. For example, if customer service is 15% of each job then the score for each employee in this category represents 15% of their total score. Individual scores within a particular department are then averaged to establish standard performance within a department. Those employees outside of this range are either above standard or below standard according to their scores. Since employees are evaluated on job tasks, it is easy for the facilities managers to rate specific job performance and provide relevant feedback to the employee. By looking for low overall ratings within department scores, specific areas can be identified where standards need to be improved. Low overall ratings also help identify training needs and objectives for the department.

Quality Control and Inspection

In order to assure that the condition of all facilities meets the quality standards set by the department, it is essential that some form of quality control be established. The entire housing operation must support the concept of establishing benchmarks for quality and not wavering from those standards. Furthermore, the standard of quality continually should be pushed higher, so that apartment turnover becomes increasingly easier as overall conditions improve within the facilities.

Quality Control

In order to establish quality measures, all departments within the housing operation must be involved. The initial quality standard should be set and agreed on by all. It is important to listen to the customer and maintenance staff when developing a benchmark. Ongoing quality complaints by tenants should be addressed as a priority. The maintenance staff is also a good resource. They are aware of many of the work order-related items that are typical as new tenants occupy apartments. If apartments do not meet this standard then they should be taken off-line until they are able to do so, regardless of occupancy rate or demand. Without this level of operational commitment, it is impossible to assure improved quality levels.

After the establishment and definition of the quality standard, it is necessary to develop some sort of checklist to help standardize inspection. Staff training is important and the number of individuals involved in the inspection process should be limited. The subjective nature of the quality standard must be eliminated whenever possible. It is helpful to separate the quality control department from maintenance and give them full authority to determine when quality levels have been met. This eliminates any conflicts of interest and helps maintain the integrity of the quality control effort.

Inspection

After residents have occupied the facilities, some form of ongoing inspection helps maintain the quality of the apartments. Semesterly or quarterly inspections provide an opportunity for residence life and physical facilities staff to partner in the inspection effort. During these inspections, residence life staff focus on issues relating to health, safety, policy concerns, and contractual violations. At the same time, physical facilities staff focus on ongoing maintenance, custodial, safety, preventative maintenance, and pest control issues. These inspections also provide an excellent opportunity to take carbon monoxide readings, change furnace or air conditioner filters, check fire and safety equipment, document problems, and make the necessary corrections to limit liability.

Facilities Management

Checkouts

Formalized checkouts for residents vacating apartments are important in order to protect investments that the housing department has made in the facilities. As with the quality standard, it is necessary to establish a standard expectation for the return of the apartment by the resident. A significant problem in the housing maintenance environment is the lack of accountability for damage and vandalism. With limited funds available for capital improvements, the failure of administration to enforce reasonable charges is extremely demoralizing and counterproductive to the efforts of the physical facilities department. Many housing operations spend a significant amount of their operating budgets repairing damages left by vacating residents.

The solution is to establish collectively an expectation or standard for the condition of the apartment upon checkout. This expectation should be reasonable and enforceable. Normal wear and tear and acceptable damage levels should be established and standardized. As in the quality control effort, the subjective nature of assessing damage or cleaning charges should be minimized. The best way to accomplish this is through staff training and structured checkout.

Once this has been established, it is critical that this expectation be effectively communicated to residents. Checkout provides another opportunity for residence life staff and physical facilities staff to partner together. By providing good checkouts and enforcing charges for reasonable damages, the bottom line of the housing operation will improve significantly. From a student development perspective, residents learn that there are financial consequences for inappropriate behaviors, activities, and lifestyle choices.

Maintenance

The maintenance department is the core of the physical facilities department. Although many departments within the physical facilities operation interact with tenants, the maintenance department has the most direct contact on an ongoing basis. For this reason, if the maintenance staff is successful, the entire department is successful. To be successful, the department must be focused on the fact that its existence is for customer service. This underlying belief provides the springboard for all other departments. A successful and focused maintenance department is easy to identify because it is supported and defended by tenants as being one of the primary reasons that they choose to live on-campus. Employees in general take pride in the work that they do. Maintenance workers are no exception. Unfortunately, many work order systems hinder the ability of the staff to provide responsive service. Instead, employees take the blame for being unresponsive, unproductive, and ineffective. It is easier for management to place the blame on the worker or the labor union than to take responsibility for systems that are not effective. Common complaints relating to the maintenance department include excessive outstanding work orders, slow service, bad attitudes, and low productivity. In most cases, it is the work order process that is the problem, not the worker or the union.

Dispatch Work Order Process

An analysis of most maintenance work order systems will uncover a process entailing numerous unnecessary steps, inordinate amounts of paper shuffling, and poor prioritization. The focus has been placed on documenting and paperwork rather than on customer service. A typical work order system is diagrammed in Figure 1.

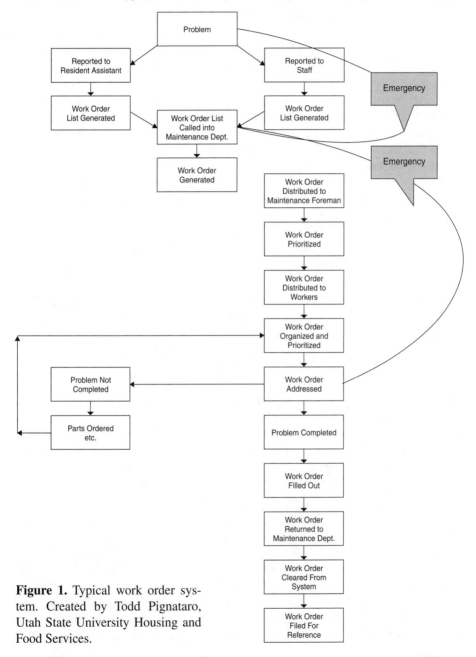

Figure 1. Typical work order system. Created by Todd Pignataro, Utah State University Housing and Food Services.

In this system, most work orders (90%) are responded to within one day of the maintenance worker receiving the work order. The problem is that in the best circumstances, it may take multiple days for the worker to physically get the work order. This, in turn, is very demoralizing and creates negative relationships between the resident life staff, maintenance staff, and tenants. The process usually results in the maintenance department or union taking the majority of the blame for the slow response. The result is a lot of complaints about the abilities and productivity of the department. Many operations seek to set productivity measures, improve prioritization, and implement extensive tracking of outstanding work. Unfortunately, these measures fail to produce any long-term improvements. In order to establish a successful work order system, the maintenance work system must be analyzed. The goal is to provide responsive service, not generate paperwork and reports. Common sense dictates that if the current staff can respond to most work orders within one day then extra help is not the answer. Most likely, the work order system is the problem, not the employee. All unnecessary steps and prioritization must be eliminated. If the work order system does not support one hour or less response to maintenance requests, then it should be changed.

By putting the maintenance system in the perspective of the production environment and applying constraint management techniques this can easily be accomplished. The key is to limit the sequential dependent steps and eliminate variability (Goldratt & Cox, 1992).

In the context of the work order system, this means getting information to the worker as quickly and in as few steps as possible. The flow chart in Figure 2 is an example of this concept.

By applying the principles of constraint management and recognizing the effect of fluctuation on sequential dependent variables, common sense solutions can be found (Goldratt & Cox, 1992). For example, if the time it takes for a maintenance worker to receive notice of a problem involves three steps, and the time required for each step varies from one hour to three days, the process can be significantly shortened and improved by limiting the steps required and the variability in the time necessary for each step. At Utah State University, these concepts have been applied to an extreme. The tenant or resident life staff calls all problems to a dispatcher. The problem is relayed directly to the maintenance worker by radio. The worker responds directly to the request and relays details of work completed back to the dispatcher. The dispatcher enters all necessary work order information into the computer without creating a hard-copy work order. This system replaced a traditional 12- to 15-step system and allows workers to respond to work requests in less than fifteen minutes on average. Productivity is monitored for each worker by tracking the number of calls responded to and average response time in a given period.

Regardless of the work order system adopted, the keys are reducing the steps required to get the work order into the hands of the worker, and eliminating the variability of the time required to do so. Any time that the worker can respond and interact directly with the tenant a great deal of variability can be eliminated. Tenants can communicate problems directly and clearly with staff and eliminate callbacks and confusion. Tenants feel important, and positive relationships with the workers are formed.

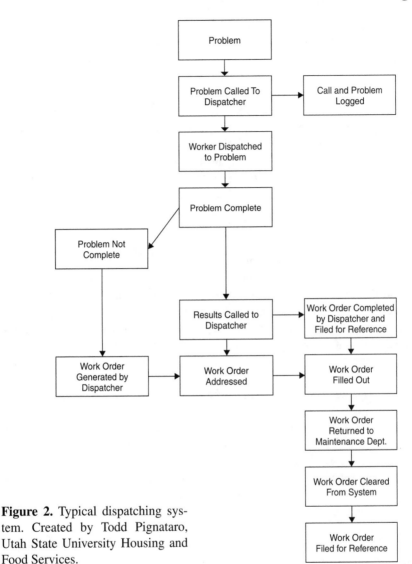

Figure 2. Typical dispatching system. Created by Todd Pignataro, Utah State University Housing and Food Services.

Apartment Turnover

In addition to the daily work order requirements of the facilities department, apartments must be turned over on an ongoing basis. This process is really a production process with the end product being clean, available apartments. As with any product, the overall quality establishes the value associated with the product by the customer. The housing operation must establish a quality standard that identifies the product the facilities department will be producing. This standard establishes the goals and objectives for the facilities department. It also helps determine the performance of the department in general. It is of no benefit to set standards that are vague or variable. Instead, the level of quality agreed upon must be clear, achievable, and absolute.

As in any production process, several objectives are universal in order to be successful and profitable. The first is to increase throughput, that is, increasing the number of apartments turned over in a given period of time. Second, operating costs associated with apartment turnover should be reduced. Third, inventory must be reduced (both the number of available and unavailable apartments in the system). At least two of these must occur simultaneously for success (Goldratt & Cox, 1992).

Many housing managers are obsessed with how quickly a particular apartment is turned over. Productivity standards are set for facilities managers based on number of days required to prepare a particular apartment. These measures are irrelevant and counterproductive. In most cases, quality is sacrificed due to time constraints. The frustration for facilities staff is that this sacrifice must be made to meet productivity standards while other apartments remain clean, ready, and unassigned. This conveys to staff that quality standards really are not that important.

It becomes easier to see the solution by putting the turnover process into the context of production. A successful manufacturer builds for demand, not for inventory. The goal for the facilities department should be to provide clean, quality apartments as needed by tenants. This means that as long as prospective tenants have an apartment, it is insignificant as to how long it took to process it. The answer to the question of how long it takes to prepare an apartment should be however long it takes to meet the quality standard. Some apartments may require hours while others may require months. The assignment process should take place only as apartments become available, not as they vacate. The facilities department should always provide the assignment personnel with clean, available apartments that meet the quality standard as demand dictates. This addresses the production principle of reducing inventory. It also reinforces the commitment to quality to all parties involved in the turnover process.

Throughput relates to moving apartments through the turnover process. One of the primary goals is to increase throughput. Since the steps of the turnover process are sequentially dependent, and their time requirements vary by apartment, there is a compounding negative effect. The solution is twofold. Most important, variation must be eliminated. Bottlenecks must be identified because they will set the pace for output. The amount of support to the bottleneck is adjusted to meet demand. Additional help for the bottleneck or division of tasks will increase the capability of the bottleneck. This will result in higher levels of throughput. By eliminating time constraints for apartment-specific turnover, staff can more effectively perform their duties and easily improve quality. If staff perform their part of the turnover process only when the apartment is ready for them, the overall time spent is considerably shorter. Consequently, the quality of the end product is greatly improved. There is a huge cost associated with sending crews back to an apartment to redo work because they were sent in prematurely. This slows the turnover process to a crawl and creates huge bottlenecks in the system. By allowing crews to work only in apartments that are ready for their services, more apartments are turned over in the same period of time with the same amount of staff.

The successful apartment turnover process should help reduce operating costs. This is accomplished in several ways: (a) by increasing the number of apartments turned over in a given time frame, (b) by limiting the number of clean, empty apartments in the system, (c) by reducing the amount of rework and improving quality, and (d) by increasing customer satisfaction. Standing firm on the quality standard reduces the number of future work orders. During turnover, many preventative maintenance items also can be addressed, reducing subsequent work orders. Standardization of equipment and supplies is another way to reduce maintenance costs and to limit inventory of parts and supplies. Repeat work by all crews is the single most expensive cost associated with the turnover process. Eliminating repeat work will have both immediate and long-term impact on the operating budget of the department.

Preventative Maintenance

For a preventative maintenance program to be effective, a distinction between preventative maintenance and capital improvements must be made. Preventative maintenance should include the regular service of equipment to prolong useful life. Capital improvements include replacing major building components and also can include renovation or replacement of facilities. Items requiring regular service should be identified and service intervals set. A log of required service for each item should be kept to assure standardized service. Equipment manufacturers and outside vendors can provide operating and maintenance manuals to assure that service is provided in accordance with manufacturers' recommendations. Care should be taken to procure service manuals as equipment is replaced or upgraded. This takes the guesswork out of the preventative maintenance service as employees change. Many operations use electronic means for tracking and notifying staff of scheduled service. Another method is simple tracking using manual techniques like calendaring. Preventative maintenance items may require outside contractors, depending on the abilities of the staff and the warranty specifications. Regardless, it is most effective to centralize the responsibility for notification of staff or vendors when service is due. The amount of preventative maintenance required varies with the type and age of equipment. Performance of preventative maintenance as scheduled helps reduce major system failure as well as future work orders.

On-Call Maintenance

An important service for maintenance to provide is after-hours or on-call maintenance. This service has been approached in a variety of ways across the country. Some operations provide service after hours for any maintenance item; others limit service to emergencies only. Staffing strategies range from full-time, on-call-only employees to regular-hours staff rotating on-call responsibility. After-hours service should be consistent with the departmental service strategy.

To determine which strategy or combination is best, the operation must first decide what level of service it wishes to provide to tenants. Costs associated with on-call responsibility should be assessed and should include hidden costs, such as the cost associated with employees taking time off to compensate for on-call hours. Further, on-call hours can significantly impact the overtime portion of the labor budget. After evaluation of these factors, a cost-effective solution can be implemented that is financially feasible. Student employees that are current residents serve as an invaluable resource in providing on-call service. By requiring student staff to live on campus, response time is shortened considerably, thus improving service. Regular staff remain fresh and available to perform daily work tasks.

In addition, unions place constraints on employers who have on-call staff. For example, if a staff member is called in for emergency maintenance or custodial services, overtime is compensated at a minimum number of hours. This guarantees an employee a certain number of hours although the job may only take one hour.

Custodial

Due to the cyclical nature of apartment turnover, the custodial department faces several unique challenges. Staffing to meet high demand creates overstaffing during slower months. Custodial staffs may rely on transient student labor to meet staffing requirements. Anyone who has actually worked in the custodial department knows that custodial work requires a certain level of skill. Due to the transient nature of custodial staff, the department is always in a state of turnover. Employees are continually being trained and retrained. A strong argument can be made that the custodial department requires the best managers in order to cope with constant change. High levels of structure and standardized procedures are necessary to assure that employees clearly understand expectations.

Apartment Turnover

During times of heavy apartment turnover, it is important that the custodial department have clear expectations and understandings of the quality objectives of the department. Since a majority of the staff is transient in nature, it is difficult to assure a high level of understanding and dedication to organizational objectives. High levels of structure and strong managers help mitigate this problem. Checklists and standard cleaning procedures help clarify expectations for student staff and should be developed by permanent staff.

As with any crew involved in the apartment turnover process, the custodial staff should be sent into an apartment only when it is their turn. A majority of rework will be in the custodial department. Any crew doing rework after custodial work has been completed will generally create additional custodial rework. This usually results in the custodial department becoming one of the major bottlenecks in the turnover process. The most effective way to reduce this bottleneck is to send the custodial staff only to apartments that are ready. All possible rework for previous crews should be completed to limit additional custodial rework. In most cases, the custodial department will set the pace for the turnover of apartments. If custodial staff can clean ten apartments per day, output will usually equal ten per day. Other crews creating custodial rework will slow the entire turnover process.

Common Space Maintenance

Many apartment complexes include common space that requires different types of custodial services on an ongoing basis. Services in these areas are repetitive and standardized in nature, possibly providing an excellent opportunity to utilize student employees. In most cases, these spaces can be maintained at odd hours that fit students' schedules. Less effort is required for training since the tasks involved generally are simpler than those involved in apartment turnover. Using student help to support full-time staff in this area helps free up full-time staff to focus on apartment turnover.

However, if housing is dependent upon full-time staff to clean these facilities, some of the challenges may include follow up or supervision of work completed. This is especially true when residents are using the commons area during cleaning times or when staff abuse the privilege of having access to these facilities for breaks or lunch.

Carpet Cleaning

A good carpet-cleaning program can reduce operating expenses by extending carpet life. All apartment turnovers should include carpet cleaning as part of the basic custodial turnover process. By making carpet cleaning available throughout the year to current tenants, turnover times can be shortened at move-out and overall carpet quality maintained. It is best to offer this service to current residents during times of low turnover, at the convenience of the resident.

Truck-mount systems are far more effective than smaller extractor systems. Although initial costs are higher, truck-mount systems will pay for themselves in a short time by reducing carpet replacement. Furthermore, a truck-mount system will clean in about one-third of the time required by extractor units. Regardless of equipment used, carpet condition and cleanliness is a major component of perceived quality and should not be overlooked. During extremely busy times, outside contractors or additional shifts may be necessary to support apartment turnover.

Window Coverings

Most apartment operations furnish window coverings as part of the standard furnishings. Apartment turnover provides the best opportunity to clean, maintain, or upgrade draperies and blinds as needed. It is most efficient to stock backup window coverings and rotate window coverings as apartments turn over. Outside contracts for dry cleaning generally are necessary for draperies. Miniblinds are best cleaned using ultrasonic blind cleaners. Of all the custodial responsibilities, blinds and draperies are the most specialized. Extensive training is required to make quality repairs. This usually becomes a responsibility within the custodial department. Other options include using an outside vendor for repairs or replacement of window coverings.

Grounds

The grounds surrounding the apartment facilities provide the initial impression of quality to the tenant. They are also an integral part of the living package being offered, becoming the front and back yards to a multitude of students and student families. This environment should be well maintained and safe. The grounds department and the quality of the grounds should be part of the overall strategy for the housing department, as important as the apartments themselves.

Landscape Management

Landscape management refers to the strategic use of the grounds department. Through proper planning, landscape management can help control issues like water damage and pest infestations. Proper planning can reduce expenses by designing low maintenance landscapes that minimize water use.

A large amount of apartment housing at colleges and universities across the country was built in the late 1950s and early 1960s. A fair amount of existing landscape was planted during that time period. One of the major problems is that the original plantings have become overgrown, full of garbage, and infested with pests. Many officials are reluctant to spend money on landscaping when huge capital improvements to facilities also are necessary. It is less clear to them how the landscape affects other aspects of apartment condition. For example, overgrown bushes and trees around apartments are the primary environments for many types of pests. As landscapes become overgrown, inordinate amounts of time must be spent in order to maintain a mediocre appearance. By replacing these antique landscapes, issues such as pest control and water damage can be addressed. Safety also becomes a concern when overgrown bushes and branches prevent proper lighting or interfere with the operation of heating and air conditioning units.

With planning, new landscapes can pay for themselves in a matter of years through reduced maintenance costs. Coupled with the landscape's ability to provide a positive first impression, landscape management becomes a key component in the facilities operation.

Snow Removal

As the seasons change, the responsibilities of the grounds crew shift focus. After the fall leaf removal and pruning is completed, most grounds crews shift their focus to snow removal. In many areas of the country, snow removal requires substantial efforts. The hours of operation for the grounds department fluctuate around snowfall and accumulation. Failure to deal with snow as it accumulates can create extra work. If snow is allowed to freeze or is compacted by traffic, it is much more difficult to remove and can create safety and liability problems.

Many housing operations that do not have their own removal crews become frustrated by the fact that housing areas generally receive low priority for snow removal. Most physical plant operations give priority to the academic areas of campus, frustrating both housing officials and residents. The best solution is to provide some form of snow removal by housing staff.

In order to have a successful snow removal program, several policies and procedures are necessary when developing landscape plans. A decision must be made as to the minimum level of accumulation before crews begin removing snow. Primary sidewalks should be designed wide enough to use plows when possible. Excessive exterior stairways and areas that require hand shoveling should be eliminated. Also, areas for snow storage must be planned so water problems and landscape damage does not occur from accumulated snow. Certain areas require salt and sand while a magnesium solution is a better option in other areas. Finally, equipment selection is another aspect of a successful snow removal program. A variety of plow types and sizes are available.

Equipment should appropriately fit the area being plowed in order to minimize landscape damage and maximize removal efforts. In many areas, the best option for snow removal is snow blowers. Additional support may be required for snow removal crews from maintenance and custodial staffs sharing snow removal responsibility as needed.

Weed and Pest Control

Grounds personnel are a good source for many aspects of the pest control program that are provided in-house. Any institution that applies chemicals for weed control should have certified personnel. These personnel also can apply pesticides with the appropriate certification. Outside contractors are another source for pest and weed control. Usually, extensive contract negotiation is necessary in order to clarify the expectations for an outside contractor. Campus housing is a unique and diversified environment that presents challenges to any pest control effort.

Many types of pests can be controlled through proper landscaping strategies and exterior chemical use. Overgrown bushes, accumulated leaves, and ground debris around buildings should be eliminated. Fields and open spaces should be mowed and sprayed. These efforts will reduce ants, spiders, mice, flies, and a variety of other insects and vermin. Many types of chemicals are more effective when applied outside of the apartment and will prevent initial infestation. The impact on tenants is less significant than when treatment is required inside the living space. The grounds and exterior of the apartment should be considered as a first line of defense.

Certain types of pests require treatment within the living space of the apartment. This is far more challenging than external treatment. Health and safety issues, tenant notification, tenant apartment cleanliness, and political resistance must be dealt with as pest control moves into student and family domiciles. Strict policies relating to treatment need to be developed and communicated to all residents. Tenants should be notified and well informed of chemicals that will be used in the treatment process prior to application. Cleanliness standards should be developed and enforced to reduce pest exposure to adjoining apartments. Initial applications and follow-up treatments of infested apartments cannot be at the option of the resident.

Purchasing/Warehouse

The purchasing and warehouse functions of the physical facilities department support all other departments within the division. Most of the accounting, inventory control, disbursement, and security measures are provided by this department. Another primary function of the purchasing department is to assure that purchases are made in accordance with state, provincial, or institutional policy. A high-quality purchasing department can help leverage buying power of the housing operation.

Facilities Management

Vendor Agreements and Contract Administration

Vendor agreements and contract administration are a major responsibility of the purchasing operation. Most facilities operations spend enormous amounts of money on supplies for various crews. Many purchasing departments are required to accept low bid or price only. Lowest price providers do not always have the best product or service. By developing clear, detailed specifications for products and services, some of these vendors can be excluded. It is also important to include specific language relating to performance expectations in the bid process. By including language allowing extensions of contracts and agreements for proper performance, the necessity to rebid is reduced. Good vendors can be rewarded with extensions while poor vendors should be replaced.

Contract administration is similar in many ways to the regular purchase of materials and supplies. It also has many unique requirements. The person responsible for coordinating the use of outside contractors must be familiar with housing policies and procedures, institutional policies, and students' schedules. Expectations for contractors should be established prior to awarding contracts. Times of operation, parking, response time, safety, and tenant interaction should be considered and spelled out in the contract. Contractors should be informed of housing policies and procedures related to issues such as right of entry.

It is most effective to have one person who administers all contracts. This helps make the coordination and communication of expectations easier and more standardized. Most problems with outside contractors arise when inaccurate expectations and communication result from too many individuals giving direction.

Stock Levels

Stock levels can have a dramatic effect on both the operating expenses and the department's ability to perform its duties in a timely manner. It is impossible to make prompt repairs if parts and supplies are out of stock. At the same time, an excess of stock and parts may become obsolete before being used. As stock levels increase, so do costs associated with warehousing them. A balance must be maintained between too much and too little stock on hand. Electronic and manual inventory control systems provide the data that warehouse personnel need to establish these stock levels.

One of the key components of reducing operating costs is inventory reduction. Many of the costs associated with inventory are hard to identify specifically. These costs include storage and handling, obsolescence, shrinkage, order costs, and tracking costs. Reorder points and safety stock levels are determined based on information gathered by the purchasing/warehouse personnel. Some operations order stock based on a periodic reorder system, others use the reorder point system (Schmenner, 1990). Under the periodic reorder system, orders are placed for materials at set intervals. This is like purchasing light bulbs on the first Friday of every month. Demand is established from historical information and adequate stock levels are established to avoid a lack of stock. The reorder point system allows stock levels to drop to a reorder point before orders are placed. Orders occur only when stock is needed. Safety stock levels coincide with material delivery lead times and historical usage information.

The best strategy is a combination of both systems, depending on the item and its frequency of use. For example, many chemicals and paper goods can be purchased with attractive volume discounts. This type of item fits well with a reorder point system since demand is more predictable. The purchase of many other items is less predictable. Smaller items that are more difficult to inventory continually are better ordered using the periodic reorder system.

Regardless of the order system used, standardization of materials and supplies is very important. Standardization helps limit obsolescence of parts and supplies by limiting the number of duplicate stock items. It also increases the buying power of the operation.

Accounting

In every facilities operation, the ability to maintain accurate accounting records is important to assure that budgets and expenditures are carried out as planned. Accurate information allows for adjustments to budgets during the fiscal year of operation. The amount of time and effort spent on the accounting function should be proportional to the amount of information derived from or utilized in the departmental decision-making process. Extreme cost accounting measures usually produce information that never is used and is costly to gather.

Many facilities' accounting processes assess costs to each individual work order. Others account for items that are specific to a particular facility as purchases are made. Stock items used are then allocated based on work orders or some other basis. Regardless of the system used, the time spent on the accounting system should be proportional to the usefulness of the information obtained. If the accounting system hinders the staff's ability to provide responsive service then it should be changed. The goal of the accounting department should be to provide essential information without negatively affecting the organization's ability to provide service. If individual work order costs are tracked and the information actually is used by management in the decision-making process, then perhaps that level of accounting is appropriate. However, if overall expenditure tracking is the level of information desired, the accounting system should focus on maintaining information at this level. It is critical that costs are accounted for in a meaningful way that supports the goal of providing responsive service.

Conclusion

Establishing productive working relationships, addressing ever-evolving customer needs, and supervising operations from an informed, enlightened administrative perspective represent real challenges to housing management. Housing administrators must ask themselves if they are prepared to lead their work teams into a more productive era of customer service amidst seemingly ever-constricting resources. Or are administrators going to keep doing the same things the same way with the same results, and wonder why things never change for the better? Students have choices about where to reside, both in an initial institutional sense and a subsequent housing sense. Will facilities managers of the 21st century provide the facilities, programs, services, and support staff that will encourage students to consciously choose to live on campus?

References

Conway, J. M., Goodman, D. F., & Jako, R. A. (1995). A meta-analysis of interrater and internal consistency reliability of selection interviews. *Journal of Applied Psychology, 80,* 565-579.

Goldratt, E. M., & Cox, J. (1992). *The goal: A process of ongoing improvement.* Great Barrington, MA: North River Press.

Harris, M. N. (1989). Reconsidering the employment interview: A review of recent literature and suggestions for future research. *Personnel Psychology, 42,* 691-721.

McDaniel, M. A., Whetzel, D. L., Schmidt, F. L., & Maurer, S. D. (1994). The validity of employment interviews: A comprehensive review and meta-analysis. *Journal of Applied Psychology, 79,* 599-616.

Schmenner, R. W. (1990). *Production/operations management from the inside out.* New York: Macmillan.

Renovation and Redevelopment of Apartment Facilities

Carey Roth
Manager of Graduate Housing
Stanford University

Renovation/Redevelopment of Apartment Facilities ————————

Introduction

As housing facilities age, the need for renovation and redevelopment of buildings increases with each year. Many apartment complexes constructed in the post-World War II era are now reaching the end of their useful lives. Other projects, constructed in the 1960s and 1970s are at a critical juncture where significant deferred maintenance must be addressed or the structures will face demolition.

The results of recent Association of College and University Housing Officers-International (ACUHO-I) student surveys clearly indicated that the immediate physical environment has a high impact upon student satisfaction ratings (Dalton & Pica, 1998). Clean, attractive, safe, well-lighted, and pleasant residential environments enhance the effectiveness of a housing program. Renovating apartments brings fresh interiors and furnishings, which can improve student attitudes, academic experiences, and housing ratings.

This chapter will address both renovation and redevelopment of apartment housing facilities. Information on these issues was obtained through surveys of large apartment programs in Michigan, Texas, California, Florida and other states. The topics reviewed in this chapter include (a) the renovation program, (b) renovation versus redevelopment, (c) capital improvement programs, and (d) references and resources (Appendix A).

A comprehensive, long-range plan that addresses a housing program's renovation and deferred maintenance requirements is essential. All too often, interior renovation and critical systems work is delayed in favor of short-term budget priorities until a crisis mode is reached. This chapter includes information to help you to develop a plan that effectively addresses these critical areas before a crisis occurs. Grimm and Dunkel (1999) also presented a comprehensive overview of renovation and new construction in residential facilities.

Renovation Program

An effective renovation program's objective is to refurbish the apartment unit and return it to a "like-new" condition, often including upgrades in information technology and cable wiring, electrical capacity, kitchen quality, and floor coverings. Management skills required for such a program include analysis, planning, directing, budgeting, and contractor supervision. Frequent and accurate communications with residents are vital to the success of any renovation program.

In 1992, Stanford University initiated an ambitious 10-year $225,000,000 capital improvement program to renovate the entire 9,355-bedspace housing portfolio. All major systems were upgraded and all units were redecorated with new carpeting, floor coverings, appliances, and blinds and drapes. Project work was completed on a tight June-July-August schedule. The size and scope of this work required solid planning and execution.

The initial site analysis should include the following:
1. Current conditions of the existing buildings.
2. Professional survey of all major building systems (electrical, plumbing, roof, communications, etc.).

3. Desirability of location if it is an off-campus site.
4. Security and safety.
5. Playground equipment.
6. Computer cluster.
7. Parking.
8. Administration space.
9. Recreational facilities.
10. Facilities management requirements.

Developing a Plan

Coordination between the housing facilities management staff, residence life, student government officers, campus capital projects department, and administrative staff are critical. Developing a plan through surveys, town meetings, and focus groups of exactly what is desired in the renovated unit will assist the architects in the development of the layout plan.

Scope of Project

The initial decision for a partial versus complete renovation program will have a significant impact upon the final product. This decision is driven by an in-depth analysis of the current portfolio status produced by a professional independent consulting company for objectivity. An outside architectural firm and the campus facilities management department are also good sources of objective information and analysis.

The major systems analysis should include:
1. Utilities and related systems (e.g., plumbing, HVAC, electrical, current costs for fiber optics).
2. Structural (e.g., square footage, roofing and drainage systems, dry rot/termite, water intrusion, seismic, foundations).
3. Interiors (e.g., appliances, furniture, floor and window coverings).
4. Common areas (e.g., landscaping, lighting, facility amenities).
5. Facilities ground work.

Financial Impact

Funding for major renovation projects will be provided by one or several sources, such as current operating funds, reserves, new debt service, and/or additional revenues via rent increases. The size and scope of the renovation program will be determined by the amount of dollars available in a multi-year budget. In most cases, newly renovated units will command a higher rental value compared to older apartments and will thus generate increased gross revenues. Operating expenses and turnover costs will decrease for the new units producing an increase in net operating income.

At minimum, a 10% contingency allowance plus a 10% "alt-add" (alternative additions) expense line should be included in the project budget. Invariably, unforeseen problems and costs will be encountered when contracting for extensive renovation of older apartments.

Renovation/Redevelopment of Apartment Facilities ──────

Project costs should be carefully tracked on a monthly basis and compared with budget projections to minimize cost overruns. On-site inspections are vital to ensure that the project is on schedule and the contracted work is being performed in a professional manner according to specifications.

Project Management Options

Three options are available to implement your renovation program: the campus facilities department, a private sector design or building firm, and in-house project management. The advantages and disadvantages of each option are listed in Table 1.

Advantages and disadvantages will vary from region to region. Today, more and more educational institutions are working with these management options on major renovation projects. By networking, housing administrators planning for renovations can benefit from the experiences of others as they make decisions about which management options to utilize. A combination of in-house staff supplemented with external contractors is a common solution.

Contracts, Policies, and Procedures

Comprehensive contract specifications for materials, design, and installation are critical for a successful project. Specific details outlining scheduling, material quantity and quality, on-site supervision, and completed segments are essential components of a renovation contract. Well-written contracts are the most effective tool for resolving performance or material quality disputes. Often, the campus capital programs and purchasing departments can provide valuable assistance with institutional liability and vendor requirements.

Carefully review the project options for design and materials. Use the highest quality materials commensurate with financial constraints. Evaluate products and materials based upon four major criteria:

1. *Durability.* Lower-cost materials often result in significantly reduced useful life versus higher quality; review the estimated product life span versus costs.

2. *Design.* Are you building an "econo-box" or are you creating an attractive living space that will be utilized for several decades?

3. *Cost versus quality.* Look for a balance between utility, durability, and budget constraints.

4. *Downstream maintenance impact.* Strive to develop a comprehensive set of material specifications that utilize light fixtures, hardware, plumbing, and appliances which will minimize operation costs for the longer run.

There is a tendency to "value engineer" out amenities that are "non-essential" and to purchase lower-cost materials in order to meet budget targets. However, the long-term consequences are increased maintenance costs and premature replacement of inferior components. For example, installing the lowest-cost hardware will enhance the renovation project manager's efforts to meet material cost limits. However, inexpensive locks wear out much sooner than quality hardware and will have to be replaced five to ten years before quality hardware would need to be changed.

Resist the tendency to meet project budget targets by shortcutting installation procedures or substituting inferior quality materials. Long-range costs always outweigh short-term budget savings. If an institution takes a perspective of 30 to 40 years of useful life, then investing in quality materials and workmanship now will pay dividends for decades of a building's useful life.

Process Control

Ensure that facilities staff or outside contractors are complying with all required Occupational Safety and Health Administration and local, state, and/or provincial health and safety codes. If utilizing in-house staff, compliance with these regulations and codes should already be in place.

Utilization of outside vendors requires weekly on-site inspections by qualified staff and professionals. Inventory security and control is critical if materials are being stored on site. Utilization of project scheduling software will assist all parties in keeping the renovation program on track.

Resident Communication

Frequent and accurate communication with residents is critical to the success of a major renovation project. Utilize newsletters, flyers, and posted notices for notification about renovation projects. Resolve conflicts in advance by contacting residents regarding problem situations. Announce and discuss the project schedule and plans well in advance of the anticipated start date. One cannot over-communicate, especially if the institution has a large percentage of international students. At a minimum, 60 days' notice should be provided to all residents involved in or impacted by the renovation project. Ideally, providing six months' advanced notice will gain significant resident support for the project.

Soliciting residents' input can also provide a positive experience for both the residents and staff involved in the project. Respond to this information and issue a memo that addresses residents' concerns before the project is started.

If possible, display a model of the newly renovated unit. Ideally, a completely renovated apartment would be available in a large-scale project for inspection. This will assist staff in building support for the inevitable disruptions that relocation of residents will cause.

A relocation allowance to cover the costs of moving, utility hook-ups, meals for one day, and childcare should be provided. It is best to issue a rent credit and allow residents to make their own relocation arrangements. Otherwise, large amounts of staff time will be spent on this process.

Project Coordination

A scenario of the work flow in an extensive renovation project would include the following steps.
1. Remove furniture, appliances, and light fixtures.
2. Complete rough plumbing, and electrical and cable systems upgrades.
3. Prepare and paint complete unit.

4. Install new cabinets.
5. Install new carpeting and linoleum.
6. Complete painting.
7. Install vertical blinds.
8. Hook up new appliances.

Careful attention to a comprehensive "punch-out" list (a final walk-through to verify that all work has been completed as originally specified) is necessary to ensure that the completed unit meets project specifications for quality and detail.

As the institution's representative, the housing services department or facilities manager has a final responsibility to ensure that the renovation project is completed on time, within the budget, and within specifications. Minimizing inconvenience to residents is essential for good public relations.

Review blueprints for conformity with project objectives. Weekly project progress meetings with housing staff, the general contractor, and the institution's capital programs staff are necessary to keep the project on track. Changed orders are costly and should be minimized by careful planning and coordination.

Project Completion and Overview

Once the project has been completed, an inspection walk-through is advisable to find any minor punch-list items. Meeting with staff to review changes and improvements for the next round of renovations is imperative. A "Lessons Learned" notebook is a valuable tool for planning future renovation projects. Review budget items with negative cost variances and analyze what could have been done to reduce or minimize cost overruns.

Document the project with "before" and "after" photographs and videotapes. Publish a notice in the community newsletter celebrating the success of the project and the lower, long-run operating costs that will result from this work in the future.

Renovation versus Redevelopment

After completing an initial assessment of the scope and costs of a comprehensive renovation project, an analysis of the redevelopment option may be warranted. If renovation costs approach 50% of the cost of new units, then a full-site redevelopment plan should be created. Buildings that are 40 to 50 years old are often at the end of their useful life. Major foundation and systems problems may be too expensive to correct. In this case, demolition of old units and construction of new apartments would be a viable option.

In 1990, at the University of California at Los Angeles (UCLA), a major renovation was slated for 647 apartments originally constructed in 1948. Total estimated costs exceeded $44,000,000 for full renovations. UCLA decided to pursue the redevelopment option and constructed 912 new one-, two-, and three-bedroom apartments in a courtyard village configuration. "University Village" was completed in 1997 and included a new community center, administration building, computer lab, and facilities operations center, as well as a new $4,500,000 child care center. Total redevelopment costs were $65,000,000. The project was completed on time and on budget.

Capital Improvement Programs

Numerous colleges and universities have instituted major apartment renovation programs in the 1990s including the University of Michigan, the University of Florida, the University of Texas at Austin, and Toronto University. In 1992, Stanford University launched a comprehensive 15-year, $275 million capital improvement program to renovate all housing and dining buildings. Programs like these can be a highly effective method to increase occupancy and reduce deferred maintenance costs.

Conclusions

In summary, apartment managers find that housing facilities should be managed with a long-run time frame in mind. Assume that a college or university will never sell the existing portfolio. The useful life of most apartment buildings is 40 years at minimum, which can be extended with a comprehensive renovation and deferred maintenance plan.

Resident preferences and expectations are constantly changing. The colors, designs, and facilities that met expectations in the 1970s and 1980s will not necessarily work in the next millennium. By developing a well-planned, financially responsible, and professionally executed renovation program, housing departments will maintain high occupancy in quality apartments with low operational costs for future generations of students.

References

Dalton, D. R., & Pica, J. A. (1998). National survey reveals influences on residence hall student satisfaction. *Talking Stick, 16*(1), 6-8.

Grimm, J. C., & Dunkel, N. W. (1999). *Campus housing construction and renovation: An analysis of cost and design.* Columbus, OH: Association of College and University Housing Officers-International.

Appendix A

Resources for Building and Renovations

Buildings (monthly magazine)
Energy Manager (monthly magazine)
Building Operating Management (monthly magazine)
Automated Builder (monthly magazine)
The Construction Specifier (monthly magazine)
College Planning & Management (monthly magazine), Peter Li Inc., Dayton, OH, 1999.
IREM Journal of Property Management (Institute of Real Estate Management)
Means Guides to Construction Management
Means Facilities Planning & Relocation
Multi-Housing News
National Association of Home Builders
Remodeling (bimonthly magazine)
ULI (Urban Land Institute)

Websites for all of these publications are currently available. Utilize Yahoo or Excite search engines under "construction" and "facilities management."

Table 1. Advantages and disadvantages of three renovation project management options.

Management Entity	Advantages	Disadvantages
Campus Facilities	University-related Professional staff Limited trades	Limited loss of control Increased overhead charges Scheduling coordination
Private Designer/Builder	Competitive bidding Lower costs Wider scope	Outside contractor Compliance management Quality of materials Subcontractor quality
In-House	Scheduling control Knowledge of buildings Design/quality control Lower risk management costs Less liability	Limited staff experience Meeting deadlines Increased workload

Multicultural Models and Campus Ecology Theory: Applications to Diversity in Apartment Communities

Silvia Echevarria Rafuls
Assistant Professor of Counselor Education

Mary Howard-Hamilton
Associate Professor and Coordinator of the
College Student Affairs Program
Department of Educational Leadership,
Policy Studies, and Foundations

Joanna Jennie
Consultant-in-Residence
University of Florida

Multicultural Models and Campus Ecology Theory ——————

Introduction

The term "diversity" generally is associated with difference, variety, distinctiveness, or uniqueness. "Multiculturalism," which generally refers to one's ethnicity, race, or culture, is often associated with diversity. In this chapter, diversity will be used to refer to characteristics or definitions related to dimensions of identity like age, gender, religion, sexual orientation, social class, and so forth (Arredondo, Toporek, Brown, Jones, Locke, Sanchez, & Stadler, 1996). The widespread and often politicized use of both terms has led to their association with efforts to experience, acknowledge, and become more aware of groups other than those to which one belongs. In order to arrive at a better understanding of diversity within and between groups, distinctions often are made in the form of labels or definitions. These labels or definitions can be both reassuring and dangerous depending on how they are used and/or interpreted.

Labels that define who we are also define boundaries which distinctly inform us of whether we belong (i.e., inclusion) or do not belong (i.e., exclusion) within certain groups. In an effort to coexist beyond these boundaries, much of the literature related to multiculturalism and diversity encourages development of "intercultural sensitivity" (Bennett, 1993), "cross-cultural competencies" (Arredondo et al., 1996; Sue, Arredondo, & McDavis, 1992), and "re-visioning" (McGoldrick, 1999). In this endeavor it is not only important to get to know others but perhaps even more crucial to get to know oneself within the context of culture. According to Pedersen (1994), the more aware we are of how we have been influenced by our own culture and background, the less likely we are to impose these beliefs and values on someone else. As individuals learn more about each other, the differences between them become the background and the similarities they share take the foreground (Leeman-Conley, 1999). These observations are consistent with the belief that in order to successfully engage individuals in a process of intercultural communication, the challenge will lie in not only making room for tolerance of difference and appreciation of uniqueness, but also in finding ways for diverse groups to connect through shared definitions of sameness.

In this chapter we undertake the challenge of promoting diversity while also acknowledging sameness through discussions of: (a) the historical context and current demographics of diversity in apartment housing, (b) the realities of globalization and institutional issues on college campuses today, (c) various theories and models which are considered useful in enhancing intercultural experiences, (d) strategies for community building and resident involvement, and (e) implications of such efforts, along with recommendations and conclusions.

Historical Context: A Tradition of Diversity

The history of apartment housing since World War II reflects the history of the campus communities and cultures in which it is situated. In the United States, the various social movements which emerged during the 1950s and 1960s contributed to the increasing diversity of predominantly White institutions. Similarly, the number of international students has increased through the years. These patterns and trends have been reflected in the demographics of apartment housing as well.

As Buchan (1999) pointed out in Chapter 1, throughout the history of the Apartments Committee of the Association of College and University Housing Officers-International (ACUHO-I), apartment housing professionals have explored issues and pursued professional development pertaining to the intercultural experience of residents and staff. Parallel to the increasing awareness of these issues in the larger community, many programs at the annual conference have focused on diversity issues which impact apartment residents, staff, and administrators.

Current Demographics of Apartment Housing

According to Whalen, Crull, Liao, Pate, & Rochford (1997), 40% of the 10,137 residents who responded to their survey were international students. The survey, whose participants represented 50 colleges and universities in Australia, Canada, and the United States, did not indicate the diversity of apartment residents who were citizens of the host country, so the full extent of diversity in apartment housing is unknown beyond the internal data at each institution. For example, at the University of Florida, 14.4% of the apartment housing residents identified themselves as Black or African American, 5.3% were Asian Americans, and 11.5% were Hispanic (University of Florida Division of Housing, 1999).

Diversity and Inclusion of Diverse Groups

As Arredondo et al. (1996) so eloquently stated, "We are all unique; we all share in the diversity of humankind making us more alike; and in this shared identity, we also find differences" (p. 44). One of the ways that they proposed to bridge experience and identity, while also acknowledging difference, was through Arredondo and Glauner's Dimensions of Personal Identity (DPI) model (cited in Arredondo et al., 1996). They presented a multidimensional perspective of identity by proposing that descriptions of self go beyond one label or one dimension, thus increasing the likelihood of finding levels of sameness throughout the model's dimensions.

The DPI model is based on the premise that everyone is a multicultural individual who possesses a personal, political, and historical culture, affected by sociocultural, political, environmental, and historical events. The model can be used as a paradigm to see people and their complexities more completely in a way that complements the discussion of multiculturalism by characterizing individuals across three dimensions (i.e., the "A," "B," and "C" dimensions of personality). Each dimension consists of characteristics based on conceptualizations of individual differences and shared identity.

The "A" dimension is associated with characteristics of self that one is born with or born into (e.g., race, age, culture, gender) that are generally fixed or for the most part less changeable (Arredondo et al., 1996). The "C" dimension situates one's experience within the context of history and time, in terms of the impact of specific sociopolitical, global, and environmental events throughout history (e.g., wars, movements, natural disasters). Like the "A" dimension, the "C" dimension is often associated with events or situations that are beyond one's control. In contrast, the "B" dimension is associated with characteristics that one may be more capable of changing (e.g., education, income, marital status, religion, geographic location, hobbies or recreational interests, etc.) and therefore, more likely to share in terms of similar experiences. Theoretically, the "B" dimension may represent consequences of the other two dimensions because it constitutes characteristics that are influenced by the rather fixed qualities of the "A" dimension, along with the legacies and history associated with the "C" dimension (Arredondo et al., 1996). For example, in terms of educational experience, more women and persons of color have pursued higher education in the last 25 years based on opportunities directly linked with legacies of the Civil Rights movement and the legislation that grew out of that time in history.

From an institutional perspective, Arredondo et al. (1996) proposed that the DPI model "can assist leaders to become more aware of how the culture of their organization may alienate, marginalize, or lose people of color, women, or other minority groups, if cultural competency is not valued and practiced" (p. 55). For this reason this model has been included as one possible template to use in an effort to serve and include the diverse groups encountered in apartment housing.

One variable not addressed in such models of individual characteristics and dimensions related to cultural context is family form (i.e., family structure). Diversity in apartment housing also occurs in terms of different family forms. Many of the diverse forms found in apartment housing, such as domestic partners, single-parent families, two-parent families, childless couples, and so forth, are a reflection of societal structure and sociocultural realities. However, each of these differing family configurations is rich in its own way, and thus family form does not constitute family substance (Walsh, 1993). In other words, each of the different configurations potentially can be as substantive as any other, which should prevent judgment or discrimination against those that may not participate in "traditional" family structures. Each family, regardless of form, will have its own issues and concerns which are often similar based on their commonalities as students or family members of students.

Educational Possibilities in Diverse Residential Environments

Reality of Globalization

Cross-cultural communication is an increasingly significant issue on our campuses, in the workplace, and in other institutions based on the reality of globalization. To subsist in today's world of technological communication, commerce, economy, and politics, intercultural communication is becoming less a matter of choice or option, and more a matter of necessity if institutions and businesses are to survive. Globalization, or concern beyond narrowly defined boundaries and labels, offers opportunities to engage in meaningful practice that affects individuals, communities, and nations all over the world. Institutions of higher learning are in key positions to engage in such opportunities and meaningful practice.

In a recent on-line report, Pivo (1999) included a presentation by Dr. Peter Likins, president of the University of Arizona, who stated, "One thing we must do is understand that when people come to us from all the countries of the world to be students in our universities, not only are they here to learn from us, they're here to teach us as well." He went on to argue that American universities "have an extraordinary opportunity to prepare students for functioning effectively in a multicultural global society because we have a multicultural American society." Thus, intercultural communication among diverse groups facilitates mutual learning and is inherent in the work already underway with the diverse cultural groups in this country.

In another on-line report, there is evidence that some institutions have taken a stronger sociopolitical stance by carrying out the mission of promoting "an understanding of the processes of globalization that advance the cause of world peace and integration" (Universidad Nur, 1999). This Danish university inaugurated a Department of Education for Peace and Integration in 1994 based specifically on the realization that in the past 50 years citizens have become increasingly dependent on one another. Simply stated, "What happens far away matters much more now" (Universidad Nur, 1999).

Diversity Issues on Campus

Apartment residents, staff, and administrators in the United States are all part of a social system in which being White historically means "overall racial superiority, physical separation, a community apart from others, and mutually exclusive long-term interests" (Bowser, Auletta, & Jones, 1993, p. 19). While a "dialogue about race" has been initiated by President Bill Clinton, racism is still viewed as something which occurs in blatant, isolated events, such as cross burnings, rather than perceived as something which is pervasive in our personal, institutional, and cultural lives (Bowser et al., 1993). Thus, the recent murders of James Byrd, Jr., an African American man in Texas, and Matthew Shepard, a gay college student in Wyoming, are considered aberrations, rather than merely extreme points on a continuum of passive and active oppression in which the dominant (White) majority engages and from which it benefits daily (Feagin & Vera, 1995; McIntosh, 1989).

In addition to overt issues, such as affirmative action, freedom of speech, and hate crimes, which challenge campuses across the United States, female students, international students, students of color, gay and lesbian students, and other nontraditional students face more covert challenges presented by unwritten rules or hidden agendas of higher education (Bowser et al., 1993). "The university system of governance is based on an informal and covert way of doing things that continues to control the extent to which racial and non-European cultural groups participate in American institutional life" (Bowser et al., 1993, p. 2). Sensitivity to these issues is critical for apartment housing administrators and staff who, along with international student services departments and programs and services for students of color, can provide guidance and support as students negotiate the hidden curriculum. Formal and informal orientation programs can establish staff members as important resources for new residents as they become familiar with this challenging terrain. The infusion of multicultural perspectives and programming in community development initiatives also will increase the credibility of apartment housing staff as a source of reliable and sensitive support (Casey-Powell & Griffin, 1999; see Chapter 3). The diversity of the staff itself sends a powerful message to residents about the apartment housing operations' commitment to and support of diversity.

Multicultural Models and Campus Ecology Theory ————

Institutional Mission and the Contribution of Diverse Residential Environments

Institutions that promote student growth, development, and involvement "share, to varying degrees, five categories of factors and conditions" (Kuh, 1991, p. 11):

1.   A clear, coherent mission and philosophy.
2.   Campus environments with human-scale attributes that use their location to educational advantage.
3.   Campus cultures that value student involvement.
4.   Policies and practices consistent with the institution's mission and students' characteristics.
5.   Institutional agents who acknowledge the contribution of learning outside the classroom to achieving the institution's educational purposes.

This section will focus on the first factor (mission and philosophy) and how it impacts the apartment community because "an institution's mission defines what a college or university is and aspires to be" (Kuh, 1991, p. 12). Questions that apartment housing administrators should ask themselves include: How do the residents in this community perceive how they fit in this environment? Does our community make a clear statement to new and old residents that they matter and that we respect the diverse perspectives they bring to the environment? The college or university housing unit conveys its perception of itself in this regard, as well as community standards, through public statements in handbooks; policy manuals; and leases, contracts, or agreements. It is important for apartment communities to develop their own mission and philosophy that reflect the understanding and respect given to the diverse perspectives within the environment. The mission statement defines what the organization aspires to be (Kuh, 1991). The philosophy "is the means (policies, practices, standard operating procedures) by which it enacts its mission" (Kuh, 1991, p.12). Four essential elements of the mission and philosophy statement are: "clarity, coherence and complementarity of mission and philosophy; high expectations for student performance; the presence or absence of status or other distinctions among people consistent with the institution's educational purposes and students' backgrounds; and an unwavering commitment to multiculturalism" (Kuh, 1991, p. 12).

When addressing the issue of clarity of the community's mission and philosophy, it is important that residents comprehend and delineate from their own world view what the living environment is attempting to accomplish (Kuh, 1991). The apartment community should have reasonably high expectations for residents' academic performance. Furthermore, to attain the educational purposes of the apartment community, "distinctions among individuals and groups are deliberately accentuated or minimized" (Kuh, 1991, p. 13). Finally, a residential environment aspiring to become a "multicultural learning community is symbolized through strong statements about the value of individual and group differences; moreover, resources are devoted to establishing and supporting multiple subcommunities" (Kuh, 1991, p. 14). Thus, the apartment community's mission and philosophy should include a bold and aggressive statement promoting diversity and any initiatives to support efforts that enhance interpersonal relationships by sharing varied perspectives. It is, however, difficult to create, write, and

College and University Apartment Housing

establish this type of mission and philosophy if housing administrators do not internalize a high level of multicultural competency and awareness.

Developing Cross-Cultural Competencies

Howard-Hamilton, Richardson, and Shuford (1998) noted that student affairs administrators and preparation program faculty should have plans in effect to educate students regarding current diversity issues and demographic transitions on campus. Numerous challenges have been issued to respond to diversity and multicultural issues in an aggressive manner (American College Personnel Association, 1994; King, 1999a, 1999b; King & Shuford, 1996; National Association of Student Personnel Administrators, 1996a, 1996b; Pope & Reynolds, 1997; Pope, Reynolds, & Cheatham, 1997). However, when attempting to present multicultural initiatives in the apartment community, are residents receptive participants and administrators knowledgeable enough about multiculturalism to successfully implement a diversity plan? Howard-Hamilton et al. (1998) suggested that higher education has failed to address student learning from a holistic perspective, thus the need for cultural competencies for students and administrators.

While there is no agreement on the knowledge, skills, and attitudes students should possess in order to become culturally competent, there is some agreement among professionals in counseling and student affairs on the competencies needed to be culturally competent in those two fields. For example, Sue and Sue (1990) stated that a culturally competent counselor (a) must have an awareness of his or her own assumptions, values, biases, limitations, and world view; (b) must understand the world view of the culturally different client; and (c) must develop appropriate intervention strategies and techniques for working with culturally different clients. For other useful models, see Pedersen (1994) and Sue, Arredondo, and McDavis (1992).

Cultural competencies also have been identified for student affairs practitioners. Pope and Reynolds (1997) developed a list of 33 cultural competencies for student affairs practitioners based on a review of the multicultural literature in higher education and counseling psychology. The cultural competencies are divided into awareness, knowledge, and skills student affairs practitioners should possess. Listed below are examples of some of the competencies identified by Pope and Reynolds (1997).

At the *awareness level,* practitioners should possess "a willingness to take risks and see them as necessary and important for personal growth and development"; "a personal commitment to justice, social change, and combating oppression"; and "awareness of cultural heritage and how it affects their world view, values, and assumptions" (p. 271). Pope and Reynolds (1997) suggested that knowledge about multicultural groups is needed regarding (a) the impact of cultural differences on nonverbal and verbal communication, and (b) the impact of "identity development models and the acculturation process . . . on individuals, groups, intergroup relations, and society" (p. 271). The effective skills that administrators should hone are: "the ability to use cultural knowledge and sensitivity to make more culturally sensitive and appropriate interventions"; "the capability to accurately assess their own multicultural skills, comfort level, growth, and development"; and "the ability to incorporate new learning and prior learning in new situations" (p. 271).

Multicultural Models and Campus Ecology Theory ———————

A set of student competencies "to enhance and promote the growth of multicultural sensitivity within college communities" was developed by Howard-Hamilton et al. (1998, p. 11). It is imperative that administrators and residents in the apartment environment work collaboratively to teach and hone these skills so that students will be prepared to communicate effectively with a diverse workforce upon graduation. Table 1 provides examples of multicultural competencies students should possess.

It is also important to reiterate that the multicultural competencies should be intricately connected to the apartment community's mission and philosophy statements, as noted by Kuh (1991). The apartment community should develop effective programs and activities that enhance the multicultural competency of its residents. For example, at the community orientation or reception, small groups can be established for residents to share information about their cultures. The facilitator can then draw upon the various comments and present how the cultures are similar and what makes them unique. This gives residents an opportunity to enhance their levels of awareness. To increase levels of appreciation and valuing, residents can review and revise the community mission and philosophy statement as well as establish goals and objectives that reflect mutual respect and inclusiveness for all residents.

As mentioned by Pope and Reynolds (1997) as well as Howard-Hamilton et al. (1998), it is critical that administrators are knowledgeable about multicultural models and theories as well as having a sense of how they assess their own levels of racial consciousness. Moreover, these models are also useful in understanding human and campus ecology.

Models and Theories

Racial/Cultural Identity Development

For nearly 30 years, models of racial and cultural identity development have flourished in the United States, beginning with Cross's 1971 Nigrescence model (Cross, 1995), which addressed the racial identity development of African Americans through a series of stages "from a self-hating to a self-healing and culturally affirming self-concept" (Cross, 1995, p. 96). Since that time, identity development models also have been proposed for biracial individuals (Kerwin & Ponterotto, 1995), lesbians (Falco, 1991), and others.

Because of the proliferation of identity development models in recent years, Atkinson, Morten, and Sue (cited in Sue & Sue, 1990) proposed a more generic five-stage model of Minority Identity Development which attempted to integrate the earlier work. (Sue & Sue [1990] suggested that the name Racial/Cultural Identity Development be used.)

1. *Conformity.* In this stage, "minority persons are distinguished by their unequivocal preference for dominant cultural values over their own" (Sue & Sue, 1990, p. 96).

2. *Dissonance.* Contradictory experiences, attitudes, and beliefs which challenge the conformity-stage individual lead to a gradual or abrupt shift to a period of questioning.

3. *Resistance and immersion.* In this stage, strong emotions provoke the rejection of dominant cultural values and beliefs and elicit the motivation to abolish oppression. Information about the minority culture is sought. The low self-esteem of the conformity stage is replaced by a more positive self-image and strong racial pride.

4. *Introspection.* Moving from the reactive rigidity of the resistance and immersion stage to a more proactive process, the introspective individual begins to develop selective trust and distrust toward both the dominant culture and his or her own minority group(s).

5. *Integrative awareness.* In this stage, the individual develops selective appreciation, that is, recognition that every culture and group has both acceptable and unacceptable qualities and conditions. The multidimensionality of identity (individual, group, and universal) is evident.

Racial/cultural identity development models also have been applied to White individuals (Helms, 1995; Sabnani, Ponterotto, & Borodovsky, 1991; Sue & Sue, 1990). Sabnani et al. suggested five stages of White racial identity development which parallel the stages described above.

1. *Preexposure/precontact.* In this stage, an individual is oblivious to White privilege and participation in a racist society.

2. *Conflict.* Anxiety and ambivalence are evoked by the dilemma of remaining loyal to the dominant culture in the face of evidence of racism and other oppressive practices and institutions.

3. *Prominority/antiracism.* In an effort to relieve guilt feelings aroused during the previous stage, individuals may adopt a prominority stance, and may also reject White values associated with internalized racism.

4. *Retreat into White culture.* If the newly zealous individual is rejected during efforts to engage with minority individuals, this reactive, defensive stage may be experienced as a result.

5. *Redefinition and integration.* This stage "is characterized by a movement toward the clear development of White racial identity and an internalization of this newfound identity into the self. This last stage is also marked by a culturally transcendent worldview and by a balance in multicultural interests and respect for cultural differences" (Sabnani et al., 1991, p. 82), similar to the "integrative awareness" stage for minority group members.

Acculturation

Another component of the diversity of apartment housing is the experience for international students and their families of acculturation to the host country. Acculturation has been defined as a form of "psychological adaptation" experienced "either as 'shifts' of pre-existing customs or habits in language, beliefs, attitudes, values, or abilities, or as 'acculturative stress,' which is generated during acculturation" (Pedersen, 1991, p. 16).

Three to five "typical" phases of acculturation have been described during the past 50 years (Pedersen, 1991). The traditional model of "culture shock" has been a U-shaped curve representing the emotional highs and lows associated with "contact, conflict, and adaptation" across time (Lysgaard, cited in Pedersen, 1991, p. 16). As Pedersen (1991) explained, "these stages progress from initial excitement and optimism in the course of contact with another culture, through a U-shaped curve to feelings of failure and depression, and then recovery to a new level of excitement and optimism" (p. 16).

Later, Gullahorn and Gullahorn (cited in Pedersen, 1991), expanded this model to include not only acculturation to the host culture but also reacculturation to the country of origin, as represented by a W-shaped curve. More recently, Lin and Yi (1997) described a four-stage adjustment process (prearrival, initial arrival, ongoing, and returning home) specific to international students from Asia. While research on these models, especially the U-shaped curve, has yielded conflicting results, counseling and foreign student affairs professionals have found them to be useful and practical paradigms, not only for the international students they serve, but also for the professionals themselves (Siegel, 1991). The models offer both groups a more objective and dynamic perspective for normalizing the sometimes overwhelming process of adapting to a new culture.

Acculturative stress. While acculturation appears to be a normal, predictable, and possibly universal process experienced by anyone who enters a new or different culture for an extended time period, international students face several challenges which can compromise their adaptive abilities and result in varying degrees of acculturative stress. Oropeza, Fitzgibbon, and Barón (1991) identified six key areas of stress. (See also Svarney, 1989, on stresses specific to foreign law students.) First, the greater the degree of cultural dissonance between the culture of origin and that of the host country, the greater the difficulty experienced by the international student. Thus, for example, Asian students may face greater challenges in bridging cultural differences in the United States and Canada than European students.

Second, international students, especially those living in apartment housing, may experience radical changes in their social and economic status. Traditionally, international students who enjoyed a higher standard of living in their home countries had greater resources available for international travel and study. However, Althen (1991) argued that international students now represent a greater range of social class and socioeconomic status in their home countries. Nevertheless, adjustment to some of the aging apartment facilities on campus can still be quite challenging (Lange & Jennie, 1999; see Chapter 10 on the interface of mental health issues and acculturative stress in apartment housing).

Expectations about academic performance constitute the third key area described by Oropeza et al. (1991). International students' unrealistically high standards, often self-imposed, but also emanating from family and cultural pride and loyalty, may generate tremendous stress. In addition, the continuation of financial aid from organizations in the home country is often contingent upon academic performance.

The degree to which international students experience isolation, alienation, and discrimination—the fourth key area—is unknown. Research reports and anecdotal evidence have indicated that international students and their families encounter all of these because of negative attitudes and a lack of sensitivity from host cultures (Lee, cited in Pedersen, 1991). One persistent stereotype is that international students will "band together," regardless of their country of origin or, if from the same country, regardless of regional differences or internal strife (Oropeza et al., 1991), thus apparently absolving host country citizens from making further efforts on their behalf. However, the more involved international students become with the host culture, the more positively they describe their experience (Prieto, 1995).

Apartment housing professionals are well acquainted with the fifth key area, family-related pressures. Oropeza et al. suggested that "the magnitude and scope of adjustment problems become multiplied by the number of members in the family" (1991, p. 281). In addition, the rate of adjustment is highly variable. Depending upon the length of stay, children may incorporate the language, attitudes, and behaviors of the host country much more quickly and to a much greater extent than their parents.

The sixth key area described by Oropeza et al. (1991) is a composite of "idiosyncratic circumstances" (p. 281) that may introduce additional acculturative stress, such as gender role differences between the home country and the host country; political developments in the country of origin; illness, injury, or death of family members; and decision making about whether or not to return home after graduation.

In spite of the daunting challenges faced by international students, apartment housing administrators, staff, and residents must resist the tendency to pathologize their experiences (Pedersen, 1991). Humans are a marvelously adaptive species, especially in supportive environments such as apartment housing with a mission and philosophy emphasizing diversity. As Pedersen (1991) suggested:

> The normal circumstances experienced by international students are that (a) warm, intimate international contacts are the exception rather than the rule, (b) the well-adjusted international student is less strongly identified with home-country values, while being more self-confident and adept in communication skills, and (c) those who remain distant from host nationals and continue to be oriented to home-culture values are more traditional. (Pedersen, 1991, p. 23)

Apartment housing residents from the host country can contribute a great deal to successful acculturation. Community programs to welcome and orient international students can be very effective (Casey-Powell & Griffin, 1999; see Chapter 3), especially when linked with a "buddy system" matching host country volunteers or long-term residents from any country with new international residents. In addition, orientation to academic advisement and medical care may be particularly important, given that international students tend to access these resources more than psychological counseling services for symptoms and concerns associated with acculturative stress Harju, Long, & Allred, 1998; Lin & Yi, 1997).

Assessing residents' abilities, skills, and interests can lead to invitations to residents, especially nonstudent spouses and partners, to get involved in the community through relevant volunteer opportunities in governance, programming, community service, and so forth.

These types of activities support the functional model of social networks developed by Furnham and Bochner (cited in Pedersen, 1991, p. 24), consisting of:

1. A primary monocultural network of close friendships with other co-nationals, to provide a setting where ethnic and cultural values can be rehearsed and expressed.

2.   A secondary bicultural network bonding the international students and significant host nationals, to instrumentally facilitate the academic and professional needs of the student.

3.   A third multicultural network of friends and acquaintances, to provide companionship for recreational and nontask-oriented activities (p. 24).

Applying Conceptual Models in Apartment Housing Contexts

None of the stage models described above are considered to be linear. Individuals may move back and forth through the stages at different points in their lives as new challenges arise. For apartment housing administrators and staff, these stage models are conceptual tools that can serve several purposes. First, using these models in training may encourage self-awareness. Training activities can be tailored to the developmental needs of the trainees. (See Pedersen, 1991, for a series of critical incidents that may be useful in increasing staff self-awareness, knowledge and skills.) Further, such self-awareness may extend into interpersonal communication and result in a greater understanding of others. Finally, as described below, these models can be applied at the organizational level (Sue, 1995) to analyze apartment housing operations relative to diversity goals and objectives.

A Systemic View of Diversity in Apartment Housing

It would be difficult to address issues of diversity in apartment housing without addressing the organizational connections that students and apartment housing staff have with other systems in the university (e.g., international student office, admissions, academic departments, and support services). Change in one aspect of an entire system does not guarantee change in others. Thus, any focus within an academic setting will require systemic thinking in terms of the impact or influence this may have on other subsystems of the university. In many cases it would behoove apartment housing administrators to consider joint efforts with these subsystems in order to increase the likelihood of success in various efforts.

A systems perspective in the area of organizational development is at the core of Senge's (1990) principles and steps in building what he called "a learning organization." Although these principles and steps were adapted within a corporate context, there is no reason why disciplines of a learning organization could not be adapted to academic structures and organizations.

A learning organization is defined as "an organization that is continually expanding its capacity to create its future" (p. 14). Senge (1990) referred to systems thinking as "the fifth discipline" that integrates five learning disciplines into a coherent body of theory and practice. In addition to systems thinking, the other four disciplines or "component technologies" are personal mastery, mental models, shared vision, and team learning. Senge (1990) believed that by actually practicing these disciplines within an organizational structure (i.e., developing proficiency through practice), organizations can enhance their capabilities for creativity and innovation in ways that will make room for crafting strategies and designing policy and structure that go outside usual, expected, and often useless organizational practices. Each of the disciplines are viewed as critical to the other disciplines' success. They could be particularly useful in apartment housing settings where there is a willingness to self-assess and plan for change as a learning organization.

If apartment housing staff and residents are to consider how best to interface with other components of their institutional structure, this model could turn out to be a rather viable one to consider. This is especially true in situations where solutions merely shift problems from one part of a system to another and therefore go undetected (i.e., those who "solved" the first problem are different from those who inherit the new problem; Senge, 1990). The use of these methods in interdepartmental change efforts also are quite feasible, given certain conditions. Creating the organizational climate to meet these conditions becomes the real challenge in most cases. For example, one of the disciplines Senge (1990) referred to is personal mastery. It is the "discipline of continually clarifying and deepening our personal vision, of focusing our energies, of developing patience, and of seeing reality objectively" (p. 7). Much like the developmental stages of cultural sensitivity and competencies that have been discussed in this chapter, personal mastery is not a discipline or practice that can be created through compulsory training or even so-called "elective" programs. Instead it needs to be fostered through an organizational climate where it is "safe for individuals to create visions, where inquiry and commitment to the truth are the norm, and where challenging the status quo is expected" (Senge, 1990, p. 172). Not only does this tell participants in the process that personal growth is valued, but it also invites an ongoing practice of "on-the-job training" vital in developing personal mastery.

The following models provide some direction for apartment housing staff to develop an organizational climate which promotes many of the principles of diversity in a learning organization.

Applying Organizational Development Principles to Apartment Housing

Drawing from a variety of sources, Sue (1995) adapted principles of organizational development and compiled developmental characteristics of organizations striving to infuse diversity in academic settings. The three stages of his model of multicultural organizational development parallel the stages of the racial/cultural identity development models for individuals.

1. *Monocultural organizations* are predominantly "Eurocentric and ethnocentric" (p. 483). Utilizing the traditional "melting pot" concept (if not excluded outright), individuals from oppressed groups are expected to assimilate to expectations of the dominant majority.

2. *Nondiscriminatory organizations* lack "a systematic program or policy addressing the issue of prejudice or bias" (p. 485). Superficial changes are made to give the appearance of a more inclusive environment but legislated or court-ordered initiatives such as affirmative action are implemented with reluctance.

3. *Multicultural organizations* incorporate diversity efforts into all aspects of the organizational environment. Equal access and equal opportunity are priorities. Organizational activities reflect the commitment to incorporate the contributions of diverse groups.

Multicultural Models and Campus Ecology Theory ———————

Sue (1995) went on to propose a three-dimensional model for increasing diversity within an organization. His model went beyond heuristic value to address how best to move an organization toward multiculturalism. This model incorporates an analysis of *"functional focus,* or where the intervention should take place (recruitment, retention, or promotion), *multicultural competencies* needed by the organization or individuals (beliefs and attitudes, knowledge, and skills), and *barriers to multiculturalism* (differences, discrimination, and systemic factors)" (p. 485). Many diversity activities, both for training new staff and for developing a sense of community among residents, may build multicultural competencies. However, in addition to the administrative focus on hiring policies, attention is also needed to barriers which may limit the effectiveness of such activities. These barriers echo the campus-wide concerns described earlier, as expressed by Bowser et al. (1993).

1. "Differences in communication styles and differences in characteristics of racial/ethnic minorities are often misunderstood . . . " (Sue, 1995, p. 487).

2. "Interpersonal discrimination and prejudice (racism and sexism) have been identified as one of the most serious impediments to the implementation of diversity into education and the labor force" (p. 488).

3. "The existence of systemic barriers in an institution may mirror the nature of race and gender relations in the United States" (p. 489).

Leach and Carlton (1997) described two levels of organizational philosophy regarding multicultural training, each with two stages. They also identified philosophical statements which are representative of each stage. Level 1 (the cultural encapsulation stage) consists of (a) *cultural entrenchment,* in which Eurocentric attitudes dominate, until external demands (e.g., legislation, lawsuits, decrees) motivate top-down changes, and (b) *cross-cultural awakening,* in which a critical mass of concerned staff and students begin to lobby for bottom-up changes.

Philosophies associated with *cultural entrenchment* in apartment housing might include the following statements: Residents have "essentially the same concerns, regardless of culture" (Leach & Carlton, 1997, p. 195). "Our organizational structure has worked well. Why do we need to become more multicultural?" (p. 195). Basic customer service skills are "universal and transcend race and ethnicity" (p. 195). "We are all human beings and all we would do is [deal with] stereotypes anyway" (p. 195).

Philosophies associated with *cross-cultural awakening* in apartment housing might include the following statements: "Perhaps multiculturalism has a place because not all traditional approaches are applicable. We have people on the [staff] who can teach multiculturalism" (p. 196). "Institutional racism probably occurs but not in our department. We just have a hard time recruiting minorities" (p. 196). The department might require professional and student staff take a training module on diversity, and the facilitator is an expert. "The demographic representation of [residents] is changing and we need to address this" (p. 197).

Level 2 (the conscientious level) consists of (a) *cultural integrity,* a transition phase in which diversity concerns receive more attention, and (b) *infusion,* in which a commitment to multiculturalism is in place.

Philosophies associated with *cultural integrity* in apartment housing might include the following statements: Staff "should be aware of their own values, prejudices, and attitudes regarding diverse [residents]" (p. 198). "The sociopolitical system, including academia, influences [residents], [staff], and organizational structure" (p. 198). Most staff "can talk comfortably about racial issues and believe such discussion is necessary for effective training" (p. 198). "We believe it is necessary to achieve financial and political support . . . to further multiculturalism" (p. 198).

Philosophies associated with *infusion* in apartment housing might include the following statements: "Our program is not equipped to provide all multicultural material, and other [programs and services] can offer valuable information" (p. 199). Most staff incorporate diversity issues into every discussion of residents' problems, needs, and services. "We believe in teaching culturally sensitive communication strategies and their relationship to traditional strategies" (p. 199). "Diversity is valued and [staff] believe that they can continue to learn cultural issues from their [residents]" (p. 200).

Regardless of the level in which apartment housing operations currently find themselves (i.e., cultural encapsulation and conscientious action), residents and staff can work together to create and promote an environment of growth and development relative to diversity issues. The contribution of the environment is elaborated further in the discussion of human ecology theory.

Human Campus Ecology Theory

The foundation of human ecology theory is Lewin's (1936) Interactionist Paradigm (B=f[P x E]), which simply states that behavior is the function of the person and the interaction with his or her environment. By specifying the important person and environment variables, individuals could be paired with the appropriate environment to promote growth and development (Huebner & Lawson, 1990). Schroeder (1979, 1981) embellished Lewin's formula by noting that:

$$\frac{HD = f\ (P \times E)}{C/S}$$

His formula emphasized that human development (HD) is a function of the person and his or her interaction with the environment mediated by the challenge and support (C/S) ratio. Thus, to grow and develop as a student, there must be an environmental fit, and beyond that there should be individuals available to challenge and support one's beliefs, values, behaviors, and so forth. Without the challenge—and with too much support in the environment—the student stagnates and does not grow. Therefore, this must be mediated with the types of programs and activities that will create enough cognitive dissonance that the individual may become open to new and interesting ideas and concepts.

The Interactionist Paradigm has become the fundamental framework and the most basic way of conceptualizing the work of student affairs, and theories of college student and adult development give the human and campus ecology model developmental substance (Rogers, 1990a). Student developmental theories cannot be applied appropriately without the person-environment interactionist perspective (Rogers, 1990a). Specifically, "student development efforts tacitly focused mostly on the person (P) and often neglected the environment (E) and the interaction (X). Similarly, in using the person-environment perspective without using developmental theories, campus ecology projects did not assess, redesign, or evaluate for development per se" (Rogers, 1990a, p. 28).

Moos (1986) explained that campuses should be viewed and assessed based upon a social ecology framework which is dissected into four areas: (a) the physical setting and features; (b) the organizational factors; (c) the human aggregate; and (d) the perceived or perceptual social climate. The physical setting refers to the natural and synthetic properties on the campus. For example, natural settings include bodies of water, terrain, and climate. Synthetic features are the buildings, roads, and campus design. Organizational factors "include size of organizational units, staff-student ratios, governance structures, political climate, and programming emphasis" (Rogers, 1990b, p. 156). The human aggregate is the collective characteristics of the inhabitants (Strange, 1996) such as people who enjoy the arts, are the same age, or come from a common cultural group. The perceived or perceptual social climate "mediates the influence of the other three factors and includes perceptions of various dimensions of interpersonal relationships, personal growth and goal orientation, and system maintenance and change" (Rogers, 1990b, p. 156).

By incorporating Moos' environmental determinants of behavior (1986) with Lewin's Interactionist Paradigm (1936), apartment administrators can begin to create a living and learning community that appreciates diversity and promotes growth and development. The next—and most difficult—step is to select and integrate the appropriate adult and/or student development theories within the campus ecology framework with the outcome as student growth and development. Rogers (1990a) enumerated the following recommendations and observations when weaving the concepts together (p. 35):

1. Use the person-environment interaction as the basic general paradigm for your work and then integrate developmental and other relevant theories into it.

2. Person-environment interaction models serve as reminders to assess three things, not just one or two of the following: (a) the *students*, (b) their *environment*, and (c) the degree of congruence or incongruence in their *interaction*.

3. Use theory, including at least one developmental theory, in making campus developmental and other theoretical ecological assessments; do not limit assessments to common-sense and atheoretical variables.

4. If *multiple types* of developmental and other theoretical frameworks are used the degree of individuation in environmental designs can be increased.

5. To determine whether or not environmental redesign is needed, use criteria derived from theories and your educational values to analyze and make judgments on the interaction data.

6. If redesign is needed, the nature of the redesign also derives from the assessment data as evaluated by theoretical criteria.

7. Evaluate outcomes of redesigned environments using measures of the developmental and other theories and atheoretical variables selected for a given project.

This process was used when evaluating the Olentangy Project at Ohio State University (Rogers, 1990b).

Strategies and Approaches to Community Building

Drawing from Moos' (1986) four dimensions, the following strategies may be useful in implementing the mission and philosophy regarding diversity in apartment communities.

Physical features. The physical setting of the apartment environment has a tremendous impact on the behavior of residents. It is important to allow community members to "formally and informally change the environment to better fit their needs" (Huebner & Lawson, 1990, p. 134). This task can be accomplished formally if residents are part of the policy-making process in designing play areas, planning placement of sidewalks and security lighting, and implementing rules for keeping the property clean and free of clutter. Informally the physical design takes place when residents move furniture and rearrange play areas to fit their needs or when gardens are planted in unused open space.

Community members should have opportunities to personalize their living space (Huebner & Lawson, 1990) so that they can maintain some cultural connectedness. Individuals also become invested in maintaining a positive atmosphere and take personal ownership and responsibility for the upkeep when there is freedom and flexibility in selecting the decor, furnishings, and colors, for example (Huebner & Lawson, 1990; Schroeder, 1979, 1981). Also when assessing the physical apartment environment, note the spaces for stimulation and privacy as well as community space (e.g., recreational spaces, areas for meditation and reflection, and places where groups of people can congregate and commiserate). Keep in mind the human aggregate of the apartment community when designing the physical environment and allow the population to have a voice in the personalization process. It is imperative that there are small spaces and human places so that community members feel connected to each other, not isolated, by living in buildings that have places for people to interact spontaneously (Kuh, 1991). Place more benches and tables in main corridors, use bulletin boards to communicate with residents, and find a space to hang the artwork of the children in the community. These efforts will lead to a perception of the environment that is positive and the belief that there is a connection between the organization and the mission.

Human aggregate. The human aggregate of the apartment community is comprised of individuals from different cultural groups, adult learners, single parents, and partners or spouses who are not enrolled as students. Typically the majority group maintains the status quo of the environment. Community members in the apartment complexes should maintain a diverse governing unit and allow for diverse perspectives to be shared continuously.

Organizational structures. The organization of the apartment community should not be so layered that residents' voices are not heard. There should be easy access to administrators and policies established so that there is a problem-solving sequence that is free of bureaucratic entanglements. Many international residents in these facilities have persevered through arduous paperwork processes in order to study in the United States. Some residents would state that because they are not traditional students, the college or university has forgotten about their needs. The organizational structure of the apartment community should not mirror the complex framework of most university departments.

Multicultural Models and Campus Ecology Theory ─────────

The organizational environment should be cognizant of four areas: (a) staffing (b) programming and governance structures (c) policies on use of space and (d) political climate (Rogers, 1990b). There should be an appropriate administrator-to-resident ratio at the complex. Since many of the residents may have special needs and are from diverse cultures, there is a need for the staff members to have close contact with small groups of residents so that their voices are heard. Additionally, staff members should be representative of the population present in the apartment community. This equal representation should be present in all facets of the living environment.

The governance and programming structures should also strive for equal representation of those living in the community. Members from all facets of the community should be involved in the programming and policy-making processes. This includes students' partners and spouses as well as the children in the community. Ongoing assessments to note the needs of the community should be administered at least semiannually. Policies should be reviewed each time there is a change of representatives on the governance board and when there are administrative moves. Concomitantly, policies should be designed to support the free expression of residents' diverse backgrounds. Moreover, the key administrator should be multiculturally competent to embrace these divergent perspectives and encourage dialogue so that community members are educated about differences rather than threatened by changes that may occur.

Some of the changes should be articulated in the printed materials that the community disperses such as the community resident manual, mission statement, newsletter, listserv, and web site. These media should always promote diversity issues. For example, when a new resident arrives, his or her special cultural rituals and traditions can be shared in the community newsletter or on the web site. According to Kuh et al. (1991) there should be complementarity between the mission statement and the physical plant, that is, to gain the trust of residents, there must be a connection between the mission of the community and the beliefs reflected in the community's physical structures. If the mission statement asserts that diversity is what makes the community unique, then this philosophy must be reflected in the type of equipment purchased and space used for publicly displaying cultural artifacts, to name some examples.

The apartment community cannot be held responsible for being the primary promoter of diversity issues. The administrators in the community environment should be active participants with the overall housing operation. Furthermore, administrators should make a concerted effort to be active participants in the programming efforts of the apartment residents. Residence hall staff could involve the traditional student population in activities in the apartment community, such as volunteering to be tutors for the children or sponsoring parties during special occasions.

Implications and Recommendations

It is quite obvious that based upon our rapidly changing society, college and university apartment housing facilities can and should create a living and learning environment that encourages the opportunity for community members to share their unique cultural perspectives. Regardless of the type of campus living facility, development is enhanced when community members are an essential part of the environment (Chickering & Reisser, 1993). According to Chickering and Reisser (1993), the following characteristics within a living environment provide the key elements for optimum student development (pp. 398-399):

1.   [The living environment] encourages regular interactions among students and provides a foundation for ongoing relationships.

2.   It offers opportunities for collaborative and shared interests, for engaging in meaningful activities, and for facing common problems together.

3.   It is small enough so that no one feels superfluous.

4.   It includes people from diverse backgrounds.

5.   It serves as a reference group, where there are boundaries that indicate who is "in" and who is "out." It has norms that inform those with different roles, behaviors, and status that they are "good" members or that what they are doing is unacceptable.

To foster the type of living and learning apartment environment in which there is an opportunity for community members to achieve the five aforementioned characteristics there should be trained leaders to promote personal and community growth, learning activities to encourage diversity programs and community dialogues, a more personalized environment which means smaller units and attractive decor, and a mission or policy statement designed to provide an environment of inclusiveness for everyone (Chickering & Reisser, 1993).

The educational benefits of a multiculturally diverse campus environment can result in "effective learning and high graduation rates" (King, 1999a, p. 6). There are several other reasons for supporting diversity initiatives (American Council on Education, cited in King, 1999a, p. 6):

1.   Diversity enriches the educational experience. We learn from those whose experiences, beliefs, and perspectives are different from our own, and these lessons can be taught in a richly diverse intellectual and social environment.

2.   It promotes personal growth—and a healthy society. Diversity challenges stereotyped preconceptions; it encourages critical thinking; and it helps students learn to communicate effectively with people of varied backgrounds.

3.   It strengthens communities and the workplace. Education within a diverse setting prepares students to become good citizens in an increasingly complex, pluralistic society; it fosters mutual respect and teamwork; and it helps build communities whose members are judged by the quality of their character and their contributions.

4.   It enhances economic competitiveness. Sustaining a nation's prosperity in the 21st century will require everyone to make effective use of the talents and abilities of all citizens, in work settings that bring together individuals from diverse backgrounds and cultures.

Diversity initiatives on college and university campuses do work and it is imperative that housing administrators provide the out-of-class experiences necessary to promote cultural dialogues that could impact the lives of those living in apartment environments. Therefore, professionals in these environments need to become "more culturally competent, to have the knowledge, skills, and attitudes needed to understand and work effectively with diverse groups of students" (King, 1999a, p. 8). Several other implications for administrators pertain to issues of diversity in the 21st century (King 1999a, p. 9):

Multicultural Models and Campus Ecology Theory ——————

1. Student affairs professionals should have a deeper understanding of the historical, legal, political, and administrative issues surrounding issues of access and student success and actively promote informed understanding of these issues in order to improve campus practices.

2. Student affairs professionals should have a deeper understanding of the types of developmental issues addressed by diverse learners, apply these understandings when working with students, and share their knowledge of student development with a range of constituent groups (faculty, staff members, students, partners, spouses) who might benefit from these insights.

3. Student affairs administrators should actively use their knowledge of student characteristics and learning environments to serve as allies for underrepresented students or those who feel marginalized.

4. Student affairs professionals should have a firm understanding of organizational and administrative issues surrounding retention and educational success for diverse learners, apply this knowledge in creative ways as they work to address these issues, and bring to the attention of campus leaders the benefits of diversity initiatives to both minority and majority students.

5. Student affairs professionals should share their resources and expertise with faculty to help create classroom dynamics that are culturally sensitive and that teach students how to interact in respective and inclusive ways.

6. In light of the changing student population and their changing needs, interests, motivations, and goals, student affairs administrators should evaluate regularly which services are offered, why they are offered, and who benefits from these services.

Administrators in apartment environments should take advantage of having large racially and ethnically diverse populations by engaging in research focused on improving the living and learning environment as well as providing essential summary data for various organizations within the college or university. Some suggestions for future research in this area are to assess the educational programs that encourage acceptance of diverse groups. Additionally, does living in an apartment environment with ethnically diverse populations positively or negatively contribute to the growth and development of the community's residents? If there is a negative impact, what types of programs can be developed to change this trend? If there is a positive impact, what are the programs, activities, and stimuli that contribute to this trend? What multicultural understandings and competencies should administrators in apartment housing organizations be required to embrace and articulate in order to be successful in this type of environment? (King, 1999b).

In addition to conducting research, housing administrators should also use technology to promote the positive aspects of apartment life. The development of web pages can provide a glimpse of the multicultural housing community and give the outsider reasons why living in such an environment could enrich a person's life. The World Wide Web and other forms of technology could be an effective advertising tool to provide students with information about the assets of living on campus and being enveloped by a multiculturally dynamic environment.

Conclusion

As the world becomes more demographically complex and the use of technology brings our cultures closer together, apartment housing administrators, staff, and residents will need to become keenly aware of the verbal and nonverbal behaviors that promote and obstruct communication. There is also the important desire for students to acknowledge their cultural heritage because pride in one's background does impact self-esteem and on-campus apartment communities should encourage positive psychosocial student development. Understanding diverse cultures does not end when the degree is conferred. Respecting and appreciating the variations and nuances within and among cultural groups is an ongoing educational process, and inevitably one cannot know everything about all diverse groups. However, administrators should enroll in coursework or professional development workshops to constantly hone their skills in multicultural awareness and remain cognizant of issues and concerns impacting students of color and international students and their families. Apartment communities can be an environmental mecca for the promotion of diversity issues and understanding of multicultural groups; do not let this educational opportunity go unnoticed.

References

Althen, G. (1991). Reaction: Some help and some myths. *Counseling Psychologist, 19*(1), 62-65.

American College Personnel Association. (1994). *The student learning imperative: Implications for student affairs.* Washington, DC: Author.

Arredondo, P., Toporek, R., Brown, S. P., Jones, J., Locke, D. C., Sanchez, J., & Stadler, H. (1996). Operationalization of the multicultural competencies. *Journal of Multicultural Counseling and Development, 24,* 42-78.

Bennett, M. J. (1993). Towards ethnorelativism: A developmental model of intercultural sensitivity. In R. M. Paige (Ed.), *Education for the intercultural experience* (pp. 26-76). Yarmouth, ME: Intercultural Press.

Bowser, B. P., Auletta, G. S., & Jones, T. (1993). *Confronting diversity issues on campus.* Newbury Park, CA: Sage.

Buchan, R. (1999). The history of apartment housing. In D. Casey-Powell (Ed.), *College and University Apartment Housing.* Columbus, OH: Association of College and University Housing Officers-International.

Casey-Powell, D., & Griffin, P. (1999). Community services and programming: A search for balance. In D. Casey-Powell (Ed.), *College and University Apartment Housing.* Columbus, OH: Association of College and University Housing Officers-International.

Chickering, A. W., & Reisser, L. (1993). *Education and identity* (2nd ed.). San Francisco: Jossey-Bass.

Cross, W. E., Jr. (1995). The psychology of Nigrescence: Revising the Cross model. In J. G. Ponterotto, J. M. Casas, L. A. Suzuki, & C. M. Alexander (Eds.), *Handbook of multicultural counseling* (pp. 93-122). Thousand Oaks, CA: Sage.

Falco, K. L. (1991). *Psychotherapy with lesbian clients: Theory into practice.* New York: Brunner/Mazel.

Feagin, J. R., & Vera, H. (1995). *White racism: The basics.* New York: Routledge.

Harju, B. L., Long, T. E., & Allred, L. J. (1998). Cross cultural reactions of international students to U.S. health care. *College Student Journal, 31*(1), 112-120.

Helms, J. E. (1995). An update of White and people of color racial identity models. In J. G. Ponterotto, J. M. Casas, L. A. Suzuki, & C. M. Alexander (Eds.), *Handbook of multicultural counseling* (pp. 181-198). Thousand Oaks, CA: Sage.

Howard-Hamilton, M. F., Richardson, B. J., & Shuford, B. (1998). Promoting multicultural education: A holistic approach. *College Student Affairs Journal, 18*(1), 5-17.

Huebner, L. A., & Lawson, J. M. (1990). Understanding and assessing college environments. In D. G. Creamer (Ed.). *College student development: Theory and practice for the 1990's* (pp. 127-155). Washington, DC: American College Personnel Association.

Kerwin, C., & Ponterotto, J. G. (1995). Biracial identity development: Theory and research. In J. G. Ponterotto, J. M. Casas, L. A. Suzuki, & C. M. Alexander (Eds.), *Handbook of multicultural counseling* (pp. 199-217). Thousand Oaks, CA: Sage.

King, P. M. (1999a). Improving access and educational success for diverse students: Steady progress but enduring problems. In C. S. Johnson (Ed.), *Higher education trends for the next century: A research agenda for student success* (pp. 5-11). Washington, DC: American College Personnel Association.

King, P. M. (1999b). Research questions on improving access and educational success for diverse students. In C. S. Johnson (Ed.), *Higher education trends for the next century: A research agenda for student success* (p. 12). Washington, DC: American College Personnel Association.

King, P. M., & Shuford, B. C. (1996). A multicultural view is a more cognitively complex view: Cognitive development and multicultural education. *American Behavioral Scientist, 40*(2), 153-164.

Kuh, G. D. (1991). Characteristics of involving colleges. In G. D. Kuh & J. H. Schuh (Eds.), *The role and contribution of student affairs in involving colleges* (pp. 11-29). Washington, DC: National Association of Student Personnel Administrators.

Lange, N., & Jennie, J. (1999). Mental health in apartment housing: A spectrum of issues and services. In D. Casey-Powell (Ed.), *College and University Apartment Housing.* Columbus, OH: Association of College and University Housing Officers-International.

Leach, M. M., & Carlton, M. A. (1997). Toward defining a multicultural training philosophy. In D. B. Pope-Davis & H. L. K. Coleman (Eds.), *Multicultural counseling competencies: Assessment, education and training, and supervision* (pp. 184-208). Thousand Oaks, CA: Sage.

Lewin, K. (1936). *Principles of topological psychology.* New York: McGraw-Hill.

Lin, J.-C. G., & Yi, J. K. (1997). Asian international students' adjustment: Issues and program suggestions. *College Student Journal, 31*(4), 473-479.

McGoldrick, M. (1998). Introduction: Re-visioning family therapy through a cultural lens. In M. McGoldrick (Ed.), *Re-visioning family therapy: Race, culture, and gender in clinical practice* (pp. 1-19). New York: Guilford.

McIntosh, P. (1989). White privilege: Unpacking the invisible knapsack. *Peace and Freedom,* July/August, 8-10.

Moos, R. H. (1986). *The human context: Environmental determinants of behavior.* Malabar, FL: Robert E. Krieger.

National Association of Student Personnel Administrators. (1996a). *The 78th annual conference monograph preview.* Washington, DC: Author.

National Association of Student Personnel Administrators. (1996b). *The 78th annual conference propositions.* Washington, DC: Author.

Oropeza, B. A. C., Fitzgibbon, M., & Barón, A., Jr. (1991). Managing mental health crises of foreign college students. *Journal of Counseling & Development, 69*(3), 280-284.

Pedersen, P. (1991). Counseling international students. *Counseling Psychologist, 19*(1), 10-58.

Pedersen, P. (1994). *A handbook for developing multicultural awareness* (2nd ed.). Alexandria, VA: American Counseling Association.

Pivo, G. (1999). *Will you be ready? The University of Arizona Global Practice Symposium* (summary). [On-line]. Available: http://architecture.arizona.edu/global_practice/sympRpt%20for%20Web.htm

Pope, R. L., & Reynolds, A. L. (1997). Student affairs core competencies: Integrating multicultural awareness, knowledge, and skills. *Journal of College Student Development, 38,* 266-277.

Multicultural Models and Campus Ecology Theory —————

Pope, R. L., Reynolds, A. L., & Cheatham, H. E. (1997). American College Personnel Association strategic initiative on multiculturalism: A report and proposal. *Journal of College Student Development, 38,* 62-67.

Prieto, S. L. (1995). International student populations and needs assessment. In S. D. Stabb, S. M. Harris, & J. E. Talley (Eds.), *Multicultural needs assessment for college and university student populations* (pp. 203-223). Springfield, IL: C. C. Thomas.

Rogers, R. F. (1990a). Recent theories and research underlying student development. In D. G. Creamer (Ed.). *College student development: Theory and practice for the 1990's.* (pp. 27-80). Washington, DC: American College Personnel Association.

Rogers, R. F. (1990b). An integration of campus ecology and student development: The Olentangy Project. In D. G. Creamer (Ed.). *College student development: Theory and practice for the 1990's* (pp. 155-180). Washington, DC: American College Personnel Association.

Sabnani, H. B., Ponterotto, J. G., & Borodovsky, L. G. (1991). White racial identity development and cross-cultural counseling training: A stage model. *Counseling Psychologist, 19*(1), 76-102.

Schroeder, C. C. (1981). Student development through environmental management. In G. S. Blimling & J. H. Schuh (Eds.), *Increasing the educational role of residence halls* (pp. 35-49). New Directions for Student Services, No. 13. San Francisco: Jossey Bass.

Schroeder, C. C. (1979). Territoriality: Conceptual and methodological issues for residence educators. *Journal of College and University Housing, 8,* 9-15.

Senge, P. (1990). *The fifth discipline: The art and practice of the learning organization.* New York: Doubleday.

Siegel, C. (1991). Reaction: Counseling international students—A clinician's comments. *Counseling Psychologist, 19*(1), 72-75.

Strange, C. C. (1996). Dynamics of campus environments. In S.R. Komives, D.B. Woodard, Jr., & Associates, Student services: A handbook for the profession (3rd ed., pp. 244-268). San Francisco: Jossey-Bass.

Sue, D. W. (1995). Multicultural organizational development: Implications for the counseling profession. In J. G. Ponterotto, J. M. Casas, L. A. Suzuki, & C. M. Alexander (Eds.), *Handbook of multicultural counseling* (pp. 474-492). Thousand Oaks, CA: Sage.

Sue, D. W., Arrendondo, P, & McDavis, R. J. (1992). Multicultural counseling competencies and standards: A call to the profession. *Journal of Counseling and Development, 70,* 477-486.

Sue, D. W., & Sue D. (1990). *Counseling the culturally different: Theory and practice* (2nd ed.). New York: Wiley.

Svarney, R. J. (1989). Counseling foreign law students. *Journal of Counseling and Development, 68,* 228-231.

Universidad Nur. (1999). Education for peace and world citizenship. [On-line]. Available: http://www.nur.edu/engnur.english/Globalization.html

University of Florida Division of Housing. (1999). *Village housing census report.* Gainesville, FL: Author.

Walsh, F. (1993). Conceptualization of normal family processes. In F. Walsh (Ed.), *Normal family processes* (2nd ed., pp. 3-69). New York: Guilford.

Whalen, D. F., Crull, S. R., Liao, T.-M., Pate, R., & Rochford, H. (1997). *Resident satisfaction in apartments.* Columbus, OH: Association of College and University Housing Officers-International.

Multicultural Models and Campus Ecology Theory ————

Table 1

Attributes of a Culturally Competent Student

	Knowledge	Skills	Attitudes
Awareness	Knowledge of self as it relates to one's cultural identity	Self reflection	Pride within one's own cultural group
	Knowledge of other cultures and how they are similar or different from one's own cultural group	Ability to identify similarities and differences across cultures and the ability to articulate that with others	No one group is better than another
Understanding	Knowledgeable about issues of oppression and the effect it has on different cultural groups	Ability to see things from multiple perspectives	Discrimination due to one's cultural status is unjust
	Knowledgeable about the interactions between multiple oppressions such as race, gender, class, lifestyle, and religion	Understands difference in multiple contexts	Assumptions about an individual can not be based solely on one's group membership
Appreciation/ Valuing	Knowledgeable about elements involved in social change	Able to challenge acts of discrimination	One must take risks in life
	Knows the effect cultural differences can have in communication patterns	Ability to communicate cross-culturally	Cross-cultural interactions enhances the quality of one's life

Note. From "Promoting multicultural education: A holistic approach," by M. F. Howard-Hamilton, B. J. Richardson, and B. Shuford, 1998, *College Student Affairs Journal, 18*(1), p. 11. Copyright 1998 by the Southern Association for College Student Affairs. Reprinted with permission.

Staff Training and Development:
A Key to a Successful Organization

Lori Patterson
Assistant Director of Housing
Louisiana State University

Jana Severson
Chief Administrative Officer-Housing Services
University of California at San Diego

Staff Training and Development

And God created the Organization and gave it dominion over man — Robert Townsend (Lawrie, 1990).

Introduction

Stressing the importance of the external organizational environment, popular authors John Naisbitt and Patricia Aburdeen (1990) noted in their book *Megatrends 2000* that "the major themes of the 1990's—technological change, compressed product life cycles, and global competition—require a leader to scan the global environment and organize the internal tasks of the organization while remaining market-sensitive" (p. 251). It is therefore essential for organizations to improve their performance by anticipating and adapting to external environmental changes.

Adjustment in organizational culture is often required. What is organizational culture? While culture has long been discussed in anthropology and in organizational development circles, popular interest in it was not aroused until the publication of two major books, *In Search of Excellence* (Peters & Waterman, 1982) and *Corporate Cultures* (Deal & Kennedy, 1982). In both books, the authors demonstrated the linkage between corporate success and the unique shared values and beliefs of an organization's employees. Culture has been defined in many different ways. Most authorities on the subject, however, would agree that culture consists of behavioral patterns, concepts, values, ceremonies, and rituals that take place in an organization.

Cultural values provide employees with a sense of what they ought to be doing and how they should behave to be consistent with organizational goals. Culture represents the feeling, emotional, intangible part of the organization. Organizational culture exists on more than one level. Superficially, culture manifests itself through an organization's logos and slogans, office layout and furnishings, and employee behavior. On a second and deeper level, it encompasses the organization's prevailing values and beliefs. And on perhaps the most basic level, organizational culture is our employees.

The total budget for formal training in 1994 by U. S. organizations was $45 billion (Lee, 1995). More than 40.9 million employees received 1.3 billion hours of formal training from their employers. A salesperson was the type of employee likely to get the most training. An office or administrative employee was likely to get the least amount of training. Unfortunately, the type of organization with the lowest average expenditure for employee training was educational services.

Apartment housing professionals certainly have dealt with the major organizational themes of the 1990s, and perhaps have been challenged by the myriad adaptations of internal and external environments even more than other areas of higher education. This chapter will provide information on these environments and what is needed to produce efficient and effective employees. The issues addressed include staffing patterns, interviewing strategies, and orientation and training, as well as performance appraisals.

Staffing

One of the most prevalent challenges faced has been staffing—and all that this seemingly innocent word implies. "Staffing" encompasses job descriptions written to specific needs, increasingly specialized job responsibilities compounded by shrinking staff budgets, staff development, and training needs. Additionally, it includes awareness of and compliance with local, state, federal, and provincial laws governing interviewing and hiring practices, and training issues specific to apartment living, such as increasing international populations and technological change.

Apartment professionals have responded to these challenges by becoming innovative in staff utilization. For instance, many institutions cross-train and utilize both undergraduate and graduate students in their housing offices as student office workers. These student employees serve as "gatekeepers" at front desks to meet the public, answer generic and specific housing questions, receive and process applications, and perform general office work such as filing and copying. They also answer maintenance phones; input maintenance requests; and perform minor maintenance, painting, and cleaning of apartments, common areas, and grounds. They deliver notices to residents, run errands on campus for professional staff, help with the details of programming, and assist in computer literacy, as many are on the cutting edge of technology. A fundamental truth of apartment housing is the heavy dependence on student staff in day-to-day operations. Students generally work from 20 to 40 hours per week during and between semesters; each institution has specific rules and regulations governing student employee hours. Remuneration ranges from minimum wage to rent credits in halls and apartments or tuition waivers. Hours of employment range from regular office hours to shift work for 24-hour desk operations and "turn-around" periods of move-outs and move-ins. The 1993 apartment housing survey sponsored by the Apartments Committee of the Association of College and University Housing Officers-International (ACUHO-I) is an excellent resource for information about employee remuneration at various educational institutions (Whalen, 1993).

Additionally, a majority of institutions hire graduate students as live-in staff. Graduate students take on the positions of resident managers, community assistants, resident assistants, graduate assistants or apartment managers, specific team members, emergency response team members, children's services coordinators, programming assistants, and recreation assistants. Remuneration varies according to individual institutional rules and regulations and ranges from tuition and/or rent waivers or credits to specific stipends, graduate assistantships, or hourly wages. These paraprofessionals' on-call duties are as varied as the communities they serve. Generally, apartment housing operations maintain daily office hours with full- or part-time professional staff on duty during business hours and some type of facility or maintenance support in the evenings and on weekends. The on-call staff serves most often as a liaison or point of contact for resident emergencies, be it a broken water main or spousal abuse. The average ratio of student staff to residents is 1 to147.

Full-time professional staff in apartment housing is another area of flexibility and innovation. Full-time employees are hired for maintenance, clerical support, office administrative managers, custodial services, assignments, program coordinators, and community directors. Budget-driven staffing results in creative combinations of full- and part-time staff for these positions. Professional staff generally report to an associate or assistant director, although many titles for similar positions have been discovered.

Housing operations in Canada, England, Ireland, and Australia have similar staffing patterns.

Budget-driven staffing decisions also require utilization of temporary employees and private vendors at substantial savings to provide service during seasonal peak demands. Before working with nonuniversity personnel, consider the following suggestions. Avoid throwing temporary assistants into the fire. Before they arrive, develop a plan for them including guidelines, goals, and deadlines. Provide orientation on their first day. Provide essential information about their environment and include discussion of the work environment and culture. Make sure to give temporary employees constant feedback to avoid lost days of misdirected work. Reward temporary staff and service providers when they do well. Finally, treat them as part of the team, not second-class citizens. The operation will reap the benefits of these actions.

For any position in apartment housing, be it a career position or a temporary employee, an accurate, up-to-date job description is essential for effective staffing. Examining a job description to see if responsibilities are clear, boundaries and expectations are sufficiently well defined, and organizational authority is adequate are all essential tests for job descriptions. Are job objectives readily identified and written in concise, detailed language? Does the job description indicate the essential job functions? Are departmental job standards clearly defined? Are they consistent with organizational goals? (See Appendix A for samples of job descriptions and responsibilities.)

Human resource management standards, particularly specific core competency skills, are a valuable tool for apartment housing professionals in developing effective job descriptions. The following core competencies are examples of specifics related to positions in the industry (Kramer, 1998):

Personal Commitment

Commitment to professional development. Keep abreast of current research in the field; attend seminars and training courses.

Confidence. Use clear and honest statements. Believe in one's own worth and abilities. Able to deal constructively with a situation.

Dependability. Meet and exceed expectations of the department regarding job description. Take the initiative to meet expectations. Can be relied on in difficult situations. Punctual, reliable attendance.

Ethics. Truthfulness; how one treats other staff members. Use confidentiality, fairness, honesty. Establish positive relationships with individuals and groups, demonstrating genuine concern, respect, and patience.

Flexibility. Demonstrate adaptability and openness to change.

High standards of quality. Show commitment to doing the best job possible. Provide encouragement that will reinforce similar behavior in others.

Independent thinking. Receptive to new approaches. Suggest ideas and make recommendations leading to improvement.

Problem solving. Anticipate and correctly assess situations and make appropriate judgments regarding course of action.

Strong customer service orientation. Seek input from customers.

Willingness to work beyond job responsibilities. Participate in committee work. Help others with their work. Take the initiative to find more work to do.

Commitment to Diversity

Awareness of needs and contributions of different cultures and lifestyles. Demonstrate an interest in monitoring a welcoming and just environment for the community. Intervene through supervision, programming or management to improve the climate.

Cross-cultural communication skills. Awareness of differing communication styles based on culture, race, and gender. Participation in foreign language classes.

Organizational Commitment

Visualize "the big picture."

Represent the department well to the university and community at large.

Support the long-term vision of the department of housing and its director.

Support the mission statement of the area and work to accomplish its strategic plan.

Team player. Demonstrate willingness to cooperate and assist others by sharing ideas, expertise, and resources.

Supervisory Skills

Ability to train staff effectively.

Communication skills. Organize and express thoughts clearly and concisely. Use verbal and nonverbal skills to encourage, hear, and understand the thoughts and feelings of others.

Conflict resolution. Able to identify conflict and effectively mediate and facilitate resolution.

Delegation. Make available opportunities for employees to take on special projects while providing guidelines and feedback and remaining available as a resource.

Leadership skills. Use good judgment, motivational skills, employee recognition. Provide feedback and appraisal in an appropriate manner.

Managerial Skills

Crisis management. Able to deal with unexpected situations in a calm and professional manner.

Prioritization. Effectively establish an order by importance or urgency.

Project management. Able to manage projects or multiple projects and apply strategic planning methods using available resources and considering long-term goals.

Total Quality Management (TQM). Understand and implement the concept of TQM.

Interview Process

Armed with a clearly defined job description which incorporates necessary core competencies, the interview process can begin. Apartment housing professionals agree that it is critical to be prepared. Ask too few questions, and be left with an incomplete picture of the candidate. Ask too many questions, especially inappropriate ones, and face a lawsuit for discrimination.

"A manager has no job more important than hiring," says Dr. Alan Weiss, president of Summit consulting, East Greenwich, Rhode Island. "A bad hire can cost a business many thousands of dollars in lost productivity and training expenses."

Consultants say it's critical to be prepared. "Most managers assume that interviewing is something they can do naturally, like breathing," says Weiss. "In reality, it requires a great deal of planning."

Here's help! Human resource specialists tell how to conduct job interviews that safely ferret out the information you need (Perry, 1997, p. 37).

Step 1. Define the performance requirements of the position. Do not fail to adequately describe the performance requirements for the job opening.

"You must define the job you are interviewing for before you can know what questions to ask," says Judy Foritano, partner in the Somerset Consulting Group of New Jersey. "Be specific in terms of what is truly a requirement, versus what is nice to have." (Perry, 1997, p. 37)

This last element is crucial. Stated requirements will be demanding enough without muddying the waters with a wish list. Furthermore, dodge legal trouble by avoiding listing unnecessary parameters for jobs (Perry, 1997).

Step 2. Ask questions that predict the applicant's performance. Is the interview supposed to judge the applicant? No.

"Anyone can make a judgment about a job applicant," says Dr. Richard Camp, who teaches seminars on strategic interviewing at the University of Michigan Business School in Ann Arbor. "Your real goal is to predict performance. And that requires an understanding of the interviewing process."

Run each question you are planning to ask through this critical filter: Will it elicit answers that measure skills required to successfully carry out the tasks of the available job? (Perry, 1997, p. 38)

Step 3. Stay out of court. Watch out for common interviewing mistakes that can spark costly discrimination lawsuits.

"The interview process is littered with legal mine fields," says Robert P. Sherman, a partner at Karr & Sherman, Columbus, Ohio. "Don't ask any questions that may be interpreted as biased against any protected group." Protected groups can be defined by age, sex, race, national origin, and disability.

Sherman offers some helpful guidelines:

1. DON'T ASK for a birth certificate, high school graduation date, or any other information that reveals age.

2. DON'T ASK about marital status. (Examples of questions to avoid: "Do you have difficulty finding babysitters?" "Are you married?" "Will your spouse be moving to another state?" "Will you need health insurance for your children?")

3. DON'T ASK for place of birth, either of the applicant or parents, or citizenship. However, you may ask for verification that the applicant is eligible to work in the United States.

4. DON'T ASK about the ability of the applicant to work on religious holidays. However, you may ask if the applicant can work on a specific work schedule, including weekends if that is necessary for the job. (Perry, 1997, p.39)

Step 4. Pose questions in the right format.

"Ask questions that elicit descriptions of behavior rather than hypothetical responses," says Jerry Shuster, associate professor of communications at Robert Morris College in Pennsylvania.

The idea is to elicit real evidence of skills rather than vague bromides. Such questions are usually variations of the following:

1. "Can you recall a situation in which (state a business problem). What steps did you take to solve the problem?" This approach is good for those applicants who have prior work experience.

2. "Suppose you were in a situation where (state a business problem). What steps would you take to solve the problem?" This approach is usable if you come up dry with the first approach or if the applicant does not have work experience. In either case, you are challenging the applicant to describe concrete solutions that reveal skills and behaviors that are required to perform the duties of the available job. The business problem or situation should always be a realistic one, and relate directly to the activities involved with the job opening. (Perry, 1997, p. 40)

Perry (1997) offered employers the opportunity to consider the benefits of various types of questions to ask during the interview.

Open questions encourage applicants to open up and talk. They are dangerous because applicants can wander into forbidden territory, such as discussions of their marital status, family, religious observance, care for elderly parents, and so forth. This in turn can lead to charges of discrimination if the applicant is not hired. (Example: "So what do you do when you aren't working?")

Closed questions probe for additional information. These are allowable, but too many can make the interview sound like an interrogation. (Example: "Explain why you think that happened.")

Leading questions direct the applicant to the correct answer. They are useless, and can reflect a lack of self-confidence on the part of the interviewer. (Examples: "You believe that teamwork is essential, don't you?" "Surely you have been tempted to skip a day of work.")

Multiple questions combine two or more questions into one. They create unnecessary confusion. Worse, they allow the applicant to answer only the easiest question. Avoid them. (Example: "Give me an example of a time where you had to accept discipline that you thought was unjust, and while you're at it let me know how *you* would handle a similar situation if you were a supervisor.")

Link questions open up new topics for discussion and can help smooth the interview. (Example: "Speaking of disciplinary procedures, suppose you were in this position and the following situation occurs . . . (describe a behavioral problem at your business). Describe the steps you would take to resolve the issue."). (Perry, 1997, p. 40)

Behavioral questions go right to the heart of the matter, eliciting information about what a candidate has done or will do, rather than what the candidate "thinks" about an issue.

[They] elicit descriptions of how the applicant would handle impor-tant business problems. They are the recommended question style. (Exam-ple: "Describe the last time your work was criticized. What did you say, and what did you do to improve your performance?") (Perry, 1997, p. 40)

To elicit the desired answers, ask the right questions; include questions that are specific to apartment housing. "Every business situation you present to the applicant should relate to the position being offered (Perry, 1997, p. 40). Create "questions that elicit information about behaviors that indicate the candidate's skills and attitudes" (Perry, 1997, p. 41).

People skills. "Can you recall a situation in which you had a difficult interper-sonal interaction? How did you handle this situation?" (Perry, 1997, p. 41).

Judgment. "The departmental policy is clear—we do not assign six students to a one bedroom apartment—but this student's mother is the president of the university, and her son really wants to live with his five closest friends. What do you do?"

Disciplinary procedures (for supervisors). "Tell me about a situation in which you had to counsel an employee for violating a rule and how you went about doing so."

Initiative. "Describe the last time you took the initiative to solve a problem in the workplace. How did you get others involved?" (Perry, 1997, p. 41).

During and after the interview, take notes. Failing to adequately record responses to questions is just as damaging as not preparing for the interview.

"Selecting the most qualified candidate is a difficult process under the best of conditions," says Shuster. "Take the time to plan out your inter-view, because you need to do everything right the first time." (Perry, 1997, p. 41)

Employee Orientation and Training

Oxford American Dictionary (Ehrlich, Flexner, Carruth, & Hawkins, 1980) de-fined the verb *train* as follows: "to bring to a desired standard of efficiency or condition of behavior . . . by instruction and practice" (p. 729). *Staff* can be defined in a number of fashions. To *develop* is "to make or become . . . more mature or organized" (p. 175). Blend them together and find concepts which are integral to a successful organization.

Apartment professionals should create, support, and utilize a staff training and development plan and policy. Begin with a simple statement. For example, "Our staff training and development plan will provide an avenue for improving our employees' work performance by establishing a structured and efficient means of identifying and fulfilling their training and development needs." Or, "Our department is committed to supporting and promoting training as staff development, recognizing that it represents an investment in the institution's most important asset: its staff."

The University of Canberra, Australia, has published on their web site the following principles supporting their commitment to staff training and development (1998).

1. To encourage and promote access to appropriate training and development opportunities which develop specific and transferable skills for current and future jobs, tasks, and roles that staff may undertake within the institution.

2. To provide and maintain a work environment which encourages and assists staff to identify their individual current and future career goals and contributes to their personal development.

3. To facilitate consultation, communication, and cooperation between managers, supervisors, and staff in identifying and addressing individual and group training and development needs.

4. To provide and maintain the skill and knowledge necessary for effective work performance in order to facilitate attainment of the institution's goals.

Having successfully completed the hiring process by defining performance requirements, asking effective questions, and selecting candidates based on their skills, take advantage of the opportunity to shape a new hire into the ideal employee. While screening for the ideal certainly takes place in the hiring process, the first formal opportunity for training with impact is during the orientation for new employees.

Orientation training gives employees essential information about their organization, work group, and job. It should introduce newcomers to their organization's work rules, benefits, and facilities. Often, it provides information in compliance with governmental, state, or union rules. It is also an excellent opportunity to expose new employees to the company philosophy and culture, organizational charts, history, mission statements, standards, and expectations. It is an appropriate arena to discuss institution-wide issues and policies on subjects such as diversity and sexual harassment. Positive and thorough orientation training lays the groundwork for a well-trained staff. (See Appendix B for a sample orientation training checklist.)

Other types of training that might be utilized include qualifying training, cross training, in-service training, second-chance training, and specialty training. Briefly, *qualifying training* overlaps conceptually with orientation training. It is designed to help individuals acquire the basic knowledge, skills, and attitudes they need to meet job requirements. Its primary purpose is to eliminate the unproductive breaking-in period that new employees endure if they are not told what to do or how to perform in the unique culture of the organization. *Cross training* prepares employees to perform critical activities in the absence of employees normally assigned to them. Today, cross training is both crucial and more difficult than ever as lean-staffed, "right-sized" organizations struggle to function with fewer people whose jobs have been enlarged and enriched. Retraining or *in-service training* keeps employees' knowledge, skills, and attitudes current with changing technologies and job requirements. Common in-service training topics include effective communication, effective working habits, stress management, time management, and new technologies. *Second-chance training* corrects individual performance deficiencies; it is geared to employees who have been trained but have not met minimum job requirements.

Staff Training and Development ──────────────────────────

In addition to the traditional types of training, an ever-changing environment requires more. The apartment professional's responsibilities are growing, staff numbers are diminishing, customers' expectations are becoming more sophisticated, communities are becoming increasingly diverse, technology is surpassing itself regularly, and employees are expected to stay safe and well in the midst of it all.

Under these circumstances educational institutions are providing training sessions covering current specialty topics by utilizing the expertise of existing resources on campus. As customers and competitors become more sophisticated, customer-service training and skills in marketing become essential not only for bringing in customers but also for resident retention. This training is essential to all employees. How quickly can excellent service at the front desk be undone by a misinformed comment from a service staff member while making a repair in a unit?

The variety and complexity of cultural differences in the United States makes apartment housing fascinating. This complexity applies to customers as well as colleagues. At many institutions, over 50% of the apartment housing population consists of international students and their families. Diversity issues are well worth addressing in specialized training sessions. Experienced managers agree that working with people who are "different" is certainly more complex than interacting with people who share the same perspectives. Are staff members trained to be cognizant of existing differences in the community and workplace?

How many professionals are using the same computer or software programs that they used at the beginning of their careers in student housing? Or, perhaps a better question, how many even had a computer when first hired? Research has shown that current technology is replacing itself every eighteen months—and this includes getting new products to market. Who has not experienced the loss of a favorite software program because of a decision made to convert all employees to the newest "wonder program," soon to be rewritten? The truth is that technology will continue to evolve, and employees will be expected to evolve with it. It is imperative that employees are provided with technology training which will allow them to be successful and efficient in the workplace.

In this increasingly litigious society housing professionals are faced with a variety of legal issues. These are best addressed locally as laws and regulations vary within states, provinces, counties, and municipalities, and even from campus to campus in the same system. The institution may even be exempt from certain laws and regulations. Staff should certainly be informed about these issues. Educational institutions mirror the increase in legal actions taken in the larger community. In an attempt to address rising worker's compensation claims and to reduce related costs, choose to develop a disability management program. Such a program might require that training be provided on established attendance standards, safety awareness programs, wellness programs, and benefits awareness programs. The development of an "early return to work" program would also be included. These programs are all designed to keep staff healthy and working—and out of the legal system.

Performance Appraisals

Once a person has been selected for a job, and training is accomplished to satisfactory levels, monitoring and maintaining a high level of performance is accomplished by frequent coaching or counseling sessions. These informal day-to-day appraisals are specified in terms of explicit goals on an ongoing basis. Additionally, most institutions utilize formal methods of annual assessment, referred to as employee reviews or performance appraisals. A properly developed appraisal instrument serves as a contract between the organization and the employee in that it makes explicit what is required of that individual. Evaluating performance is necessary because it serves as an audit for the organization about the effectiveness of each employee. Such a control system, based on key standards, enables a manager to specify what the employee must start doing, continue doing, or stop doing. It is the combination of performance feedback and the setting of specific goals based on this feedback that enables the performance appraisal to fulfill its two most important functions, namely the counseling (motivation) and development (training) of employees. These are the primary purposes of performance appraisal because it is on the basis of an employee's motivation and training that decisions are made regarding that employee's retention, promotion, demotion, transfer, salary increase, or termination (Latham & Wexley, 1981).

Employee reviews are an essential part of supervision. When handled effectively, reviews can be a tremendous help in closing the gap between what employees do and what they are expected to do. The four most commonly used types of evaluation tools are goal oriented, management by objectives, trait based, or behavior anchored rating scales (Latham & Wexley, 1981; Morisey, 1976).

Goal-oriented performance appraisal focuses on how to motivate workers to contribute input to their jobs. This type of appraisal system explains what types of goals are most effective in producing high levels of motivation and performance; it also explains why goals have these effects. Managers evaluate their employees based on the goals employees have achieved over a specific period of time. The setting of goals has a directive effect on what people think and do. Goals regulate energy expenditure. Specific goals lead to higher levels of performance than obscure goals or a lack of goals. Whenever one group of employees is required to have specific production goals, they automatically increase their productivity over other groups that did not set goals. When managers set goals for employees, it is important that employees accept and meet these goals. Goal setting works best when a high level of feedback is involved.

Management by objectives (MBO) is a results-oriented rating method. MBO involves setting goals to establish objectives and to evaluate the employee based on how difficult the objectives were and how the objectives were met. In MBO, performance goals or standards are usually set in terms of cost-related targets. Emphasis is placed mainly on tangible results that are perceived to be easily measurable. As a result, some employees feel that there is an overemphasis on quantitative goals because the same employees are not evaluated on—nor do they receive credit for—important aspects of their jobs that cannot be measured in quantitative terms. The objective of MBO is to make sure that the goals selected contribute to the effectiveness of the organization as a whole.

Staff Training and Development

Trait-based performance appraisals are evaluations based on personal character-istics such as personality, skills, or abilities that are deemed appropriate to job perfor-mance. A trait-based performance appraisal is undefined in terms of observable em-ployee behaviors. It refers to potential predictors of performance. Trait-based performance appraisals can foster misunderstandings and disagreements between man-agers and their subordinates. This appraisal system does not indicate exactly what the employees must do differently on the job.

Behaviorally anchored rating scales (BARS) are subjective measures on which specific work-related behaviors are evaluated. BARS attempt to overcome the problem of interpretation by careful definitions of what each scale point signifies. Each scale point corresponds to a specific work-related behavior. A potential problem with BARS can occur when the employee demonstrates behaviors corresponding to more than one scale point at the same time. Also, this type of performance appraisal system can take a significant amount of time to create and use. (See Appendix C for samples of employee evaluation and assessment forms.)

Staff development and training is a very complex responsibility of apartment housing professionals. The process of creating specific job descriptions, followed by effective interviewing and careful hiring practices leads up to thorough training and regular appraisals of employees. It is likely that a manager will confront some portion of this process each day. How this responsibility is handled can have a major impact on employees' long-term success and productivity.

Mitchell (1997) believes that there are four widely held myths that can impede training efforts.

Myth 1: You can teach anyone anything. In reality, some people are simply inca-pable of learning what you need to teach them despite your best and most sincere ef-forts. When this happens, it is important to cut your losses rather than hang on to an employee who will always be substandard.

Myth 2: If you say the same thing the same way again and again eventually the trainee will "get it." In reality, adults learn in different ways. Some learn by hearing, some by visual instructions. Adjust your style to fit the needs of the individual.

Myth 3: Technology has become commonplace; people are used to working with it. The truth is that many trainees are fearful of new technology and may have no expe-rience in a high-tech environment. Assure your staff, when appropriate, that equipment is rugged and has built-in safety features to prevent untrained personnel from causing permanent damage.

Myth 4: Once employees are able to do the job, your work is done. In truth, it is necessary to update and upgrade employees' skills regularly. In our rapidly changing environment, your company is falling behind if your employees are standing still.

Take into account the individual needs of staff members. This will encourage co-operation from employees and better ensure their success.

Motivate them, train them, care about them, and make winners out of them.—J. W. Marriott, Jr. (LeBoeuf, 1994)

References

Deal, T., & Kennedy, A. (1982). *Corporate culture.* Reading, MA: Addison-Wesley.

Ehrlich, E., Flexner, S., Carruth, G., & Hawkins, J. (1980). *Oxford American dictionary.* New York: Avon Books.

Kramer, P. (1998). *Core competencies for housing employees at the University of Colorado at Boulder.* Boulder, CO: Office of Employee Development.

Latham, G., & Wexley, K. (1981). *Increasing productivity through performance appraisal.* Reading, MA: Addison-Wesley.

Lawrie, J. (1990). Differentiate between training, education and development. *Personnel Journal, 69*(10), 44.

LeBoeuf, M. (1994). *How to win customers and keep them for life.* New York: Putnam.

Lee, C. (1995). The budget blahs. *Training, 29*(10) 31-38.

Mitchell, E. (1997). Dispelling myths about training. *Leadership for the Front Lines,* Issue 301.

Morisey, G. (1976). *Management by objectives and results in the public sector.* Reading, MA: Addison-Wesley.

Naisbitt, J., & Aburdeen, P. (1990). *Megatrends 2000: Ten new directions for the 1990's.* New York: Avon Books.

Perry, P. (1997). Hire right: Three steps to a great job interview. *College Services Administration, 20*(5), 37-41.

Peters, T., & Waterman, R., Jr. (1982). *In search of excellence: Lessons from America's best run companies.* New York: Harper & Row.

University of Canberra. (1998). *Training and development policy—general staff.* [Online]. Available: http://www2.canberra.edu.au/hr/policies/gentd.html

Whalen, D. (Ed.). (1993). *1993 Apartments survey report.* Columbus, OH: Association of College and University Housing Officers-International.

APPENDIX A

Samples of Job Descriptions and Responsibilities

Assistant Director—Community Relations

Assist with the development and implementation of staff selection and training.

Develop, participate in, and direct staff meetings.

Functional supervision of Community Development Advisors (CDAs).

Provide unit coverage in absence of Complex Director on tasks as assigned.

Schedule Help Line duty.

Provide training and leadership for the CDAs in problem resolution and community development.

Assess resident problems and strategize the appropriate response level and strategies.

Provide leadership for the problem resolution and conflict management component of University Apartments Residence Life (UARL).

Provide emergency and immediate intervention when necessary.

Provide support and back-up to CDAs.

Involve CDAs in mediations as appropriate.

Conduct intervention, mediation, or confrontation on serious problems and work with campus and local resources to provide needed services.

Maintain records of all activities; document events, incidents and actions; handle all formal correspondence and filing of action; and other administrative responsibilities.

Represent the UARL area in campus, community, and departmental meetings.

Develop appropriate liaisons with necessary campus offices and local agencies.

Complete additional tasks as needed and assigned.

Assistant Director—Community Services

Participate in staff selection and training.

Participate in and direct staff meetings.

Provide support and back-up for programming efforts of CDAs.

Involve CDAs in UARL programming and community development.

Maintain records of all activities, programs, and events; handle all formal correspondence.

Coordinate resident orientation and community development of University Apartments.

Assist with selection and training of Service Center staff.

Coordinate and develop facility operations.

Maintain program budget and staff payroll.

Supervise the Give or Take Center operation.

Select, train and supervise Recreational Aides.

Develop appropriate educational and social learning activities for University Apartments.

Supervise directly or through Recreation Coordinators (RCs) and CDAs all programming efforts conducted in University Apartments.

Maintain work and payroll schedules for RCs

Manage records of participation, agreements to participate, liability and safety guidelines, and other administrative records necessary to assure organized, documented, and safe programs.

Represent UARL area in appropriate campus and community meetings.

Coordinate, develop, and provide programming information for Residence Life Service Center (1434).

Provide administrative support to the unit and to adult, graduate, professional, family, and international (AGPFI) students.

Community Development Advisors

Participate in staff meetings, one-on-ones and task forces as assigned.

Participate in staff selection and training.

Provide coverage of the UARL Help Line on assigned days throughout the year.

Provide personal orientation to new residents (and families).

Develop and implement programs, activities, and events for University Apartments.

Respond appropriately to residents' needs for information and assistance with problems as needed.

Maintain a complete logs of activities which is submitted at designated times.

Maintain awareness of and handle appropriately all community issues and environmental concerns.

Provide mediation and judicial services as appropriate.

Participate in unit and area training.

Complete other tasks as needed and assigned.

Recreation Coordinators

Attend regular staff meetings and training sessions.

Provide direct coordination of a variety of programs occurring seven days per week, during the day and evening hours, as well as during vacation periods.

Maintain appropriate safety and behavioral standards at all programs and activities.

Participate in program preparation and clean-up activities.

Manage the opening and closing of facilities for assigned events.

Provide on-site supervision of programs and activities.

Direct programs as assigned.

Complete other tasks as needed and assigned.

Facility Supervisors (Supervised by Facility Coordinator)

Provide direct supervision of all facility spaces in University Apartments as assigned.

Provide entrance and lock-up for program participants where applicable.

Staff Training and Development ————————————

Maintain proper adherence to facility usage regulations by program sponsors and participants.

Maintain the proper condition of all facilities and an inventory of all equipment and supplies.

Monitor events during occurrences as well as provide checkout at conclusion of events.

Complete other tasks as needed and assigned.

Give or Take Center Staff

Manage the organization and distribution of used goods donated to the center.

Follow administrative accounting procedures relative to distribution of items.

Consistently maintain an inventory which is well organized, and a center which is convenient and helpful.

Cover the hours posted for center operation.

Complex Director (Full Time)

Develop and supervise the entire UARL operation.

Effectively monitor and evaluate all activities.

Conduct staff selection and training of UARL staff.

Provide regular formal and informal evaluation of staff activities.

Conduct staff meetings.

Jointly train staff.

Select, supervise, and direct the work of senior staff (2 Assistant Directors).

Select, supervise, and direct the work of CDAs and other UA support staff (2 administrative aides, 2-3 facility staff, 2 recreational aides, and 3 Give or Take Center staff).

Manage the problem resolution and conflict management component of UARL.

Manage the database on resident problems and conflict management.

Develop and direct the programming and activities provided for residents.

Develop and manage the payroll of UARL operations and programming budgets.

Administer judicial system.

Hear contract release applicants.

Edit the "Community Update" newsletter.

Conduct mediations and train staff in mediation and conflict resolution.

Conduct contract hearings.

Coordinate the overall facility operations.

Develop and maintain liaison relations with relevant university and community offices such as the CPO, University Apartments management, school personnel, and others.

Share administrative coverage of unit and of AGPFI.

Advise the University Apartments Advisory Board.

Complete other tasks as needed and assigned.

(Michigan State University, Department of Residence Life)

ASSISTANT DIRECTOR FOR COMMUNITY RELATIONS

University Apartments
Job Description

I. *Basic Function*

The Assistant Director for Community Relations for University Apartments is a member of the senior staff of University Apartments Residence Life (UARL). The Assistant Director for Community Relations works with the Assistant Director for Community Services and the Complex Director to provide leadership for the programs and services offered to residents of University Apartments.

II. *Responsibilities*

The Assistant Director is primarily responsible for the conflict management and problem resolution activities of the office through direct intervention, assessment and referral, consultation, mediation, and collaboration with University and community staff and agencies. The Assistant Director lives in an assigned apartment in University Apartments.

Specific responsibilities include daily monitoring of the Help Line, ongoing consultation with Community Development Advisors (CDAs) and others, strategic planning for response to identified concerns, and developing and maintaining liaisons with other services providers.

III. *Characteristic Duties*

    A. Problem resolution and conflict management
1. Review daily the Help Line log of calls and follow up as appropriate.
2. Develop and institute action plans for responses to individual and community concerns.
3. Consult and collaborate with others.
4. Coordinate individual or neighborhood mediations as appropriate.
5. Conduct neighborhood or bay meetings to address community concerns.
6. Assist CDAs in conflict management and problem solving as appropriate.
7. Establish strong networks of resources and agencies for problem management.
8. Develop and implement protocols for resolving individual/neighborhood problems.
9. Log, track, and report cases to appropriate staff.
10. Assist the Complex Director in managing individual and neighborhood crises.

    B. Information resource and referral
1. Maintain regular office hours; be available to respond to requests for information and assistance.
2. Maintain a consistent interest in and concern for the welfare of residents.
3. Provide students and staff with information regarding university resources, policies and procedures.

4. Provide information for "Community Updates" (newsletter).
5. Provide information regarding academic, campus, and community resources.

C. Emergency response
1. Provide back-up coverage to the Help Line.
2. Answer phones in the Help Line system one night each month as assigned.
3. Respond appropriately to neighborhood and individual emergencies.

D. Program direction
1. Assist in providing direction to UARL operation through active participation in the central UARL staff.
2. Represent UARL as assigned; serve as liaison to specific office and agendas as assigned.
3. Provide unit coverage in the absence of the Complex Director or Assistant Director for Community Services.
4. Represent resident concerns as appropriate.

E. Staff responsibilities
1. Participate in the selection and training of UARL staff as assigned.
2. Assist in the development of training for UARL staff.
3. Attend senior staff, UARL staff, and one-on-one meetings with supervisor; and other required training programs as directed. UARL staff meetings are regularly scheduled on Wednesday afternoons from 3:00 p.m. to 5:00 p.m.

F. Other duties
1. Carry out responsibilities and other duties as needed and assigned, for example administration of surveys, committee assignments, assisting with special programs, newsletter articles, and information dispersal.

IV. *Supervision Received*

The Assistant Director reports to and is supervised by a Complex Director. The Assistant Director is expected to keep his or her supervisor regularly informed of activities and issues. Regular and frequent verbal contact is expected. Written reports may be expected concerning specific situations. Periodic evaluations are conducted throughout the year.

V. *Conditions of Employment*

REQUIRED: Previous experience with problem resolution and conflict management; cross-cultural skills and experiences; administration, organization and leadership experience. Successful Assistant Directors possess integrity, creativity, maturity, energy, sensitivity, a sense of humor, and a commitment to helping individuals as well as to building a better community.

A counseling or social work license; training in mediation and conflict resolution; experience working in student affairs; a Master's Degree in Counseling, Community Relations, or Student Personnel; and a working knowledge of Microsoft Office (Word, Excel, Access) are preferred.

The Assistant Director for Community Relations must live in a designated apartment and area of University Apartments while holding the position, and vacate this staff apartment upon leaving the position; be able to make a full-year commitment; and work approximately 29 hours per week.

VI.   *Remuneration*

The Assistant Director receives a waiver of the monthly apartment rent, plus $750 per month for the duration of their appointment. Appointments are typically made for 12 months. Periodic evaluations are conducted throughout the year.

(Michigan State University Department of Residence Life)

Duties and Rounds Expectations

1.   Live-in staff must be enrolled full time and must work 20 hours per week. Resident Advisors (RAs) and Resident Directors must be graduate students and cannot have any other job including within the University. They may be pursuing their Master's or doctoral degree and can be either U. S. or international students.

2.   The House Manager must have a background in property management. Maintenance and housekeeping staff must join the union and have seniority to the position. Each building is staffed with one manager, one graduate coordinator, one mechanic, and two custodians. Central workers coordinate paper work, the general manager handles all problems, and there is one budget officer and one director of housing. Managers rotate weekend duty from 4:00 p.m. to 8:00 a.m., seven days a week.

3.   The live-in staff of seven RAs have duties of programming (30%), office hours (40%), and in-complex and other responsibilities (30%). All are undergraduates, but may be either U. S. or international students. Duties: one time a week, one weekend every 6 to 7 weeks, three rounds daily between 8:00 p.m. and 12:00 midnight, and carry an emergency pager and cell phone when on duty.

4.   Community Assistants are live-in graduate students or undergraduates with 50% being international students. They hold duties in the apartment complexes and residence hall facilities such as: minor maintenance; policy enforcement; crisis management; on-call duty; outside rounds; emergencies; advising, counseling, and mediation; blackouts; lockouts; opening Community Center rooms; administrative duties; and calling outside tradespeople.

5.   RA duties include two weeks of training, weekly meetings (two hours each), facilities management, and keeping the director informed of problems and concerns. There are two RAs per night, making three rounds per night (four rounds on the weekends), and two back-up RAs on duty for the weekends.

6.   The apartment supervisors must check residents in and out of apartments; ensure that apartments are ready for occupancy; provide lock-out service; clean stairwells, laundry rooms, and storerooms; check area regularly for health and safety hazards; and hire and supervise apartment student custodian when needed. They must also act as a liaison between residents and the apartment office, refer tenants to appropriate resources, and post emergency and general notices as needed.

7.   The duties of the Assistant Director are to develop, participate in, and direct staff meetings; provide training and leadership for the CDAs in problem resolution and community development; maintain a record of all activities; document events, incidents and actions; handle all formal correspondence; coordinate and develop facility operations; and maintain work and payroll schedule for Recreation Coordinators. CDAs' du-

ties include participating in staff meetings; providing personal orientation to new residents; developing and implementing programs and events for residents; and participating in unit and area training.

8. Community Assistants (CAs) are paid $100 per month. They work five hours per week, make weekly deliveries, conduct one program for 40 to 50 units per semester, complete two hours of office work per week, and assist other programs in the community. CAs spend 40% of their time in the apartment office helping with lockouts, service requests, and applications. They spend 10% planning social gatherings and another 10% getting to know all of the residents.

9. CAs assist full-time staff and residents to provide services and information. They are subject to emergency calls after regular hours, on weekends, and on holidays Their duties consist of administrative responsibilities, checking parking lot for violations, taking care of lockouts and basic maintenance problems, organizing one community project per term, and informing new students of special services and events. To be eligible for a CA position, one must be a full-time resident of university apartments, have at least junior status, and a 2.4 cumulative GPA or better.

10. CAs' duties consist of policy enforcement, rounds, break duty, programming, and mediation.

(Michigan State University, Department of Residence Life)

HOUSING SERVICES EMERGENCY ON-CALL RESPONSE TEAM MEMBER

University of California, San Diego, Housing Services Department Job Description

General Team Purpose

To respond to emergencies which threaten our residents or properties during non-business hours. This may mean responding in person, but more often will mean acting as a conduit for referrals for assistance.

Types of Incidents Requiring Response

Death, Violent Crime, Suicide
Fire
Flood, water breaks, overflows
Custodial response
Lock and key emergencies
Broken glass
Contacting Psychological Services
Contacting Student Safety Awareness
Confirmation of residents
Hotel arrangements

Communication

1. Assess each situation to determine emergency status, who to contact in the chain of command, and when.

2. Report incidents or problems occurring during nonbusiness hours to the appropriate campus resource.

3. Assess each situation to determine if senior management staff should be notified immediately or if it is appropriate to leave a message for their return.

4. Communicate accurately and immediately to area manager or Affiliated Manager detailed information about any situation or occurrence which is potentially or actually detrimental to the welfare of residents.

5. Maintain working relationship with various departments including campus police department, private security firm, property management company, customer service center, and office staff.

6. Notify appropriate party if system fails. Assess (as a team) the breakdown in system or communication and take corrective action.

7. Act as a resource for guidance to the private security firm.

8. Contact answering service and campus police dispatch confirming on-call status at beginning of each shift.

Administration

1. Maintain sufficient contact with and attend all meetings called by the immediate staff supervisor.

2. Maintain appropriate confidentiality regarding on-call response incidents.

3. Maintain highest level of security for all keys assigned to them or entrusted to them.

4. Insure immediate and accurate reporting in response to all requests from the immediate staff supervisor and senior management.

5. Maintain accurate records relating to contacts while on-call, including necessary follow up.

6. Review Affiliated Manager's weekend updates at beginning of shift.

Physical Response

1. Response appropriately to crisis situations (such as fire, medical emergency, serious maintenance problems, personal crisis), but in no instance in such a manner which would endanger her- or himself. Appropriate reactions in such situations include informing residents of danger and contacting the proper authority.

2. Assist campus security officials in matters related to the safety, welfare, rights of students, and protection of university property.

3. Accept responsibility for facility coverage on designated week nights and weekends throughout the term of employment.

4. Respond by telephone to all pages and telephone calls within five minutes. Be available to respond physically at the site within 30 minutes.

5. Address every page, even if it is not an emergency and simply requires redirection or general information.

6. Respond to emergency situation if assigned on-call member cannot be reached.

7. Tour each affiliated site once per week while on duty. Make appropriate reports or recommendations.

8. Travel to sites to assist with access or customer service when appropriate.

Formal Qualifications

To be an on-call team member:

1. You must have been an employee of Housing and Dining Services for a minimum of two years.

2. You must have excellent administrative skills.

3. You must have knowledge of campus and community resources.

4. Your most recent Housing and Dining Services Employee Evaluation must be above expectations.

5. You must use tact when dealing with the public.

6. You must use impartiality, sensitivity, and open-mindedness.

7. You must be a self-starter and work well under light supervision.

Conditions of Employment

1. Must live in assigned Affiliated Housing Complex.

2. Employment is for a one-year term, contingent on satisfactory performance as evaluated by the on-call coordinator and Affiliated Manager.

3. Must be available to cover duty every fifth week. Team members who are unable to take scheduled duty must arrange with another team member to substitute for them, and must have the change approved by the on-call coordinator.

Remuneration

1. $450.00 toward rent on one unfurnished two-bedroom apartment in an Affiliated Housing site. Balance of rent to be paid by employee.

2. Gas, water, and electricity provided by the university.

Period of Employment: July 1 to June 30

Position is renewable for additional one-year terms based on performance in the program and in the traditional position held with the Housing and Dining Services department.

APPENDIX B

Employee Orientation Checklist
Human Resources Development
University of California, San Diego, Housing Services Department

Name:_____Date:_____

_____ Overview of University Housing and Dining Services, and Housing Services
Organizational Chart and History

_____ Map of Campus

_____ Customer Service
Mission Statement and Goal
Identifying Our Customer
Housing Services Product and Themes
Standards

_____ Communication
Chain of Command
Unit Bulletin Board

_____ Sexual Harassment Information

_____ Employee Handbook
Payday
Attendance Standards
Meals/Meal Periods
Rest Periods
Holidays/Vacation
Sick Leave
Scheduled Work Shutdowns
Personal Appearance
Uniforms
Smoking Policy

_____ ID Photo

Benefits Orientation Date:_____

The above has been explained to me and I have no further questions at this time. I
have received a copy of the Housing Services Employee Handbook.

Employee Signature:_____Date:_____

Orientation Trainer:_____Date:_____

APPENDIX C

Employee Evaluation Samples
Louisiana State University Department of Residence Life

Associate Director—Residence Education
Candidate Evaluation Form

Candidate: _____

Evaluator: _____

Rate each of the five categories below from 1 (poor) to 10 (excellent).

I.   Residence education management skills   SCORE:_____
    A. Residence hall management.
    B. Resident Assistant selection and training.
    C. Developmental programming.
    D. Crisis management and judicial affairs.
    E. Knowledge of student development theory.

Comments:_____

_____

II.   Leadership   SCORE:_____
    A. Team building.
    B. Collaborate in decision making.
    C. Work well with diverse staff.
    D. React well under pressure.
    E. Ethical decision making.
    F. Projects well in front of groups.
    G. Ability to motivate others.

Comments:_____

_____

III.   Management skills   SCORE:_____
    A. Supervision of large staff.
    B. Budget development and management.
    C. Manage day-to-day operations.
    D. Understand and interpret policies.
    E. Long-range planning.
    F. Handle difficult personnel issues.
    G. Organizational ability.

Comments:_____

_____

IV.   Interpersonal skills   SCORE:_____
    A.   Thoughts articulated in a concise manner.
    B.   Service-oriented.
    C.   Can adequately represent Residence Life to external constituencies.
    D.   Listening skills.
Comments:_____

_____

V.   Can this person work well   SCORE:_____
    A.   With current Residence Life staff?
    B.   With students?
    C.   With university community?
Comments:_____

_____

General comments:_____

_____

_____

_____

                                          TOTAL SCORE:_____

EVALUATION OF PERFORMANCE FACTORS

Performance Factors: Examples of Key Performance Indicators

I.   Work habits

A. *Manages workload.* Submits completed work on time consistent within priorities. Commits time as necessary to fulfill responsibilities of position in a competent manner. Manages work in an orderly and efficient manner. Operates with a clear sense of priorities. Shows a high capacity to adapt quickly to change, shortening the response time of processes and systems. Eliminates bureaucratic practices to accelerate all aspects of work.

B. *Attendance/use of time.* Keeps appointments on time. Maintains appropriate office hours. Makes effective use of time. Returns telephone calls m a timely manner. Employee is dependable and has a minimum of unplanned absences.

C. *Ethics/professionalism.* Follows generally accepted standards and guidelines for the profession and area of work. Performs job duties in accordance with university policies and procedures, ethical standards and practices, and in accordance with relevant laws and regulations. Reaches decisions based on the highest ethical standards. Fosters a culture of trust and respect for others by behaving in a fair and ethical manner toward others.

D. *Commitment to work.* Commits fully to the job. Concentrates on outcomes, works across departmental boundaries, avoids turf issues, and eliminates unnecessary work to achieve right results. Self-motivated with a strong work ethic.

E. *Flexibility.* Adapts to change quickly. Applies rules and policies flexibly. Adjusts behavior to fit the situation or person as appropriate. Modifies plans and goals to meet changing institutional demands and opportunities.

F. *Value-added orientation.* Capitalizes on opportunities to reduce costs, improve customer service, increase productivity, increase customer satisfaction, improve decision making, and reduce waste. Encourages flexibility and personal initiative by others.

II.   Analyzing problems and making decisions

A. *Initiative.* Reviews alternatives, considers department's resources, and suggests a recommended course of action when bringing a problem to the supervisor. Requires minimum supervision. Applies what is learned in one situation to a subsequent similar situation. Improves working skills and abilities. Keeps technically updated by applying current technical data and practices, department policies, guidelines, and regulations. Accepts change and addresses problems by a "how can we" (positive) rather than a "we can't" (negative) approach.

B. *Information and viewpoint gathering.* Listens to and considers the views of others. Considers the advantages, disadvantages, usefulness, potential results, and other relevant factors of alternatives.

C. *Judgment.* Assumes ownership of problems and avoids finger pointing. Resolves problems with minimum impact on staff and public with satisfactory results. Maintains a firm, fair, objective, and unbiased approach in determining the most appropriate action. Anticipates internal and external forces that will impact the future effectiveness and efficiency of the unit and responds with needed change.

III.   Communication

A.   *Writing skills.* Has effective writing skills. Writes in an understandable manner which is free of grammatical, spelling, or sentence structure errors.

B.   *Oral communications.* Speaks effectively. Conducts an effective meeting, that is, prepares an agenda, defines the purpose of the meeting, encourages group participation, listens and considers group recommendations, adjourns on time and follows up on suggestions. Gives clear directions.

C.   *Informing supervisor.* Uses appropriate communication channels. Consults with supervisor about actual or potentially sensitive issues. Assumes responsibility for communicating relevant information.

IV.   Interpersonal work relationships

A.   *Conflict resolution.* Steers conflict away from people and toward issues. Tries to understand the views of others. Looks for a basis of agreement, seeks solutions, and reaches agreement on a course of action.

B.   *Team relations.* Maintains good working relationships with coworkers, superiors, and the public. Listens attentively, considers employee views, avoids interrupting unnecessarily, assists employees when they request help, and recognizes superior contributions. Disseminates needed information to staff. Functions well with administrative peers, that is, has a manner of dealing with people that encourages joint problem solving, openness and candor. Has open communication style, that is, shares information in a timely manner, sets others at ease in conversations, and encourages positive interaction. Contributes to problem solving and policy formulation in meetings.

V.   Client service orientation

A.   Responsive to customers and projects a desire to solve problems in a way that makes customers feel that their concerns or issues have been understood and will be acted upon.

B.   Continually assesses customer wants, needs and priorities and makes continuous improvement a part of the management of all systems and processes.

VI.   Institutional and technical knowledge

A.   Understands and complies with university policies and procedures.

B.   Demonstrates technical competence in performing duties.

EVALUATION OF MANAGEMENT ACTIVITIES

**(Do not complete this section unless the employee
has management or supervisory duties.)**

Management Activities: Examples of Key Management Indicators

VII.   Administrative and leadership skills

A.   *Communication skills.* Demonstrates effective mediation and negotiation skills.

B.   *Group management skills.* Employees are trained, encouraged, and held accountable for streamlining work processes, solving problems, planning for performance, and creating new ways to satisfy students and other customers. Encourages participatory decision making. Shares information and keeps people up to date. Solicits input, ideas, and expertise of others. Builds team spirit and promotes employee accomplishment to others inside and outside the work group. Resolves conflict quickly to restore team effectiveness. Works as a facilitator and coach, building cross-functional relationships and a shared sense of governance.

C.   *Develops others.* Designs jobs around core competencies and capabilities of individuals. Practices active learning. Develops all employees for skill diversification on a continuous basis. Identifies staff development needs, formulates development plans, and assesses the impact of plans on performance results.

D.   *Resource management.* Attracts top talent. Uses automation and reengineering continuously to improve efficiency and effectiveness. Directs resources to high-value activities.

E.   *Strategic focus.* Directs unit resources and activities toward high-value work, contributing directly to institutional mission and goals.

F.   *Manages effectively in a climate of uncertainty and ambiguity.* Operates with a clear sense of priorities.

G.   *Action oriented.* Initiates actions to avoid potential problems before they occur and/or to increase the probability of achieving desired results.

H.   *Promotes and effectively manages diversity.* Creates a work culture that embraces diversity. Recruits for a diverse workplace. Develops, evaluates, and rewards employees consistent with the goal of creating a diverse work force.

I.   *Builds pride in the unit and the institution.* Provides employees with the conditions, incentives, and resources for doing a good job. Recognizes and appreciates the contributions of others.

J.   *Technology.* Encourages innovation and use of new technology.

K.   *Employment laws and regulations.* Understands and complies with laws and regulations that impact employees. Institutes discipline and grievance-handling policies as needed.

Student Worker Job Performance Evaluation

This evaluation is based on the student's job performance according to the job description in the Student Staff Handbook. Please use the following descriptions:

Outstanding (O)—Goes above and beyond what is required.

Very Good (VG)—Meets requirements and does well.

Good (G)—Meets but does not exceed requirements.

*Fair (F)—Meets *some* requirements.

*Needs Improvement (NI)—Does not meet minimal requirements.

Not Applicable (N/A)—Hall does not require.

*Must explain in comments section.

Name:_____Date:_____

JOB PERFORMANCE	N/A	NI	F	G	VG	O
Corresponds with desk on a daily basis						
Attends DA meetings						
Enforces and follows hall rules and regulations						
Availability						
Participation in training sessions and events						
Accuracy and detail on forms and documents						
Ability to adapt to new policies						
Punctual						
Professionalism						
AVERAGE FOR JOB PERFORMANCE						

COMMENTS: _____

_____

EMPLOYEE/RESIDENT RELATIONS	N/A	NI	F	G	VG	O
Ability to work with others						
Contribution in meetings						
AVERAGE FOR EMPLOYEE/RESIDENT RELATIONS						

COMMENTS: _____

_____

Staff Training and Development

COMMUNICATION	N/A	NI	F	G	VG	O
Ability to communicate effectively						
Effective interpretation of departmental and university policies to residents						
Regular communication with staff concerning incidents, problems and progress						
AVERAGE FOR COMMUNICATION						

COMMENTS: _____

_____

LEADERSHIP/MOTIVATION	N/A	NI	F	G	VG	O
Ability to work with staff						
Ability to exercise good judgement						
Respects confidentiality						
Initiative on the job						
Overall attitude						
AVERAGE FOR LEADERSHIP/ MOTIVATION						

COMMENTS: _____

_____

Areas of special strength:_____

_____

Areas needing improvement:_____

_____

If this person were to apply for this position again, would you recommend this student based on his or her performance to date?   YES_____   NO_____

Would you recommend for a higher position?   YES_____   NO_____

Overall Evaluation

NI	F	G	VG	O

Signature of Evaluator:_____Date:_____

Evaluator's Position:_____

This report has been discussed with me.

*Employee's Signature:_____Date:_____

*Your signature indicates that this evaluation has been shared and discussed with you, and does not necessarily indicate agreement with its contents.

On a separate sheet, the student employee should comment on how he or she feels about his or her evaluation. The student will sign, date, and return this separate comment page only if he or she feels it is necessary to be placed in the permanent file.

Staff Training and Development

Performance Evaluation Form for Classified Employees

Name:_____Social Security #_____

Department:_____Anniversary Date:_____

The supervisor should be prepared to discuss each section of the form during the performance review. Following the review the supervisor and the employee should sign the form. A copy of the form should be given to the employee and another copy sent to Human Resource Management (HRM) *within 10 days*. If you need more space for any item, please use a separate sheet of paper and attach it to this worksheet.

Section I—Reviewing the job requirements. Make note of any important changes that have occurred in the employee's responsibilities since the last performance review. Also note any changes occurring in the next 12 months that are likely to affect the employee's job responsibilities.

Supervisor's Comments: _____

_____

Supervisor: The odds are that some important changes have occurred, or will occur, in the employee's job responsibilities. Let the employee know what changes you see occurring in the work situation so that the employee knows what job assignments are most important and relevant. Document significant job changes on the job description and send the update to HRM.

Section II—Obstacles to effective job performance. Note "trouble spots"—things that happened that made the employee less effective than he or she could be. Obstacles to effective performance may come from resource limitations, the performance of subordinates or others, breakdowns in communication, the employee's own attitudes or performance, or factors that are beyond the employee's control. Note any suggestions you have for removing these obstacles.

Supervisor's Comments: _____

_____

Section III—Performance rating. Competencies represent the set of knowledge, skills, abilities, and work habits the employee must possess to successfully perform his or her job. By assessing the employee's performance on key competencies, you are better able to make decisions concerning the employee's career development, readiness for new assignments, and job performance. Using the chart below, rate the employee on each of the core performance factors/competencies listed. Examples of performance indicators/factors to consider for each competency area are available in a separate attachment. All employees must be rated on Performance Factors 1 to 6; additionally, supervisors must be rated on Performance Factor 7 below. Circle the appropriate numerical rating for each performance factor.

Evaluation of Performance Factors
Applying to All Classified Employees

PERFORMANCE FACTORS/ COMPETENCIES	RATING SCALE		
	Improvement is essential for job success	Performance on target	Key contributor who consistently performs at a high level
Work habits	1 2	3	4 5
Analyzing problems/making decisions	1 2	3	4 5
Communication	1 2	3	4 5
Interpersonal work relationships	1 2	3	4 5
Client service orientation	1 2	3	4 5
Job knowledge and technical skills	1 2	3	4 5
Overall rating: Sum the factor ratings and divide by 6. Record the overall rating in the space provided: (If you are rating a supervisor, do not sum the ratings, continue below.)			

Administrative and leadership skills (supervisors only)	1 2	3	4 5
Supervisor's overall rating: Sum the factors and divide by 7. Record the overall rating in the space provided:			

Supervisor: Indicate below what you and the employee will do between now and the next appraisal to further develop the employee's core competencies.

Professional Development Goals for the Coming Year

1._____

2._____

Section IV—Objectives and future plans. Make notes concerning the employee's performance plan for next year. The ideas will serve as the basis, in part, for the objectives you and the employee will develop for the coming year. Here are some important questions to keep in mind when setting objectives: How satisfied are you with the quality of work produced? Are there ways the employee could do the work that would decrease the current rate of mistakes, better meet deadlines, improve the quality of the work, and/or increase customer satisfaction with the work? In terms of technology, what does the employee need now? What will he or she need in the future? What can the employee do to reduce costs, serve the client better, and improve productivity or quality?

   Supervisor: Thinking through your discussion with the employee concerning his or her job responsibilities, contributions, obstacles to effective performance, and the needs of the department, list below the performance objectives for the coming year. You and the employee should spend enough time discussing these objectives to assure they are realistic and in line with other goals of your department.

Future Performance Objectives

1._____

2._____

Supervisor's Comments: _____

_____

_____

MERIT RAISE RECOMMENDATION

_____RECOMMENDED   _____NOT RECOMMENDED

---

*Employee's Signature:_____Date:_____

Supervisor's Signature_____Date:_____

---

*Your signature indicates that this evaluation has been shared and discussed with you, and does not necessarily indicate agreement with its contents. If your overall score from Section III is less than 2.5 (i.e., improvement is essential), your merit increase must be denied and you are ineligible for promotion. You will be reevaluated again within the next three to six months.

Student Governments Within Apartment Housing Operations

M. Katherine Carr
Assistant Director for Resident Life
University of Utah

Student Governments within Apartment Housing

Introduction

Student government in an apartment environment can be the solution to many communication problems and programming challenges. Many of the apartment complexes at colleges and universities around the world have some form of student or resident government, either formal or informal. The style of student governance systems will vary depending on the needs of the organization.

This chapter is based on more formal, specific student or resident government structures and their selection modes, funding, and impact on apartment operations, as exemplified by the Resident Council of the University Student Apartments Resident Association (USARA) at the University of Utah. Criteria selected for review include: (a) the history of the model; (b) the model; (c) the purpose of a resident council form of student government; (d) positions and duties; (e) funding; (f) honoraria, stipends, and support systems; and (g) election processes. In addition, the successful, long-lived student or resident governments from four other institutions (Iowa State University, University of Calgary, University of Florida, University of Michigan) are summarized. Readers may find it helpful to use one of the structures as a guide, or a combination of several, to better serve the needs of the residents in their unique apartment complexes.

History of the Model

The University of Utah campus at Salt Lake City has had family housing since Stadium Village opened in 1945. The original one-level apartments were constructed quickly and cheaply to house the great influx of students with families at the end of World War II. Involvement in the university's student government from those families was informal. The student government system for the apartments started in 1973, and was formalized with a constitution in 1978.

The Model

Over the years, the Resident Council has seen many changes in management, resident officers, and issues. These changes have included adversarial situations regarding how the apartments should be run, who should approve rental rate increases, how student government activities could be funded, and even who should pay for and publish Resident Council information. The original constitution was full of confusing language that referred to the group as a Village Board, and/or a Resident Caucus without clear language to define duties and privileges.

After struggling to make sense of the existing constitution's meaning and being frustrated with attempts to amend it, a decision was made in 1992 to rewrite the document. Over a period of several years, the elected student officers wrote and rewrote drafts of a new constitution with the assistance of the appropriate administrators. When the document reached a point of acceptable structure and content, the new constitution was submitted to the University of Utah Student Involvement Center for approval and support. With some revisions, the new constitution proceeded through the review and approval process, which included the University of Utah President's Cabinet and the Board of Trustees, and formal approval was granted in December, 1992. During the next two years, amendments and minor changes were made and the final constitution was approved by the Board of Trustees in July, 1995 (see Appendix A).

The USARA constitution has been a very successful document. With its clear and consistent language, the guidance it provides for the student government is invaluable. It provides enough flexibility that each new Resident Council has its own identity and the ability to accomplish a variety of differing goals from year to year.

The Purpose of a Resident Council

The Resident Council at the University of Utah Student Apartments serves as representative group for the residents both within the housing operation and in the university community at large. Internally, the Resident Council is instrumental in an advisory capacity to administration. It is included in deliberations for improvements to the facilities, changes in policy, rental rate increases, eligibility issues, and programming. Administrators are well advised to include this group in all issues that will affect the population. Experience has shown that students care a great deal about their environment but generally lack the time to get involved unless there is a negative or threatening issue at hand. The Resident Council is in a position to be the eyes and ears of the community. It can bring information into planning discussions that helps staff provide better and more appropriate service and improvements.

The Resident Council takes an active role in the external organizations of student governing bodies, such as the Associated Students of the University of Utah (ASUU), the Resident Hall Students Association, and the Greek Panhellenic Council. These organizations are directly related to the university's Department of Student Affairs. The Resident Council also participates in campus-wide programming. This allows the Student Apartments to take advantage of the fund sharing available from student fees. The Mayor and other Council members frequently are invited to participate in special planning committees and task forces for other university organizations such as parking, new construction, campus events, and child care.

Positions and Duties

The governing bodies of the USARA include the four-member Resident Council, the seven-member Executive Committee, and the 10-member Advisory Board. By means of the constitution, the membership and governing bodies are clearly defined with powers and duties set forth therein. Membership is limited to eligible residents of Student Apartments. Eligibility is established when one of the responsible household members is a student and completes a minimum number of credit hours in at least two of the three semester each year. This requirement is set specifically for housing at Student Apartments. It is important to note that this does not parallel academic requirements.

The *Resident Council* consists of four elected members: the Mayor, Facilities Council member, Financial Council member, and Program Council member. The four members of the Resident Council carry equal voting rights.

The *Executive Committee* includes the four-member Resident Council, the director of Student Apartments, and two assistant directors. The Executive Committee meets weekly to discuss issues, share information, and address residents' concerns. The director and assistant directors do not have voting privileges.

The *Advisory Board* includes all members of the Resident Council and the Executive Committee, plus three additional administrators from departments of the University of Utah as assigned by the Vice President for Administrative Services. These members are selected to provide objective advice and guidance to the Resident Council and the Executive Committee. Advisory Board members might include the director of parking services, the director of student health, the director of plant operations, the manager of the risk management office, the director of the International Center, the director of the Student Involvement Center, and others whose policies and procedures have an impact on—and are impacted by—Student Apartments residents and the Resident Council.

Only the four members of Resident Council and the three members from campus departments have voting privileges at the Advisory Board's monthly meetings. The Advisory Board votes on procedures and proposals made by the Resident Council. It also may vote on advice it presents to the administrators of Student Apartments, such as rental rate increases and how they may be best implemented, changes in parking rules and regulations, eligibility changes, and other issues that impact Student Apartments residents.

Individual responsibilities of the four Resident Council members are detailed in the constitution. The terms used are broad in scope to allow flexibility in procedures. However, the language for specific duties is clear. For example, the *Mayor* is, in broad terms, responsible for coordinating the Resident Council's activities, which vary from year to year. The Mayor also is the officer in charge and chairs meetings, establishes meeting agendas, arranges for minutes to be taken, and calls special meetings as needed.

The duties of the *Facilities Council member* include reviewing facilities and environmental issues pertaining to Student Apartments. The Facilities Council member also coordinates projects and tasks that relate to facilities concerns, such as the garden plots adjacent to three apartment villages. The coordination of organizing, distributing, and cleaning up the garden plots is the responsibility of the Facilities Council member. As issues arise from residents or others about the physical environment for their families, the Facilities Council member organizes the information, researches options for solutions, to problems and makes proposals to the Resident Council, the Executive Committee, and/or the Advisory Board for action. Examples of concerns that might generate requests for policy changes are smoking in the apartments, the number of occupants allowed in each apartment, traffic and parking problems, and recycling projects.

The *Financial Council member* is responsible for the management of the Resident Council's financial account in accordance with administrative and fiscal policies of the University of Utah. The Financial Council member is expected to provide financial advice for the Resident Council regarding the best use of budgeted funds. In addition to standard costs associated with doing business, regular yearly projects must be accounted for on an ongoing basis. These projects include a biweekly publication called "Classified Ads," a dedicated telephone line with voice mail, advertising and funding of Resident Council programs, and other expenses that may arise. The Financial Council member accomplishes his or her duties with good record keeping and regular financial reports at weekly Resident Council and monthly Advisory Board meetings. A yearly budget is presented to the Resident Council, Executive Committee, and Advisory Board for their recommendations, which are included in the Student Apartments budgeting process. It is important to note that the Resident Council has the power to change, increase, or dissolve any of the projects or programs inherited from a previous Council as long as the funds are adequate. The Financial Council member, in cooperation with the Mayor, applies to the ASUU for a share of student fees that are collected by the university at large.

The *Programs Council member* plans and coordinates programs and activities for residents. All four members of the Resident Council support the implementation of the programs under the leadership and supervision of the Programs Council member. To accomplish this work, the Programs Council member prepares and proposes a yearly programs and activities agenda with estimated costs for each. He or she also coordinates publicity for the activities. A list of vendors is kept in a programming file for current and future use. Many of the programs are produced in cooperation with the Resident Assistants team. The Programs Council member acts as the liaison and coordinator of those activities. When resident volunteers are needed, they are solicited for and work under the direction of the Programs Council member.

Even though the duties of each Resident Council member are defined, the work is shared. Depending on the projects and goals of each Resident Council, regular duties are divided by the group to balance the time involvement whenever possible. For the Resident Council to function appropriately, it is important that the adviser not inject too much advice nor strongly influence decisions. The Resident Council is encouraged to maintain a close working relationship with staff, but also to remain independent in order to have the power to make a difference for residents and for the community.

The Assistant Director for Resident Life is the adviser to the Resident Council and is available to clarify the parameters set by university and Student Apartments rules and regulations.

Resident Council Funding

Funding for the Resident Council is accomplished through a line item in the Student Apartments budget. The funds are approximately .35% of the annual gross revenue budget which is approximately $1.50 per month per apartment. The Resident Council is regarded as an important and essential part of the Student Apartments culture. The Resident Council also provides financial support for specific programming events. Some of these events are eligible for funding from the ASUU student fee disbursal. ASUU-supported activities include funding for a parents' night out with the Student Apartments child care center, supplies and training for the "Neighborhood Watch" program, and safety training with the fire department. ASUU funds are not automatically forthcoming and the Resident Council must apply for specific activity financing every year.

The only controls on the Resident Council for spending their budgeted funds are dictated by University of Utah guidelines which impact all student groups. Through training and counseling, the adviser informs the Resident Council when they may be out of compliance with the rules of the university.

The monthly accounting of funds spent and funds available assists the Resident Council to stay within the budget. However, if it should find that a project that exceeds the budget, the Resident Council may wish to have fundraising events and/or solicit additional money from the Student Apartments general budget. In addition, philanthropic assistance from the community may be solicited, within the rules for donors set by the university. This happens rarely—and only with Advisory Board approval. To date, funding practices have been very successful.

Resident Council Honoraria and Support Systems

Each Resident Council member at Student Apartments receives a monthly honorarium. This amount is designated as part of the Resident Council's budget and must be approved yearly by the Advisory Board members. The recommended formula is calculated by taking the average of what the part-time Resident Assistants are given as a rent reduction for their services. Time commitments and expectations are similar for both groups. Currently, the honoraria encompass just over 50% of the budget.

Student Apartments has been able to effect the honoraria through an exchange-of-service rent reduction arrangement to eliminate the need for transfer of money. Tax requirements do not apply to the rent reduction, because it is neither compensation nor payment but a requirement of the position. The benefits of having dynamic Resident Council members who are committed to quality performance is well worth the nominal cost to residents.

The issue of control has been discussed many times. The perception might be that since Student Apartments funds the Resident Council there is an element of administrative control. The possibility certainly is present, but the practice and guidelines provided by the USARA Constitution and the Advisory Board keeps a healthy level of separation from administration. The fact that the administration has an advisory role without voting privileges assists in the separation of control. Genuine differences of opinion are considered to be healthy. Discussions develop with questions, answers, and solutions being explored. The conclusions that result from such interactions are generally positive for residents and for management.

Student Apartments' Resident Life staff also provide limited secretarial and staff assistance as negotiated with each Resident Council. For example, the biweekly "Classified Ads" require a central drop-off point for residents and efficient processing and printing. The clerical work does not relieve the Resident Council from monitoring, proofreading, and approving each publication. They also pay for printing services and paper. The Resident Assistants participate by delivering "Classified Ads" door to door with their regular weekly deliveries. The Resident Council may choose not to utilize this service with no repercussion from administration. Again, independence and objective interaction are important elements of the group.

The Resident Council may conduct resident surveys from time to time and do so with or without any additional financial support unless they propose a cooperative effort with another group. That group, from time to time, may be Student Apartments' administration as the need to gather objective information from the residents is recognized. In such instances, administration may request and fund the survey with participation or sponsorship of the Resident Council, which may or may not agree to participate. If it does not wish to be involved in a project there is no pressure for involvement and no retaliation for the rejection. This practice of doing business ensures continuing communication and support from year to year.

Each Resident Council is different in how it wishes to operate. Some groups are very dependent and need to be encouraged to stand apart from administration. Such groups find comfort in the clerical support and administrative decisions being made for them. This practice is consciously discouraged and avoided. Other Resident Councils may be adversarial and need to have a great deal of information available. The more information they have provides them with a broader picture of how the apartment complex is operated. Their suggestions for changes and/or improvements are more realistic and valuable to facility planning and budget projections. Past experience with the various Resident Councils provides evidence that the more involved a Resident Council is with making recommendations based upon valid and complete information, the greater possibility there is for cooperative effort and agreement.

Resident Council Election Process

The rules for electing a new Resident Council are clearly defined in the constitution. Standard requirements of residency, eligibility, and accountability are included. To ensure an unbiased and objective election, however, the procedures for each election are placed in the hands of an Election Committee that is separate from any Student Apartments staff and from Council members running for reelection. The chair of the committee is one of the Advisory Board members from campus. General information regarding dates, procedures, and contact points are delivered door to door to all residents by the Election Committee or its designee(s). Advertising or promotion of candidates is not allowed by staff members, Resident Assistants, noncandidate Council members, or Election Committee members. The goal is to have an election that represents the will of the residents and not that of the existing resident government or administration. To accomplish this goal, the Election Committee, with the support of the constitution, provides a grievance process for resolution of protests.

Previous Election Committees have prepared packets of election procedures which are passed to the new Election Committee which may use, change, or recreate the process while at all times being in compliance with the constitution. The hands-off position of current Resident Council and Executive Committee members has, over the years, allowed new Councils to maintain the healthy independence that is needed to have quality interactions.

Elections may be filled with emotion, and it may be tempting for a sitting Resident Council and/or administration to get involved and influence the results. It is strongly recommended that this not occur. The attitude to "take what you get" has proved to be extremely valuable for both administration and councils. The paradoxical experience has shown that many Resident Council candidates who give the impression that they may be challenging and difficult to work with if elected have been excellent leaders and ultimately the strongest advocates for needed administrative programs and changes. Because of this structured, constitutional approach, as well as the honoraria, Student Apartments has experienced interest and service from many of "the best and the brightest."

Student Governments within Apartment Housing —————

Former Resident Council members have reported that there were two main reasons they were attracted to the elected position and the election campaign. One reason was the opportunity to serve and the benefits that will be realized by the residents and themselves. The second reason—and a realistic motivator—is the honorarium. Jeremy Baker, the 1998-1999 Mayor, explained the value of the honoraria in this way (personal communication, February, 1999):

> Knowing that there is compensation for work performed makes me know that I must be accountable. It also gives me the feeling that my work and contributions are worth something, that they have value enough to merit some payment. I know that the amount is not much, but the psychological impact is still there. The combined motivation of service and compensation, and that I have an opportunity—even the responsibility—to make a difference in the residents' lives while they are living in student housing is very satisfying. Working by the rules and procedures set forth in the US-ARA Constitution is great training for my future also.

Most student or resident governments found in apartment complexes do not have honoraria or other significant means of monetary reward for their officers. Having experienced both approaches, the University of Utah Student Apartments administration is convinced that the amount allocated to the officers of Resident Council has a very high return for the cost. The honorarium lends credibility to and requires accountability from those in office.

Amendments and Bylaws

As time passes and needs of the organization change, the Resident Council is called upon to make adjustments in how it functions. Provisions for amendments are clearly defined in the constitution. The different University of Utah groups who must review and approve amendments are specifically identified. Changing the review process would require an amendment to the constitution. But, because of the confusion experienced when using the previous constitution, it was deemed necessary to have this section of the current document be more specific to avoid omission of any groups during a review process.

The final section of the constitution detailing the right to create bylaws gives the greatest amount of flexibility to the Resident Council. Herein they may establish rules and procedures as the times and student culture may require. The Election Committee rules and procedures would fit nicely into this category if the Resident Council and Advisory Board decided to formalize them. Bylaws would also be helpful if student governments of the University of Utah became more interactive and had more responsibility in other university groups. The flexibility is built into the constitution to do what is necessary with utilization of the bylaws section.

Additional Models of Resident Government

Many colleges and universities with on-campus apartment housing support resident governance systems similar to the Resident Council at the University of Utah.

Four North American universities with long-term, successful resident government systems are described below.

Iowa State University

The Community Council is comprised of a Mayor and a Chairperson who are elected at large during annual campus-wide elections, with two persons elected by the residents of each housing area for a total of six members. The Mayor appoints an Information Director, Treasurer, Magistrate, and Family Advocate for Programming, with the Community Council's approval. The election procedure specifies that these officers must be residents of the housing complex. There is no limit on the number of times each member may serve.

For funding, half of the vending revenues from both resident halls and apartments are designated for the Community Council. Fundraisers are conducted with local merchants as well as with in-house projects such as assembling and selling a residents' cookbook.

Each Community Council decides how much of the budget will be designated for such expenditures as child care during meetings and similar support needs. Currently, members receive a stipend that ranges from $100 to $250 per academic year, depending on the position.

The Community Council is bound by the university's ordinance system and operates in an advisory capacity. The Council has significant impact on housing administration by means of resident support. Within the set parameters, the Council operates by means of a constitution. There are also bylaws and standing rules of order specifically for Community Council that are not binding to the administration.

The student governing body is self-disciplined. The Magistrate and/or the Community Council's Resident Life adviser hear discipline cases and make final decisions regarding conduct, parking, and other concerns.

University of Calgary

The student government consists of 18 volunteer members, of whom five of these are elected as officers (chair, two executive assistants, secretary, and treasurer). Members receive no compensation, honoraria, stipends or other benefits. One representative from administration meets with the officers one week prior to the full Council's monthly meeting. Special subcommittees are formed for special activities from non-elected resident volunteers.

Funding is established through a mandatory $20 annual levy from all of the 250 apartments. In addition, $1.00 per month per apartment from rent for a summer recreation coordinator. The budget money is placed into a special account that is controlled by the Council. If a resident does not pay the annual $20 levy when it is billed, the Council is responsible for collection of those funds. The Council is accountable to the residents for budget and activities.

The Council operates with a constitution which is binding upon members. Other rules of conduct are contained in the lease agreement. The Council is self-disciplined through an addendum which establishes guidelines for the Peer Review Committee. This committee is established by need.

The Council is autonomous from housing administration, but is recognized by the Board of Governors of the University of Calgary as an official student government. The relationship with administration is best defined as "friendly influence." The Council meets regularly one week prior to the administrators' meeting and then meets monthly with administration. One resident life person is designated as adviser to the Council.

University of Florida

The Mayors Council of the University of Florida's Village Housing is comprised of five mayors (one elected from each of the five housing areas) and an Executive Board (chair, secretary, and treasurer). A student senator (a resident who is elected to represent Village Housing in the University of Florida student government) also attends the monthly meetings. The Coordinator of Village Community Services serves as adviser.

Each mayor presides over a village commission which may be structured in one of two ways. The commission may be comprised of representatives who volunteer or are appointed by residents of each building (one commissioner per building), or it may be an open structure in which any resident may participate. Each commission has a secretary and a treasurer. Mayors, officers, and commissioners may be students or spouses; all Executive Board members must be students. The chair of the Mayors Council receives a $50.00 rent reduction; the other officers, mayors, and commissioners receive no compensation.

Each mayor convenes the commission monthly, reporting on previous Mayors Council activity and noting information and issues to be presented at the next Mayors Council meeting. All issues, including those presented by administration, are addressed by the Mayors Council. After discussion, the Mayors vote on what they will recommend to administration. The Council's approval regarding administrative operations, policies, and procedures is not binding but is considered seriously by administration in planning for the community growth and changes.

Mayors Council is funded annually by monies collected by the university-wide student government (approximately $15,000) and by a percentage of vending revenues from the apartments (approximately $15,000). Student government funds are allocated for specific preapproved projects, programs, and activities; vending revenues support programs and activities for all villages, such as the annual Village Olympics, as well as specific projects in each village, as approved by each commission.

A constitution guides the Mayors Council but is not binding on administration. Decisions that are made regarding procedures and rules affecting the Council are binding upon the Council. Since the Mayors Council is a student-government-registered organization, issues of discipline are addressed by the student government; there is not a separate disciplinary group within the Mayors Council.

University of Michigan

The University of Michigan's Residents Council operates by means of a constitution. The Council has the capacity for 11 to 15 members; the size of the Council varies depending upon the interest and number of volunteers during any one year. During the past four years there have been six to twelve volunteer members. A residence life staff adviser meets with the group at least once a month.

Council members are selected from the volunteers to accommodate representation from each of the Community Aide areas. Officers are selected from the Residents Council membership. The term of each Council member is for one year but may be longer or shorter depending upon the need for planning and the willingness of the members to stay involved. Recruitment may be ongoing. Through the monthly newsletter and other in-house media, the residents are invited to get involved.

Funding is appropriated in response to a needs-based budget request to apartments' administration from the Residents Council. The administration generally allocates $5.00 per apartment per year from rent revenues for operation costs. The Council also petitions for funds from the student fee pool of the University of Michigan's student government. The members do not receive honoraria or stipends, but child care may be provided for members while they attend Council meetings.

The administration consults with the Residents Council to gather feedback from residents regarding administrative policy recommendations and issues that affect lifestyle changes, facility upgrades, and rental rates. The Council's advice is given strong consideration, and there is traditionally a strong working relationship between the Council and administration.

The constitution and bylaws guide the Council's operation and is registered with the University of Michigan's student organization office. There is no formal avenue for appeals, policy, or eligibility issues, but residents may request a mediator to review committees and mediate disagreements.

A dialogue group is formed by the Council to deal with campus interactions and education programs, and to bring resident issues to the forefront. The Council participates in philanthropies and important causes that affect the housing complex. The goal is to enhance community development.

The strength of any particular Council depends on the number of volunteers and the quality of work. Leadership training is provided by residence life staff.

Establishing New Resident Government Systems

The following questions may be useful during the formation of a new student or resident government.

1. How will the student or resident government be selected: election, appointment, volunteers?

2. How many may serve at a time and for how many terms are they allowed to serve?

3. How will the student or resident government be funded: from rental revenues, other residence life funds, the institution's student government fees, self-motivated funds (fundraisers), charges for activities, and/or special donations?

4. What powers will the student or resident government have?

5. What is the expected impact (liability and/or benefit) of the government on apartments administration?

6. Will the student or resident government be recognized as an official representative of resident issues?

7. What will be the duties, responsibilities, and authorities of, and benefits for, the officers?

8. Will members receive compensation such as honoraria, rent reduction, and/or special services?

9. Will the student or resident government operate with a specific constitution, with rules of conduct, bylaws, disciplinary procedures, and/or an appeals or grievance process?

Summary

The University of Utah model and the other institutional summaries presented in this chapter offer a variety of approaches to and structures for student or resident government systems. Readers may wish to select one form of government—or a combination of several—while putting together a plan that will best serve residents. Opinions vary on the value of honoraria. Some institutions believe it takes away from the pure attitude of the volunteer who does the work for the love of serving. Others see it as a budgetary concern. The University of Utah views it as an incentive for "the best and the brightest" to come forward. The precious little time student residents have usually is spent trying to carve out a living while pursuing a degree. For Resident Council members, the honorarium makes the commitment financially worthwhile, and their record of service is impressive on a resume as well.

The suggestions in this chapter are designed to encourage institutions with apartment complexes to create meaningful student or resident government programs. Regardless of the style developed, establishing a governing body of student residents enhances the total postsecondary student experience.

Appendix A

Constitution
of the University Student Apartments Resident Association
at the University of Utah
(Approved by Board of Trustees, July 10, 1995)

PREAMBLE

We the residents of University Student Apartments (Student Apartments) at the University of Utah, in order to form a community government which represents the interests and concerns of the residents, proposes policies consistent with those interests, and provides programming for residents, do hereby establish this Constitution for the University Student Apartments Resident Association (USARA).

ARTICLE I
MEMBERSHIP AND ORGANIZATION

Section 1 - Membership

1.1   Membership of USARA shall be limited to eligible residents of Student Apartments at the University of Utah.

1.2   Student Apartments policies and procedures shall define resident eligibility.

Section 2 - Governing Bodies

2.1   The governing bodies of USARA shall consist of the Resident Council, the Executive Committee, and the Advisory Board.

Section 3 - Resident Council

3.1   The Resident Council shall consist of four resident members of USARA holding the positions of Mayor, Facilities Council member, Financial Council member, and Programs Council member.

Section 4 - Executive Committee

4.1   The Executive Committee shall consist of the Resident Council, the Student Apartments Director, and appointed members of the Student Apartments administration. The Director shall appoint a member of the Student Apartments administration as an advisor to the Resident Council.

Section 5 - Advisory Board

5.1   The Advisory Board shall consist of the Resident Council and three appointed representatives of the University of Utah administration. The Student Apartments Director and appointed members of the Student Apartments administration serve on the Advisory Board in a nonvoting capacity.

ARTICLE II
RESIDENTS

Section 1 - Residents' Responsibilities

1.1   Residents shall abide by the policies and procedures of Student Apartments and the University of Utah.

1.2   Residents shall be subject to disciplinary action by the Student Apartments administration for:
    (a)   violation of the terms and conditions of the rental agreement,
    (b)   violation of Student Apartments or University of Utah policies and procedures, or
    (c)   failures to maintain resident eligibility.

1.3   Residents shall have the right of appeal to the Special Hearings Committee, the Financial Appeals Committee, or the Student Apartments Director.

Section 2 - Open Access to Meetings

2.1   The Executive Committee and Advisory Board meetings shall be open to residents of Student Apartments in a nonvoting capacity.

ARTICLE III
RESIDENT COUNCIL

Section 1 - Resident Council

1.1   The Resident Council members shall:
    (a)   represent interests and concerns of residents,
    (b)   propose policies consistent with resident interests,
    (c)   provide programming for residents,
    (d)   regulate policy governing resident use of the Community Centers,
    (e)   serve on the Special Hearing and Financial Appeals Committees,
    (f)   serve on the Executive Committee and as voting members of the Advisory Board,
    (g)   serve as directed by the Resident Council,
    (h)   attend Executive Committee and Advisory Board meetings,
    (i)   provide or assign representation at the meetings of other student associations and campus organizations,

(j) submit a proposed yearly budget to the Student Apartments administration as required, and

(k) authorize Resident Council expenditures.

Section 2 - Mayor

2.1 The Mayor shall:

(a) coordinate Resident Council activities,

(b) chair Resident Council, Executive Committee, and Advisory Board meetings,

(c) establish meeting agendas,

(d) be responsible for the minutes of all meetings,

(e) appoint a member of the Resident Council to act as Chair in the Mayor's absence,

(f) have the authority to call special meetings of the Resident Council, the Executive Committee, and the Advisory Board, and

(g) cast the deciding vote, as Chair of the Advisory Board, in the event of a tie.

Section 3 - Facilities Council Member

3.1 The Facilities Council member shall:

(a) review and make recommendations on Student Apartments facilities and environmental issues, and

(b) coordinate projects and tasks with members of the Student Apartments administration as designated by the Director.

Section 4 - Financial Council Member

4.1 The Financial Council member shall:

(a) ensure that the financial accounts of the Resident Council are managed in accordance with the administrative and fiscal policies of the University of Utah,

(b) provide financial advice on Resident Council expenditures,

(c) provide financial reports each month, and

(d) prepare the proposed yearly budget.

Section 5 - Programs Council Member

5.1 The Programs Council member shall:

(a) plan and coordinate programs and activities for residents,

(b) prepare a proposed yearly programs and activities agenda,

(c) coordinate publicity for Resident Council sponsored activities,

(d) supervise Resident Council programs,

(e) establish and maintain a vendor list, and

(f) keep records of Resident Council programs.

Section 6 - Compensation

6.1 Resident Council members shall be compensated out of Resident Council's operating budget.

6.2 Honoraria shall be recommended by the Resident Council and approved by a majority vote of the three members of the University of Utah Administration appointed to the Advisory Board.

Section 7 - Vacancies

7.1 Should the position of Mayor become vacant, the Advisory Board shall appoint a member of the Resident Council to fulfill the position for the remainder of the current term.

7.2 All other Resident Council vacancies shall be filled either by:
(a) special elections or
(b) appointment by a Nominating Committee.

7.3 The Nominating Committee shall consist of a minimum of four members of the Advisory Board, at least two of which must be members of the Resident Council.

Section 8 - Term of Office

8.1 All members of the Resident Council shall be elected by eligible members of USARA for a term of one (1) year to begin on the first (1st) day of the month of June with a maximum of two (2) elected terms.

ARTICLE IV
EXECUTIVE COMMITTEE

Section 1 - Responsibilities

1.1 The Executive Committee shall meet no less than twice monthly:
(a) to review the interest and concerns of residents and
(b) to review Resident Council sponsored programs and operations.

ARTICLE V
ADVISORY BOARD

Section 1 - Responsibilities

1.1 The chief responsibility of the Student Apartments Advisory Board is to review and advise the Student Apartments Administration on:
(a) policies and procedures and
(b) resident concerns.

1.2 Additional responsibilities of the Student Apartments Advisory Board shall be:
(a) to review actions of the Executive Committee and the Resident Council,

(b) to appoint an Elections Committee,

(c) to validate Resident Council election results, and

(d) to coordinate efforts between USARA and other University of Utah departments and agencies.

ARTICLE VI
SUSPENSION/REMOVAL FROM OFFICE

Section 1 - Suspension/Removal from Office

1.1 Members of the Resident Council may be suspended or removed from office for:
(a) failure to fulfill duties of office,
(b) actions unbecoming of a Resident Council member,
(c) violations of by-laws,
(d) consecutive unexcused absences from meetings, or
(e) failure to comply with all provisions of the Rental Contract and Handbook of Terms and Conditions of Occupancy for University Student Apartments (the "Rental Contract") as it may be updated and revised from time to time.

1.2 A petition for suspension or removal from office of a Resident Council member from office may be brought by:
(a) members of the Resident Council or
(b) petition signed by a minimum of 50 USARA members.

1.3 Hearings to suspend or remove a Resident Council member from office shall be conducted by the Advisory Board.

1.4 The conditions of suspension or removal from office shall be determined by the Advisory Board.

1.5 A Resident Council member under suspension shall forfeit all rights and privileges for the period of suspension determined by the Advisory Board.

1.6 A Resident Council member who has been suspended or removed from office shall have the right of appeal to the Associated Students of the University of Utah (ASUU) Supreme Court.

ARTICLE VII
ELECTIONS

Section 1 - Eligibility and Registration

1.1 Resident Council members shall be elected in a USARA general election to be held prior to the first (1st) day of June in accordance with this Constitution and the election rules and procedures.

1.2 All eligible USARA members may vote during Resident Council elections.

1.3   Candidates for the Resident Council must register by completing an election packet and by submitting any necessary documents prior to the deadline set.

1.4   Neither employees of Student Apartments nor Resident Assistants shall serve on the Resident Council.

Section 2 - Votes and Election Results

2.1   The candidate receiving the most votes is the winner.

2.2   In the event of a tie, a run-off election shall be held.

2.3   If one of the two candidates in a run-off election withdraws, the other candidate shall be declared the winner.

2.4   The Advisory Board shall confirm the election results.

2.5   Election results shall be posted at the Student Apartments main office upon confirmation by the Advisory Board.

2.6   Candidates serving as members of the Advisory Board shall not participate in the administration of the election.

2.7   Newly elected members of the Resident Council shall take office on June 1st of the new calendar year as set forth in Article III, Section 8.

Section 3 - Election Committee

3.1   An Election Committee shall be appointed by the Advisory Board to oversee and administer the elections, and shall be comprised of five members as follows:
(a)   USARA members or retiring Resident Council members and
(b)   one University of Utah administration member of the Advisory Board to serve as Chair of the Election Committee.

Section 4 - Protests

4.1   Any Election protest(s) not resolved by the Election Grievance Committee must be submitted in writing to the Advisory Board within forty-eight (48) hours after posting the election results.

4.2   Written protest(s) submitted within forty-eight (48) hours after posting the election results shall be resolved by the Advisory Board.

ARTICLE VIII
RATIFICATION AND AMENDMENTS

Section 1 - Ratification

1.1   This Constitution shall become effective upon the approval of:
(a)   the Student Apartments Advisory Board,
(b)   the Student Apartments Administration,

    (c) the University of Utah administration,

    (d) the Committee on Student Affairs,

    (e) the Board of Trustees, and

    (f) a majority vote of the ballots cast by the USARA members.

Section 2 - Amendments

2.1   Amendments may be proposed by:

    (a) at least five (5) of the seven (7) Advisory Board members or

    (b) a petition signed by at least 100 residents and presented to the Chair of the Advisory Board.

2.2   Amendments must be ratified by a majority vote of the USARA members in a general USARA referendum following approval of the Board of Trustees. Board of Trustees approval will be preceded by review and recommendations by such University organizations as the Board of Trustees may require.

2.3   Proposed amendments shall become a valid part of this Constitution upon ratification as set forth in Article VIII, Section 2.2.

Section 3 - Bylaws

3.1   Bylaws not in conflict with this Constitution may be adopted, amended, or repealed by a majority vote of the Advisory Board.

Mental Health in Apartment Housing:
A Spectrum of Issues and Services

Nancy Lange
Assistant Director of Residence Life
Michigan State University

Joanna Jennie
Consultant-in-Residence
University of Florida

Mental Health in Apartment Housing

Scenario: Late one sleepless night, as her two children sleep nearby, a single mother in her final year of an undergraduate degree program makes the decision to take her life. After years of struggle, she is unable to go on with the seemingly insurmountable challenges of being a good student, a good mother, and a good person. Exhausted from the unrelenting pressures, her despair has driven her to the point where leaving her children alone seems like yet another failure. She decides that her son would be all right living with his father, but her daughter would not. She quietly suffocates her five-year-old daughter and just as quietly takes pills to join her.

Scenario: A graduate student with a transcript full of courses and grades—but no clear progress toward a degree—comes into the office to request yet another apartment change. His complaint is always the same: At night, sounds that cannot be heard by others—but which are very real to him—come out of the walls, and strangers enter his room and put transmitters in his teeth.

Everyone has heard his stories. He complains to the management team about unlawful access. Maintenance staff examine the pipes in the storage room next door and find nothing amiss. However, no one is satisfied with the outcome. His complaints about noise and safety escalate as he notifies his department chair, the director of housing, and the president of the institution that apartment staff members are unresponsive, ineffective, and prejudiced toward him.

Scenario: As students arrive home and begin to prepare dinner, a man in a nearby apartment begins shouting angrily. A woman responds in a low, placating voice. A child in the apartment starts crying. As the man begin shouting again, something crashes in the apartment and the woman screams. A moment later, the apartment door opens and the woman rushes out, clutching a small child. Both are sobbing.

Scenario: From the moment they arrive at the airport and the nice women from the university pick them up and take them to the housing office, there is nothing but noise, strangeness, and confusion. Although they have studied English for ten years, they are quickly exhausted from the effort involved in paying careful attention to everything. The student and his wife are entering the world of higher education in the United States. Both graduated with honors from the most prestigious university in their country. After graduation, the couple married and prepared to come to the United States so that the husband could get a graduate degree in electrical engineering.

When they finally receive their apartment keys and enter their new home, the newlyweds find only minimal furniture—and remnants of the last residents lingering in the apartment. With crumbs in the corner, a stale odor in the refrigerator, and pencil marks on the kitchen wall, this apartment is nothing like the simple, clean quarters they left behind in his mother's house, and no mother welcomes them home from their long journey.

The husband contacts his department and learns that the orientation for new students has begun. He immediately leaves for the departmental office while his wife remains at home. The apartment is utterly foreign to her. She knows no one and she feels unsure about leaving the apartment to look around without her husband.

Each day is similar, with the husband leaving to work in his department, and the wife waiting until he returns to go out. Soon her discomfort leads to depression. She often is crying when her husband comes home. He encourages her to get out of the apartment to meet the neighbors, but she is immobilized with fear and sadness. He becomes impatient with her as each day he meets more people and gains more confidence about navigating in this new culture. The distance between them increases and neither knows how to reach out to the other.

Introduction

These scenarios highlight some of the most serious mental health issues and crisis situations which occur with increasing frequency in college and university apartment communities, just as they occur in every segment of society. How can institutions and, more specifically, apartment housing staff assist students and their families *before* a difficulty becomes a crisis? Should living on campus in apartment housing provide students with services and supports that are different from what is available in off-campus housing? What kinds of staffing and response protocols are institutions developing to respond to these questions, and to the mental health issues and crisis situations that evoke them?

The goals of this chapter are (a) to examine the shifting role expectations and needs of apartment housing residents and staff, especially as they pertain to the larger institutional mission and interests, (b) to identify patterns of difficulties experienced by residents, and (c) to highlight two models of current trends in staffing and interventions in support of the emotional well-being of residents. The final section of the chapter is devoted to a discussion of implications of these trends for training and research. During the preparation of this chapter, 10 apartment housing administrators in the United States and Canada participated in an informal survey via electronic mail about current trends and needs of apartment residents and staff regarding mental health issues and crisis situations; their comments appear in italics throughout the chapter (Lange & Jennie, 1998).

Shifting Role Expectations

As the make-up of the traditional student is changing and more nontraditional students are pursuing advanced degrees or returning back to school in order to finish their degrees or keep pace with the advancement of technology, apartment communities have to be prepared for the ever-increasing demands of programs and services for students and their families. Much more funding, commitment, collaborative partnerships of university resources and respect for staff have to be applied to the work we do. University leaders who have the positions of power must recognize this element.
—Housing administrator in Michigan (Lange & Jennie, 1998)

In 1995, almost half of all college students in the United States were age 25 or older (Chronicle of Higher Education, 1998). Over 30% were identified as minority students and 3% as international students (Chronicle of Higher Education, 1998). In contrast, on-campus apartment housing, with an international student population averaging almost 40%, presents a far more diverse demographic picture, with unique characteristics and challenges not necessarily found in residence halls for single undergraduates (Whalen, Crull, Liao, Pate, & Rochford, 1997). Apartment communities on campus offer residents the opportunity to live and raise children in the most culturally diverse environment they will ever enjoy. With such diversity, unique ways to address concerns must be developed which match the uniqueness of the residents themselves (Rafuls, Howard-Hamilton, & Jennie, 1999; see Chapter 7).

Most apartment complexes on campus are home to a number of populations, often very different from one another with respect to age, academic level, cultural background, family status, and interests. Large numbers of international students, graduate students, and professional and postgraduate students seek convenient, low-cost housing on or near campus. Single graduate students, families with young children, childless couples, and single parent families also add to the demographic mix. In other words, campus apartments are home to all segments of the campus population, including an increasing number of single undergraduate students.

This diversity is one of the hallmarks of apartment life. It also can present challenges every day to one's beliefs, customs, and comfort zones, particularly regarding spousal and family relationships, child rearing, problem resolution, and communication. While it is intriguing and immensely enriching to view other cultures so closely, it also may be irritating when others' customs interfere with one's life. Cross-cultural conflicts can occur over such everyday issues as normal conflicts between children, sharing toys or other personal possessions, cooking aromas, parking spaces, tastes in music, and the uses of shared space.

Another unique characteristic of apartment housing is the year-round presence of residents on campus. The marked flow of students at "opening" and "closing" typically seen in undergraduate residence halls is muted by the fact that many students and their families remain throughout the year, taking classes, doing research, or taking a term off, while still maintaining their apartments. Apartment communities are "home" to many residents. Students from countries around the world often are limited by their financial circumstances in their ability to visit their home countries. Residents with children establish apartments as their permanent residence while going to school since moving frequently is disruptive to family life.

These diverse residents do share some commonalities. They all share the common experience of working toward a greater goal, often deferring gratification, savings accounts, homes, and vacations while pursuing their (or their family member's) academic dreams. Often they share with other residents the challenges of living on a reduced income, in a smaller space, and with greater time demands, higher stress, greater need for cultural and lifestyle adjustments, and the challenge of balancing multiple tasks with limited resources.

In the first monograph on what was then commonly referred to as "family housing (Gore, 1992a), several authors touched upon services and needs pertaining to mental health issues and crisis situations. Moen (1992) summarized the literature concerning married students, who occupied the majority of on-campus apartments for most of the post-World War II period. He observed that married students accessed campus resources much less than single undergraduates living in residence halls. Whalen (1992) cited research on the psychosocial needs of apartment residents, and noted a shift in occupancy to include more single students. Conneely (1992) discussed the potential of community development activities to reduce residents' stress. Shere (1992) included social work services, with an emphasis on conflict resolution, as one component of a comprehensive approach to community services. Gore (1992b) expanded upon the traditional student development model derived from residence halls to include a family-oriented model of development and services. All of these authors pointed out the distinctive characteristics and needs of the diverse, multinational, multigenerational population occupying apartment facilities. However, little research has been conducted with this dynamic, diverse population since then.

With the continuing shift in the demographics of the higher education student population to a more diverse age range, postsecondary institutions and facilities increasingly are interested in providing services tailored to the unique needs of nontraditional students (Baker, 1992; Champagne & Petitpas, 1989; Marlow, 1989; Senter & Senter, 1998). What those services should be is not always apparent. Even if needed services are identified, they may not be utilized because of some of the additional complexities of getting the service to the person at a particular time, in a specific language, at a low cost, and in an accessible location. Barker, Felstehausen, Couch, and Henry (1997) observed that the nontraditional students in their study preferred very specific programs and services related more to academic resources than to social supports or mental health. The expansion of any services may necessitate new staffing structures, a potentially daunting challenge in an era of shrinking budgets and increasing demands. Retention is also a concern. Villella and Hu (1991; cited in Allen, 1998) described the tremendous growth rate of nontraditional students—and their significant attrition rate as well (32% by their estimation).

Who is Responsible?

Because they are situated in small communities within or between the institution and the city, it has not always been clear to which jurisdiction on-campus apartment residents and their problems belong. Institutions have provided housing but not always staffing or supports, sometimes relying on the larger community to address residents' needs as bona fide citizens. At the same time, local municipalities providing the "address" to these apartment dwellers perceived the institution as better equipped to handle the needs and demands of these residents. In some communities, the institution pays no property taxes and ostensibly contributes little direct income to the coffers of city government.

This territorial debate often results in apartment residents living partially in both worlds and partially in neither. Though an interesting conundrum, it is disturbing in situations where emergency services are needed and each "landlord" looks to the other entity to respond. Of particular concern are emergency services involving counseling, health care, and public safety.

An institution must first determine its mission with respect to apartment housing residents. The housing staff can then direct their resources toward providing appropriate supports. Many institutions see apartment residents as self-maintaining and, to a large degree, they are. However, the scenarios described in the introduction are all too real and occur with alarming frequency. An institution may also find it necessary to consider the Americans with Disabilities Act of 1990 in its responses to such scenarios. The language of apartment leases or rental contracts (including criteria for eviction), the role of judicial affairs, and risk management variables all need to be examined more closely, not only by housing staff but also by legal counsel to clarify the institution's role in response to mental health issues and crisis situations (Luskin, 1999; see also Chapter 4).

Patterns of Mental Health Issues and Crisis Situations in Apartment Housing

For the purposes of this chapter, mental health needs are conceptualized broadly to result from (a) family life cycle concerns, (b) acculturation stress, (c) interpersonal relationships, (d) diagnosed mental illnesses, and (e) crisis situations. This concept of mental health is obviously arbitrary since significant overlap can occur among the categories. For example, an international student experiencing interpersonal difficulties may also be addressing family life cycle concerns and acculturation stress.

Family Life Cycle Concerns

My gravest concern is that many students who make the choice to be a parent and a student are not always prepared to deal with the consequences of their decision. . . . These parents often feel that our programs and staff should be surrogate parents.—A housing administrator in California (Lange & Jennie, 1998)

Residents of apartment facilities are at various points in the family life cycle. Carter and McGoldrick (1999) outlined six stages of the family life cycle: (a) leaving home (single young adults), (b) joining of families through marriage (the new couple), (c) families with young children, (d) families with adolescents, (e) launching children and moving on, and (f) families in later life. While undergraduates living in residence halls consist primarily of individuals in the first stage (leaving home), apartment facilities may include residents who are experiencing four or more of these stages.

Each of these developmental stages presents unique opportunities for growth as well as unique challenges for adult residents and their children. Complications arise in the form of marital separation and divorce, the end of committed relationships, and single parenting. In addition to the typical challenges faced at each developmental stage, single parents may also experience unique stressors, both personal and institutional, which impede their progress toward a degree, as depicted in the first scenario (Herbold, 1996; Huff & Thorpe, 1997; Quinnan, 1997).

Acculturation Stress

I'm concerned about international students and how they utilize our services. I know that it is a cultural thing. We usually get involved when things get really bad.—Housing administrator in Florida (Lange & Jennie, 1998)

The couple described in the third scenario above experienced different degrees o acculturation stress, a developmental process unique to international students. All students coming from other cultures face the challenge of making the adjustments necessary to maintain their sense of self while using new skills, languages, and coping strategies to survive. Prieto (1995) and others have observed at least three phases of acculturation in international students studying in the United States: a "honeymoon" period, disillusionment, and adaptation (Rafuls et al., 1999; see Chapter 7). While this developmental process is not a mental illness in and of itself, when complicated by other stressors it may lead to depression, anxiety, or other emotional difficulties. In apartment housing on campus, how visible is the shift from predictable acculturation stress to serious clinical depression? In their desire to "put their best foot forward" in a competitive and demanding academic environment, students and their families often do not want to disclose that they are having emotional difficulties. In addition, most non-Western cultures have nothing like the wide array of counseling services and service providers found in the United States. Psychosocial difficulties are not aired in public; instead, they are either borne in stoic silence or entrusted to the extended family or spiritual leaders for resolution. Thus, those who are in a position to be of assistance may not be able to observe the signs of diminishing well-being.

In contrast, the experience of international students can be improved by developing social support systems with host country residents as well as home country peers and other international students (Hayes & Lin, 1994; Lin & Yi, 1997; Pedersen, 1991; Rafuls et al., 1999; Rodriguez and Casey-Powell, 1998). The diversity in apartment housing and the philosophy of community development offer many opportunities to alleviate acculturation stress through staffing and programming, as described below (see also Chapter 3).

Interpersonal Relationships

We would love to have a full-time social worker and a domestic violence expert on staff.—Housing administrator in North Dakota (Lange & Jennie, 1998)

The negotiation and maintenance of healthy adult (and adult-child) relationships is of great relevance to achieving academic goals. "Date rape," domestic violence, child abuse and neglect are grave interpersonal concerns which occur in apartment communities and involve legal ramifications which can lead to the termination of a perpetrator's status as a student and/or resident, as well as seriously jeopardizing a victim's well-being and academic progress. Although overall campus crime rates have declined in recent years (Grimm, 1996), difficulties with interpersonal relationships—whether neighbor disputes, spouse or partner abuse, or child abuse and neglect—have become more visible. Whalen et al. (1997) noted that about 33% of apartment residents surveyed reported that neighbors' actions produced stress "sometimes" or "often" (p. 10). Otherwise, little has been written about the effects of interpersonal conflict and violence in apartment housing.

The recent occurrence of several deaths in college and university apartment housing in the United States merits detailed analyses that address crisis prevention as well as crisis response. Powell (1998) and Taylor (1998) have already described processes and procedures used at two U.S. institutions. The apartment housing listserv also is an important resource for sharing policies and procedural information and offering support to colleagues who are managing challenging situations. For example, a recent question about domestic violence elicited discussions about the specific wording of housing policies and contracts, local ordinances and the role of public safety officers, counseling services, and domestic violence shelters and other community resources (Apartments & Family Housing List, 1999). Apartment housing staff and administrators also need to be familiar with campus "trespass" orders and court-issued restraining orders. Developing a policy for disseminating and updating this information, as well as understanding institutional policies and local statutes, is critical in the case of domestic violence, stalking, harassment, and other interpersonal concerns.

Diagnosed Mental Illnesses

We have more residents coming to us with different mental health issues, backgrounds, experiences with mental health counseling, medications, dealing with others, violence, etc. . . .—Housing administrator in Florida.

The mental health issues our student families experience mirror those in the larger community.—Housing administrator in California (Lange & Jennie, 1998)

Among apartment residents, the extent of mental illness, as classified by the *Diagnostic and Statistical Manual of Mental Disorders* (American Psychiatric Association, 1994), is not known. Most residents who have been diagnosed with a mental illness have developed adequate coping strategies and personal, medical, and psychological supports. However, apartment housing staff regularly meet students (such as the individual in the second scenario) with extensive histories of treatment and functional difficulties who may be diagnosed as anxious, depressed, schizophrenic, or suffering from posttraumatic stress, attention deficits, and other disorders.

Crises

Full-time professional counselor/educator and social service staff members . . . would be trained to recognize what "red flags" were there and educate residents on how to deal with these situations. If a crisis did develop, they would be on call to assist, along with the student apartment manager, public safety, and me.—Housing administrator in Missouri (Lange & Jennie, 1998)

A crisis is "an acute emotional upset arising from situational, developmental, or sociocultural sources and resulting in a temporary inability to cope by means of one's usual problem-solving devices. A crisis does not last long and is self-limiting" (Hoff, 1995, p. 4). While some crises, such as natural disasters, may occur unexpectedly, many arise only after a long incubation period, when an individual's coping strategies have been exhausted, as depicted in the first scenario. This gradual process suggests that housing staff may have multiple opportunities to intervene, as described in the Michigan State University model below. In addition, the impact of self-injurious behavior (e.g., attempted or completed suicide) and interpersonal violence on other residents in the apartment community, while generally acknowledged, has not been researched. However, housing staff typically assess and respond to crises not only as they impact specific individuals, but also with the wider community in mind, often drawing on general knowledge of post-traumatic stress (Lange & Jennie, 1998).

Staffing Patterns in Apartment Housing

The first student affairs staff hired to work with apartment residents were often part-time workers who were residents themselves. They were asked to assist other residents in planning and participating in activities, welcoming new residents, and introducing residents to their new community and to other residents. Potluck dinners were planned, babysitting cooperatives were established, resident governments were formed, and new residents were greeted with friendly faces and orientation information. Staff activities were often of the "good neighbor" variety. If serious situations developed, apartment management staff took over. If the emergency involved a mental health crisis, administrators looked to other institutional or community resources to respond to the immediate crisis. Often ad hoc response teams were developed. Their membership differed from campus to campus and reflected the specific community or university resources available. More ongoing mental health or emergency services, especially within the campus apartment staff, did not appear to be justified by the occasional event, however traumatic it was.

Front-line staff often can identify individuals who are "acting strangely" or who might be involved in emotionally charged situations. Beyond offering a listening ear and a referral to a campus or community agency, they are not hired or trained to provide interventions. This leaves them—and the institution—waiting for those horrendous "somethings" to happen. If the worst-case scenario takes place, professionals from other agencies often are available to assist. Once the pain and chaos of these situations subside, everyone goes back to their usual responsibilities.

Because of the great breadth of issues that apartment residents present, staffing models have developed over time to address "a little bit of everything." Live-in staff have had to be "Jack or Jill of all trades," and subsequently could not be master of any. The needs and demands of apartment residents have been consistently wide ranging. Due to the diversity of the populations, the staff have been expected to be culturally sensitive, familiar with adult and child development, knowledgeable of local and campus resources, and creative in bringing a very diverse group of people together around common goals and concerns.

As incidents of campus violence, domestic conflict, suicide, and assault have increased on campuses across the country (Siegel, 1994), a greater awareness of what could happen has led to an increased responsiveness to allocating resources to address such problems before they become personal tragedies as well as front-page news. The challenges of working with residents who represent ages from birth to middle age, from single to single parent, from Sierra Leone to Costa Rica call for unique models of staffing to provide support and prevention services to residents.

College and university housing operations have developed various internal systems of responses, having determined from their own experience that trained and dedicated staff can make a difference in emergency situations. Support for this type of staffing has developed as the occasional crisis has become a more frequent event. They also can provide assessment of situations where there is a question about the stability or coping resources of residents as these concerns are first expressed at the local level. They can institute preventive or support programs for individuals experiencing similar transitions in their lives, such as acculturation, new marriage, childbirth and parenting, and divorce. If an emergency does occur, trained and skilled staff can work with the community in its grief, confusion, or anger, as well as coordinate the necessary resources from fellow professionals to provide essential after-care to family members, neighbors, and cultural groups. To illustrate in greater detail the programs and services which have been developed to meet the mental health needs of apartment residents, two models are presented below. Although both universities incorporate elements of community development and clinical triage and networking, each is described more from one perspective than the other.

A Focus on Community Development

The primary responsibility is to provide a customer-friendly and supportive atmosphere for families. This means to exercise active listening, refer residents to agencies or persons who can assist them, and to periodically touch bases to assess the resident's progress.—Housing administrator in California (Lange & Jennie, 1998)

Michigan State University's (MSU) Community Aide program was designed in 1976 and served for years as a "good neighbor" program, with part-time residential staff welcoming and orienting new residents, delivering flyers and newsletters about community events, sponsoring social and recreational programs, developing child care cooperatives, and hosting potluck dinners. All of these activities were directed toward creating a sense of community among residents, and a connection to the university at large (Lange, 1997).

As residents' problems became more complex, the staff relied on making referrals to agencies within the university (which often were not geared to nontraditional students' needs) or to community agencies (which were not always responsive to the needs of the more transient students and families living on campus). Residents made use of some of these services, but often they remained within the apartment community, dealing with their problems when they had the time and energy to do so. Child abuse and neglect, domestic violence, global politics, divorce and custody issues, cultural adjustment and transitional concerns, and poverty all presented issues that were beyond the capacity of the friendly "hello," the potluck dinner, or the local movie night to address.

As an intermediate step between the Community Aide program and the present residence life program, staff members were hired to provide more specialized services. Some were hired only to develop, implement, and supervise programs and group events. Others were hired to provide welcoming and orientation and to mediate neighborhood disputes. These staff members were more focused on developing relationships with residents, improving relationships between residents, and connecting residents to institutional and community resources.

This staffing model has evolved to include a full-time director of apartment residence life and two part-time assistant directors (30 hours per week each), one to coordinate programming and the other to address individual and neighborhood problems. The latter individual is required to have a background—and preferably a license—in counseling or social work, as well as familiarity with student life, family life issues, world cultures, cross-cultural adjustment, and campus and community resources. Ten Community Development Advisors (CDAs) are still very involved in welcoming activities, local or neighborhood activity development, and neighborhood problem resolution. However, they now have the additional responsibility of staffing a 24-hour Help Line which provides a mechanism for residents to reach a staff member for assistance at any hour of the day. Problems that cannot be resolved quickly are referred to the director and assistant directors or to the campus police or emergency services.

The inclusion of a staff member with skills in psychological assessment and intervention provides ongoing support to the CDAs as they respond to residents' problems during home visits or through calls to the Help Line. In this way, they may observe behavior which is out of the ordinary. Thus the residence life staff provides an invaluable service to residents when serious problems are identified early, and support, interventions, or referrals are provided before a crisis occurs. This model has expanded the ability of staff closest to residents to have ongoing consultation with others who are not only skilled in assessment and intervention, but also are aware of the context and lifestyles of residents because they are a part of the community. Excellent support can be found with the resources of the institution when critical situations occur. The MSU model allows staff to be more active in the very important arenas of prevention, early intervention, and follow up (Lange, 1997).

A Network of Services

The campus has an emergency response team and University Police Services to deal with crises.—Housing administrator in Ontario

[We] also feel that strong partnerships with university services, such as the Counseling Center and Legal Aid are critical.—Housing administrator in North Dakota (Lange & Jennie, 1998)

Once mental health needs or crises have been identified in apartment housing, most institutions activate existing collaborative or partnering relationships with multiple university resources, particularly counseling facilities, health care services, and public safety offices. In addition to providing direct services for apartment residents, these cooperative relationships also serve as training resources for staff.

The University of Florida (UF) has created a Consultant-in-Residence position based in the apartment communities to work closely with apartment staff and campus and community resources, and to provide (a) psychoeducational programming; (b) individual, couple, and family consultation; and (c) crisis response to the 1000 apartments on campus. The consultant also participates in crisis interventions in the residence halls on campus, which house over 7000 single undergraduate and graduate students.

This half-time graduate assistantship, filled by a doctoral student eligible for licensure in marriage and family therapy and with a subspecialty in multicultural counseling, is part of a network of services developed to address the emotional well-being of all students at the institution. The consultant is supervised by the Counselor-in-Residence, a licensed mental health counselor with a doctorate in counselor education, who serves the undergraduate residence hall population, in addition to his clinical duties at the university's Counseling Center.

Both individuals participate in the UF Trauma Response Team (TRT), which is composed of representatives from myriad university programs and services, as well as the Campus Ministry Cooperative, and representatives from the local community college, crisis services, and city and county law enforcement offices (Griffin, Lewis, Probert, Rollo, & Sandeen, 1997). The TRT evolved from working relationships that developed during the student murders which occurred off campus in 1990 (Siegel, 1994), and now provides campus-wide crisis response and meets monthly to debrief recent incidents that involved or impacted students, and to exchange information about emerging issues.

Both individuals also are members of the University Counseling Resources Network (UCRN; Dunkel, Griffin, & Probert, 1998), which is a component of the campus-wide disaster management plan. The UCRN is designed to coordinate mental health counseling resources on campus for victims of large-scale human and natural disasters and for the service providers who assist victims during such emergencies.

The primary referral sites for apartment residents needing counseling services are UF's Student Mental Health Service and the Counseling Center. Both offices provide brief individual, couple, and group therapy services, as well as consultation and outreach programs; the Student Mental Health Service also offers psychiatric consultations. These services are free to all students. The Counseling Center's Residence Life Liaison Program (RLLP) is designed to promote an active, collaborative working relationship between the Counseling Center and the Division of Housing. The RLLP's objective is to facilitate the utilization of consultation and educational services to enhance the learning and community life experience for students living on campus. Counseling Center faculty meet with residence life management teams to develop a "covenant of understanding" appropriate to the distinct needs of each residence life community. This agreement may include (a) periodic meetings with the management or area staff of the residence life community, (b) consultation, and (c) collaboration in the presentation of in-service or educational programs for area staff or residents.

Other campus resources available to apartment residents and staff include the Center for Assault Recovery and Education, the Center for Dispute Resolution, the University Police Department's victim advocate, and the Department of Counselor Education Family Therapy Clinic. In addition, the UF College of Medicine at Shands Hospital offers emergency, inpatient, and outpatient psychiatric services for adults and children, as well as specialty clinics conducted by the Department of Clinical and Health Psychology. Community resources include the guidance programs in the local public schools, the Gainesville Family Institute, the Veterans' Administration Hospital, the Alachua County Crisis Center, the Alachua County rape/crime victim advocate, an adolescent shelter, and a domestic violence shelter. The Consultant-in-Residence for UF's apartment communities is familiar with all of these resources and collaborates frequently with residents and staff to facilitate referrals when indicated.

Together these two models illustrate the wealth of resources available in apartment housing, on campus, and in the community to enhance the emotional well-being of residents and staff and thus promote academic success. While formal relationships such as the UF Counseling Center's RLLP may not always be necessary, apartment housing staff's awareness of campus and community resources and key personnel is essential.

Implications

We plan to build additional apartments on campus and as our communities grow I expect increases in mental health and crisis issues. We will continue our relationships with the appropriate campus offices but I would want to add a trained staff member to deal with those issues. It is also important to have protocols and procedures in writing so everyone knows how to respond.—Housing administrator in Pennsylvania (Lange & Jennie, 1998)

With greater recognition of shifting role expectations and patterns of mental health difficulties comes greater clarity about staff development and research needs for apartment housing facilities on campus. Whether offering support from a community-based perspective or from a more clinical, triage-oriented one, housing administrators continue to seek support for innovative staff development and resident support services. The following suggestions address critical incidents, diversity, needs assessment, and research.

Staff Development

Scenarios as critical incidents. Use the four scenarios presented at the beginning of this chapter for staff development. The following questions may be useful to guide discussions.

1. If any of these incidents occurred at your institution, how would apartment staff or housing administrators most likely learn about it?

2. What procedures would then be followed, and for what purposes?

3. What other programs or agencies would be involved?

4. What interventions would be indicated for family members, friends and neighbors, and/or other students, faculty, and staff? Who is responsible for providing such interventions?

5. Who is responsible for media relations subsequent to an incident similar to the first scenario?

6. What procedures are in place to protect the privacy and confidentiality of victims and other residents to the fullest extent of the law? Can staff adequately respond to requests for information within the parameters of those procedures?

7. If similar incidents occurred on campus in the past, have all of the subsequent recommendations been implemented? Why or why not?

8. How could similar incidents be prevented or their severity decreased in the future? Develop an action plan.

9. What new resources are needed and who is responsible for advocating for them?

10. What additional training needs become apparent as each scenario is discussed?

Diversity. Given the diversity of apartment housing residents, cross-cultural awareness and training for staff is essential, not only for daily apartment management transactions, but also in times of crisis when communication skills may deteriorate and coping strategies may vary widely across cultural groups. The following questions may be useful to assess current training modalities and facilitate increased cultural awareness (see also Chapter 7).

1.   What is your staff's level of cross-cultural awareness and training? How is this evaluated?

2.   How do staff demonstrate respect for differences in beliefs about health and illness?

3.   How well does the residence life program facilitate the development of positive, neighborly relationships, particularly between residents from the host country and international students and their families?

4.   How visible and familiar are campus and community agencies to apartment housing residents? How do staff facilitate referrals, especially for nonstudent family members?

5.   How do staff learn about and demonstrate an understanding of the particular needs of women from other countries?

6.   How do staff and administrators demonstrate sensitivity to language difficulties, which may be exacerbated during periods of heightened emotion?

7.   How can the use of current technologies (e.g., web pages, listservs, and e-mail) improve communications with residents and increase their awareness of campus and community resources?

Needs Assessment of Residents

Assess residents' needs from a resource-based orientation (Kretzmann & McKnight, 1993). Every new resident brings interests and skills that can be shared with the apartment community. Increased involvement may reduce isolation by constructing support systems, particularly for nonstudent spouses, and bring residents in contact with staff who can offer referrals and resources to address difficulties before they become crises (Jennie, 1997; Jennie, Buchan, & Casey-Powell, 1997).

Research

In recent years, Whalen and his colleagues (e.g., Morris & Whalen, 1989; Whalen, 1989; Whalen, 1992; Whalen et al., 1997; Whalen & Winter, 1987) have almost single-handedly brought the apartment resident population into sharper focus through their research efforts. However, the current literature on the mental health needs of students at colleges and universities includes nothing specific to residents of apartment communities. While much can be learned from perusing the growing literature on international students, "adult learners," and "nontraditional students," the unique resources and needs of apartment housing staff and residents merit further research.

One way to increase research may be through greater collaboration with academic departments on research protocols to learn more about acculturation, developmental concerns, relationship issues, economic barriers, mental illness, and institutional obstacles that impede the academic progress of apartment housing residents. For example, if international students undergo a predictable process of acculturation, do similar processes occur in other populations in apartment housing, such as newly married couples, new parents, and newly single parents? If so, can more specific community development activities and mental health interventions be designed to ease those transitions in some way?

Another line of research may be to investigate how residents make use of campus and community resources. When is the best time to provide orientation programs or other forms of information about resources for stress, adjustment, and family or relationship concerns that arise from the pressures of academic life? How often do residents with pre-existing or emerging conditions, such as depression, anxiety, and other mental health concerns, come to the attention of apartment staff? What kinds of follow-up are useful after residents have accessed campus or community resources?

More research also is needed to identify exemplary staff development programs on diversity and cross-cultural awareness. A recent study by Harju, Long, and Allred (1998) offered one model for this type of research. They created a questionnaire addressing international students' utilization of and satisfaction with student health and counseling services.

Conclusion

As colleges and universities respond to changing student demographics, as well as local and global needs, housing operations will continue to support student residents and their families with evolving prevention and intervention programs to address mental health issues and crisis situations. Developing a comprehensive strategy will position the apartment housing staff to be able to educate and respond to residents in a timely and effective manner.

Acknowledgments

We would like to express our appreciation to the 10 housing officials who participated in our electronic mail survey. We also appreciate the input of Dr. Ellen Amatea and Dr. Wayne Griffin from the University of Florida Department of Counselor Education, who commented on earlier versions of this chapter.

References

Allen, B. A. (1998). The student in higher education: Nontraditional student retention. *Community Services Catalyst* [On-line], *23*(3). Available: http://scholar.lib.vt.edu.ejournals/CATALYST/v24n3/eaton.html

American Psychiatric Association. (1994). *Diagnostic and statistical manual of mental disorders* (4th ed.). Washington, DC: Author.

Apartments & Family Housing List. (1999). *Domestic disputes* [On-line]. Available E-mail: annb@saffairs.msstate.edu

Baker, H. K. (1992). Service needs of traditional age and adult graduate students. *NASPA Journal, 30*(1), 20-29.

Barker, S., Felstehausen, G., Couch, S., & Henry, J. (1997). Orientation programs for older and delayed-entry graduate students. *NASPA Journal, 35*(1), 57-68.

Carter, B., & McGoldrick, M. (1999). Overview: The expanding family life cycle: Individual, family, and social perspectives. In B. Carter & M. McGoldrick (Eds.). *The expanded family life cycle: Individual, family, and social perspectives* (3rd ed., pp. 1-24). Needham Heights, MA: Allyn and Bacon.

Champagne, D. E., & Petitpas, A. (1989). Planning developmental interventions for adult students. *NASPA Journal, 26*(4), 265-271.

Chronicle of Higher Education. (1998). Almanac issue. *Chronicle of Higher Education, 45*(1).

Conneely, R. (1992). The development of community. In V. Gore (Ed.), *ACUHO-I Family Housing Monograph* (pp. 29-35). Columbus, OH: Association of College and University Housing Officers-International.

Dunkel, N., Griffin, W., & Probert, B. (1998). Development of coordinated mental health counseling resources in time of disaster. *NASPA Journal, 36*, 147-156.

Gore, V. (Ed.). (1992a). *Family housing.* Columbus, OH: Association of College and University Housing Officers-International.

Gore, V. (1992b). Family housing: Challenging the residence hall paradigm. In V. Gore (Ed.), *Family housing* (pp. 75-81). Columbus, OH: Association of College and University Housing Officers-International.

Griffin, W., Lewis, L., Probert, B., Rollo, J. M., & Sandeen, A. (1997). *The Trauma Response Team: A campus-wide approach to crisis management.* Workshop presented at the meeting of ACPA/NASPA, Chicago.

Grimm, J. C. (1996). The campus crime rate: Some light at the end of the tunnel. *Journal of College and University Student Housing, 26*(1), 7-10.

Harju, B. L., Long, T. E., & Allred, L. J. (1998). Cross cultural reactions of international students to US health care. *College Student Journal, 32*(1), 112-120.

Hayes, R. L., & Lin, H.-R. (1994). Coming to America: Developing social support systems for international students. *Journal of Multicultural Counseling & Development, 22*, 7-16.

Herbold, H. (1996, January). Single mothers on campus. *Monthly Forum on Women in Higher Education, 15-20.*

Hoff, L. A. (1995). *People in crisis: Understanding and helping (4th ed.)*. San Francisco: Jossey-Bass.

Huff, D. D., & Thorpe, B. (1997). Single parents on campus: A challenge for today. *NASPA Journal, 34*, 287-302.

Jennie, J. (1997). *Resident Resource Network*. Gainesville, FL: University of Florida.

Jennie, J., Buchan, R., & Casey-Powell, D. (1997). *It takes a village to raise expectations: Mapping and mobilizing residents' assets*. Paper presented at the meeting of the ACUHO-I Apartments Conference, Estes Park, CO.

Kretzmann, J., & McKnight, J. (1993). *Building communities from the inside out: A path toward finding and mobilizing a community's assets*. Chicago: ACTA Publications.

Lange, N. (1997). The *AGPFI program: A residence life program for the "other" populations at Michigan State University*. Unpublished manuscript.

Lange, N., & Jennie, J. (1998). *A survey of apartment housing administrators' perceptions of mental health issues and crisis situations in apartment housing*. Unpublished report.

Lin, J.-C. H., & Yi, J. K. (1997). Asian international students' adjustment: Issues and program suggestions. *College Student Journal, 31*(4), 473-479.

Luskin, E. (1999). Legal, safety, and operational issues. In D. Casey-Powell (Ed.), *College and university apartment housing* (in press). Columbus, OH: Association of College and University Housing Officers-International.

Marlow, C. (1989). Identifying the problems and needs of nontraditional students at your institution. *NASPA Journal, 26*(4), 272-277.

Moen, C. (1992). Development of family housing. In V. Gore (Ed.), *Family housing* (pp. 1-18). Columbus, OH: Association of College and University Housing Officers-International.

Morris, E., & Whalen, D. F. (1989). The impact of social distance on community in university apartments. *Journal of College and University Student Housing, 19*(1), 22-27.

Pedersen, P. B. (1991). Counseling international students. *Counseling Psychologist, 19*(1), 10-58.

Powell, J. D. (1998). Responding to death in the residence halls or family housing. *Talking Stick, 16*(2),15-16.

Prieto, S. L. (1995). International student populations and needs assessment. In S. D. Stabb, S. M. Harris, & J. E. Talley (Eds.), *Multicultural needs assessment for college and university student populations* (pp. 203-223). Springfield, IL: C. C. Thomas.

Quinnan, T. W. (1997). *Adult students "at risk": Culture bias in higher education.* Westport, CT: Bergin & Garvey.

Rafuls, S. E., Howard-Hamilton, M., & Jennie, J. (1999). Multicultural models and campus ecology theory: Applications to diversity in apartment communities. In D. Casey-Powell (Ed.), *College and university apartment housing* (in press). Columbus, OH: Association of College and University Housing Officers-International.

Rodriguez, C., & Casey-Powell, D. (1998). *International students coping with acculturative stress in U.S. university settings.* Manuscript submitted for publication.

Senter, M. S., & Senter, R., Jr. (1998). A comparative study of traditional and nontraditional students' identities and needs. *NASPA Journal, 35*(4), 270-280.

Shere, L. (1992). Philosophy of community services. In V. Gore (Ed.), *Family housing* (pp. 37-44). Columbus, OH: Association of College and University Housing Officers-International.

Siegel, D. (1994). *Campuses respond to violent tragedy.* Phoenix, AZ: Oryx Press.

Taylor, K. S. (1998). Death of a student: Response team process. *Talking Stick, 16*(2), 16.

Whalen, D. (1989). Live-in staff for apartment housing. *Journal of College and University Student Housing, 19*(2), 12-15.

Whalen, D. (1992). Research in family housing. In V. Gore (Ed.), *ACUHO-I Family Housing Monograph* (pp. 19-27). Columbus, OH: Association of College and University Housing Officers-International.

Whalen, D., Crull, S. R., Liao, T.-L., Pate, R., & Rochford, H. (1997). *Resident satisfaction in apartments.* Columbus, OH: Association of College and University Housing Officers-International.

Whalen, D. F., & Winter, M. (1987). Neighbor interaction and stress in family housing. *Journal of College and University Student Housing, 17*(1), 28-34.

A Look into the Future of Child Care Options in Apartment Housing

Su-Fen Lin
Director of Children's Services
University of Michigan

Future of Child Care Options in Apartment Housing ———

History of Higher Education Institutions' Involvement in Campus Child Care

Higher education interests in family issues have evolved as part of demographic, economic, and workplace trends that affect society. The first major family initiative on campus was the introduction of married student housing after World War II. With married students in apartment housing, young children residing in these communities as well. However, after the war, there was no interest in developing programs or resources for children and parents because many women returned home to take care of the household and the children. In the 1960s, the establishment of Headstart programs, along with research indicating that by the age of three or four, 50% of brain development had occurred, the interest in early childhood education flourished. Colleges and universities started to establish early childhood education programs in departments of education, home economics, psychology, and other related fields. As the number of working parents and nontraditional students increased in higher education settings, the need for full-day child care programs for staff and students and their children led to an increase of service-oriented care on campus (Friedman, Rimsky, & Johnson, 1996).

In the mid-1980s, the U.S. Department of Labor released a report called *Workforce 2000* (Friedman et al., 1996). The authors of the report predicted an increasingly diverse labor market comprised of women, minorities, and aging workers. Across the country, many colleges and universities admitted nontraditional students who were just starting their studies, returning to complete their degrees, or pursuing postbaccalaureate programs. As a result, children were more likely to be present in those households. Therefore, more and more campuses looked into the options of providing on-campus child care.

Currently there are over 170,000 young children in child care programs on America's college campuses (Neugebauer, 1998). Two out of every three colleges and universities in the United States now provide some type of preschool program for young children. Since providing care for children of students is one of the missions of most campus programs, apartment housing is one of the logical and ideal places to establish child care for students. However, there are many complex issues involved in providing excellent care for young children.

This chapter includes a review of the current apartment housing child care programs of four institutions, a discussion of various models, and a consideration of the present and future challenges of child care on campus. The four institutions included in this chapter are the University of British Columbia, the University of Colorado, the University of Michigan and the University of Wisconsin. The history, licensed capacity, ages of children served, and funding for each institution's child care facility will be described.

The Current State of Apartment Housing Child Care Operations

Currently there are many different types of child care operations in apartment housing. Nevertheless, only a handful of child care operations are directly affiliated with apartment housing around the United States. The types of child care programs offered usually depend upon the needs of the apartment housing residents, the target population apartment housing chooses to serve, and the abilities of the apartment housing administration to support programs with space and funding. Some facilities offer limited services such as parent and child play groups or after-school programs; others try to meet the needs in a broader scope by providing full-day and year-round child care services. "Child care" is a general term used to describe a wide range of services for children; other terms commonly used in the field of early childhood education are defined below.

1. *Full-day child care.* This type of program usually operates daily on a calendar-year basis.

2. *Part-time preschool program.* This type of program is only open part of the day, and children may not attend every day.

3. *Flexible-scheduled child care.* This type of program offers parents choices of different schedules on different days based on needs. Some centers have minimum or maximum days per week or hours per day that children need to be enrolled.

4. *Drop-in child care.* These centers offer the freedom to bring children in when needed, if space is available.

5. *Evening/weekend child care.* As the name indicates, this type of program operates in the evenings or during the weekends.

6. *Before- and after-school program.* This type of program offers care for elementary school-age children before and after school.

7. *Cooperative.* This type of program is run by parents, and participating families are responsible for the organizational aspect of the program. Normally, at least one professional teacher is hired to lead the class, and the rest of the staff is volunteer parents.

8. *Summer camp.* Type of program operates only during the summer and can be for either preschoolers or elementary school-age children.

9. *Parent and child play group.* This type of program requires a parent to accompany a child to participate in the activities.

Models

University of British Columbia

History. The first child care program at the University of British Columbia (UBC) was run by nonprofit parent societies, using renovated World War II army barracks. As these facilities aged, the university, students, and parents worked together to raise funds for the construction of new child care buildings. With the new buildings, however, came the need to formalize the relationships between the university and the parent-run, nonprofit societies. The university sought to ensure that priority for admission would be given to students, staff, and faculty of the university, and that the societies would assume financial responsibility for utilities and repairs. Unfortunately, the umbrella association, which held the license for care, was unable to come to an agreement on behalf of all the smaller, parent-run, nonprofit societies for each center. As a result, the university gave notice that it would assume responsibility for operation of all child care centers in university buildings. On July 1, 1991, nine child care centers trans-

Future of Child Care Options in Apartment Housing ─────

ferred management to UBC under its Department of Housing and Conferences. In addition, two more centers were opened in a newly constructed space. Moreover, when the faculty of education decided to close its child study center, the space was offered to Child Care Services to operate four additional part-time programs.

Licensed capacity. The total licensed capacity for child care services is 330 children.

Ages of children served. Infants, toddlers, preschoolers, and kindergarten children are served. After-school care also is provided.

Funding. UBC contributes to the management cost of the central administration office by paying the salaries of the administrator, the assistant administrator, and a full-time clerk. The university also provides a support grant from ancillary revenues. For example, in 1997-1998, utilities, maintenance and housekeeping costs, totaling $159,000 (Canadian) were paid for by ancillary revenues. These contributions totaled over $303,000 annually. Parent fees and government subsidies account for nearly $2 million (Canadian) per year.

(Information for this section was provided by Elizabeth Marshall, residence life manager.)

University of Colorado

History. The child care program is located in the child care centers near the university apartment housing on the University of Colorado-Boulder campus (UC-Boulder). Historically, all child care programs at UC-Boulder have been administered by the university's housing department, maintaining close alignment with the apartment housing operation. The child care program began in 1972 with university sponsorship of a cooperative within the community. In 1975, the university built a new facility to serve children and to house child care administration at the Newton Court apartments. In 1986, the university expanded the program by building a new toddler center, also at Newton Court. In 1991, the university remodeled a single-story duplex at Smiley Court. Most recently, in 1995, the university added a second remodeled single-story duplex at Smiley Court.

Licensed capacity. Licensed capacity for the four centers is 138 children. The percentage of children by parent group is as follows: 52% are children of apartment housing residents (students), 23% are children of nonresidents (students), and 25% are children of staff and faculty. Currently, no children from the community are enrolled.

Ages of children served. The children served include 48 toddlers (12 months to 36 months of age) and 90 preschoolers (37 months to 72 months of age).

Academic program relationships. At UC-Boulder, the child care program has an informal relationship with the university academic community. From time to time, the child care program cooperates with faculty in the psychology and speech and communication departments to provide programs involving undergraduate students volunteer assignments.

Rate structure. UC-Boulder does not contract with an outside firm or organization for child care services. UC-Boulder does not offer drop-in child care services. The child care centers are open year round, five days per week, from 7:00 a.m. to 5:30 p.m. Services offered and fees charged are for predetermined (assigned) time slots only. Assigned slots range from a minimum of two half days per week up to five full days per week. Current enrollment figures indicate that 54% of the children served are enrolled in the full-time option. The fee structure is organized in three categories as follows: (a) student (apartment housing resident), (b) student (nonresident), and (c) university staff and faculty.

A portion of the rents paid by UC-Boulder apartment housing tenants is used to subsidize the child care centers' operation, which accounts for the program's lower monthly rates. Additionally, eligible parents may participate in the Boulder County Social Services child care assistance program and the Colorado preschool program administered by the Boulder Valley School District. Child care scholarships also are available and are administered by UC-Boulder financial aid department.

Funding. The UC-Boulder children's centers are supported by user fees plus a subsidy from apartment housing facilities; funding for equipment come from the housing bond fund group. Colorado's health food program, social services contracts, preschool program, and parent fundraisers also contribute to the center's budget. UC-Boulder children's centers do not receive financial support from state-appropriated funds or any university source other than the housing department. In 1996, the UC-Boulder apartment housing children's centers' annual budget was approximately $714,000. Income was received from the following sources: (a) parent fees and tuition (79%), (b) apartment housing subsidy (14%), (c) federal food subsidy (4%), and (d) miscellaneous (3%). (Information for this section was provided by Jo Copeland, Director of Child Care Services.)

University of Michigan

History. Children's services were established in 1985 in response to the need for child-oriented programs in family housing at University of Michigan (UM). At that time, services included an after-school program and summer camp for elementary-school-age children, and two parent and child play groups for children 2 to 3 years of age. Classes were held in an apartment that had been converted into a classroom. With the construction of the Family Housing Community Center in January, 1991, the Family Housing Child Development Center (FHCDC) also opened its doors to parents who live in family housing. The FHCDC provides year-round child care services and offers parents choices of either part-time or full-time programs.

Licensed capacity. The FHCDC is licensed for 60 children and currently provides child care services to approximately 90 families per semester. The percentage of children by parent group for 1998 was as follows: 87% were children of family housing residents, 9% were children of UM faculty and staff, and 4% were children from the community.

The summer camp program serves 39 children during each of the four two-week session throughout the summer. The parent and child play groups offer programs three times a year for children 1 to 3 years of age. Each session is 8 to 10 weeks long.

Ages of children served. The FHCDC serves children 2-1/2 to 5 years old. Children in the parent and child play groups are 1 to 3 years old. Children who are 5 to 10 years old participate in the school-age children's programs.

Future of Child Care Options in Apartment Housing ———————

Relationships with academic programs. The FHCDC has a formal relationship with the academic community. It currently serves as a training site for student teachers from the education department. The program also accommodates UM students participating in volunteer services or class assignments which require working with young children.

Rate structure. Fee structures are based on parents' eligibility as family housing residents, staff and faculty, or the general public. Since the rent paid by the family housing residents contributes to the total operational cost of the Community Center where the FHCDC is located, parents who live in family housing have lower monthly rates.

Funding. User fees and some overhead support from family housing contributes to the FHCDC.

University of Wisconsin

History. Eagle Wing child care and education programs started in 1992 with a license for 16 children. Summer programs for children 6 to 12 years old were opened in 1993. An after-school program for up to 20 kindergarten through fifth grade students was added in 1996. A before-school program also was added in 1996, with transportation provided to bus up to 13 children to and from the public schools. A prekindergarten-plus program for 4 year olds was added in 1997. In the same year, all classrooms were moved into one common building using seven apartments for classroom space and one apartment for office space.

Licensed capacity. Currently the program is licensed for 107 children. Ninety-four percent of the children are family housing residents and 6% are children of staff and faculty.

Ages of children served. Children's ages range from 2 to 12 years old in the program.

Rate structure. The center is open from 7:00 a.m. to 5:30 p.m., and family housing residents pay a reduced rate for the service.

Funding. Each year the Division of Student Housing provides a subsidy ranging from 3% to 13% of the total expense. (Information for this section was provided by Debb Schaubs, Manager of Children's Services.)

Common Challenges in Apartment Housing Child Care Operations

In an effort to respond to the demographic changes of the labor force and the student pool, a growing number of apartment housing operations in the United States and elsewhere are exploring various options of providing programs to support families living in the housing community. Since affordable housing is an ongoing consideration for many colleges and universities, providing high quality and affordable child care in apartment housing is also a challenge. The National Association for the Education of Young Children has developed specific guidelines for quality programs (Bredekamp & Willer, 1996). Based on the guidelines, the indicators of a quality program for young children include: (a) child/staff ratios, (b) group size, (c) educational level of staff, (d) a safe and clean environment with ample equipment and supplies for children, and (e) on-going training programs for teaching staff.

The quality of a child care program depends on the quality of the interactions between children and teachers, the level of understanding of the teaching staff for each child, and the knowledge and skills of the teaching staff to plan a developmentally appropriate programs for children. Therefore, child/staff ratios, the number of children in each group, and teachers' educational levels are interrelated in establishing a high quality program for young children.

In addition to the quality of the program, child care operations, even well-established ones, continually struggled to find solutions to several key issues regarding cost, funding, and staff.

Cost

From the indicators of a quality program discussed above, it is easily understood that quality child care is labor intensive and therefore expensive. Frequently, for good quality care programs, salaries and benefits can make up as much as 80% to 90% of a center's budget. People tend to believe that those who use the service pay for the total cost of the service. But, in reality, most child care programs, even high quality ones, cannot compensate their staff adequately for their laborious efforts. Most child care programs are in essence 'subsidized' by their staff. The National Center for the Early Childhood Work Force (1997) reported some compelling data on child care staff in the United States:

1. Approximately 3 million child care teachers, assistants, and family child care providers in the United States care for 10 million children each day.

2. Only 18% of child care centers offer fully paid health coverage to teaching staff.

3. Child care teachers are better educated than the general population even though they earn lower wages.

4. One-third of all child care teachers leave their centers each year.

The true cost of a child care program is a complex issue. To establish a good program for children the center must adequately compensate the teachers. However, the tuition charged by a high quality program might be out of reach for student parents. Thus, when addressing the issue of child care cost on campus, it is important to recognize that the true cost of excellent care for children must be shared by parents, the institution, and the community.

Funding

How can child care administrators locate funding for high quality programs for children on campus? The strategies are as varied as each program. Based on a survey of 1,800 campus centers conducted by the National Coalition for Campus Children's Center, most colleges and universities in the United States provide some combination of subsidies to campus child care centers (Neugebauer, 1998). The most common types of support are buildings (85%) and utilities(81%), followed by salaries and benefits

(52%) and supplies (36%). Fewer than 9% provide no subsidy at all. Other strategies include:

1.   Contribute a percentage of student registration or activity fees to serve student families (similar to the University of Michigan's program).

2.   Apply for grants from state or federal programs for low-income families.

3.   The chancellor or students affairs office may allocate funds for child care centers.

4.   Academic departments may be willing to contribute funding to establish programs in a center for practicum students.

Other indirect supports are provided in the form of volunteers, facility maintenance, and central purchasing and accounting.

Staffing

The training, skills, and education of the teaching staff are also major indicators of quality. The need for a predictable, enduring relationship between teachers and children is very important. However, low wages and poor benefits make it very difficult to attract and retain qualified staff with degrees and training. Many centers experience high levels of staff turnover, and children experience inconsistent care as a result. The stability and continuity of staff are determined by the salary, benefits, and support the they receive (Willer, 1990). Therefore, the staffing issue is directly connected with the funding issue. A continual challenge is finding ways to make quality child care affordable for parents while offering adequate salary and benefits to qualified staff.

Implications for the Future

The confluence of demographic and workplace trends makes it likely that family supports on campus will grow in the future. Therefore, child care will become an even more important issue to be addressed in institutions of higher education. "Today, half of all Master of Business Administration students are women" (Freidman, et al., 1996, p. 119). The fastest-growing family type is the single-parent family headed by a father. Some of these families are living in apartment housing communities. Concerns have been raised among apartment housing administrators regarding children being left alone without adult supervision. Since finding affordable quality child care is an essential need for many residents, apartment housing operations are in a position to take a leadership role in finding solutions for student's child care needs.

Assisting in child care issues not only will make apartment housing an attractive choice for students but will benefit the institution financially. Therefore, it is important to take a proactive approach to solve child-related issues that are experienced by students on campus. Apartment housing operations also can pursue other short-term programs that are affordable and very desirable to residents, such as summer camps, care for mildly ill children, and various types of emergency care.

1.   *Summer camp programs for school-age children.* This type of program operates only during the summer months. Camp counselors can be recruited from students on campus.

2. *Care for mildly ill children.* The purpose of this type of program is to provide an option for parents who have a mildly sick child at home that may result in a student not being able to attend classes. Contact can be made with local health care providers to provide care for children when students are in class.

3. *Emergency well-child care.* The purpose of this type of program is to provide back-up child care for students when the primary child care provider is unavailable or when there is a need for other short-term child care. College students can staff this type of operation.

4. *Holiday or snow day child care.* The purpose of this type of program is to provide child care for students on days that public schools are closed for children, including teacher work days, holidays, and snow days when the university remains open.

The key to implementing programs effectively lies in gathering information and knowing what works well. Needs assessments, surveys, and focus groups among residents are effective means to collect information for appropriate actions as well as gaining support and funding from the campus community. The National Coalition for Campus Child Care provides a wealth of information regarding needs assessment and other aspects of child care operations on campus (Keyes & Cook, 1988). Networking with colleagues on other campuses who have experience in providing child care for apartment housing can be very helpful in sharing ideas and concerns.

In developing any kind of program for children, many issues, such as how to offer and maintain a high quality program, must be addressed. When quality components are missing, the quality of services for children is compromised. Finding solutions for child care issues in apartment housing is certainly not an easy task, but it is a challenge well worth undertaking.

References

Bredekamp, S., & Willer, B. A. (1996). *National Association for Education of the Young Child (NAEYC) Accreditation: A decade of learning and the years ahead.* Washington, DC: NAEYC.

Friedman, D. E., Rimsky, C., & Johnson, A. A. (1996). *College and university reference guide to work-family programs.* New York: Families and Work Institute.

Keyes, C. R., & Cook, R. E. (1988). *Campus child care issues and practices: Collection of conference presentations 1975-1987.* Milwaukee: National Campus Child Care Center.

National Center for the Early Childhood Workforce. (1997). A profile of the child care work force. *Child Care Bulletin, 16,* 2.

Neugebauer, R. (1998). Kids on campus. *Child Care Information Exchange, 122,* 20-22.

Willer, B. A. (1990). *Reaching the full cost of quality in early childhood programs.* Washington, DC: National Association for Education of the Young Child.

Future Trends

Martha Castleberry
Manager, Christopher City Apartments

Peter Rejto
Coordinator of Community Development
The University of Arizona

INTRODUCTION

The most prominent future trend in apartment housing is change. Some of the change will be in familiar areas of apartments operations, such as the demographics of the population served. Some of the change will branch out into less familiar areas such as the involvement of academics and social services in the apartments environment. This chapter continues a discussion of some of the changes anticipated to be future trends.

From Family Housing to Apartment Housing

The residents served by housing administrators will continue to change. The shift from "married housing" to "family housing" to "apartment housing" continues so as not to exclude single-parent families or the growing number of single students living in apartment facilities. The types of residents projected for the future include the traditional student and spouse with children, in addition to single parents, single students, faculty and staff, visiting scholars, roommates, gay and lesbian couples, and extended families with grandparents, aunts, uncles, siblings, and so on. The ages of the residents living in the apartments—from newborns to retirees—will be as diverse as ever, with a growing number of older residents. Although most apartment communities will continue to house a high percentage of international students, shifts will occur in the countries of origin of those students. The shifts will be influenced both by world politics and by the fields of study offered at specific institutions. "Accounting for a diverse, potentially complex life course is one of the major challenges future planning presents us" (Cooney, 1993, p. 52).

Apartment housing staff will be asked to do much more than provide social activities for residents. Support services will include health care, child care, social services, tutoring, recreation, and referrals to campus or local agencies. The invitation to privatize management of these services has been met with some resistance but is likely to continue in the future.

The fact that most institutions are dealing with aging facilities will not change, but more institutions will respond either by renovating or by building new facilities. Funding will continue to be an issue.

Demographic Trends

Family Demographics and Sociological Trends

The term "family" is socially constructed and the meaning of family changes in response to a wide variety of social, economic, political, cultural, ethnic, and personal conditions (Coltrane, 1998). According to the U.S. Bureau of the Census (DeVita, 1996, cited in Coltrane, 1998), the composition of U.S. households has changed since 1970. The biggest changes include fewer households with children, more people living alone, fewer married couples with children, and more single-parent households. The number of families taking care of aging parents has also increased. People in different types of households adjust their definition of "family" to accommodate changes in their marital status, living arrangements, amount of contact with spouse or parent, and concomitant emotional attachments (Coltrane, 1998).

Other interesting demographic changes will shape the makeup of apartment communities. The minority population is increasing. According to the U.S. Bureau of the Census (1995), by the year 2020, an estimated 118 million Americans will be of minority background, an increase from 26% to 36% of the population. According to Ahlburg and DeVita (1992, cited in Coltrane, 1998), there are currently twice as many dual-income families as traditional ones with the husband as breadwinner and the wife as homemaker. There are almost as many "other" families (single-parent families, couples in which only the wife is employed, no workers, and other related people living together) as dual-income families. But by the year 2010, there will be even fewer traditional families and a wide number of others (Ahlburg & Devita, 1992, cited in Coltrane, 1998; Hayge 1990, cited in Coltrane, 1998; see Figure 1).

Since the 1980s, the acceptance of different types of family arrangements has leveled off. Americans seem to have become less worried about the negative impacts of mothers working and day care on children, which can be supported by the dramatic

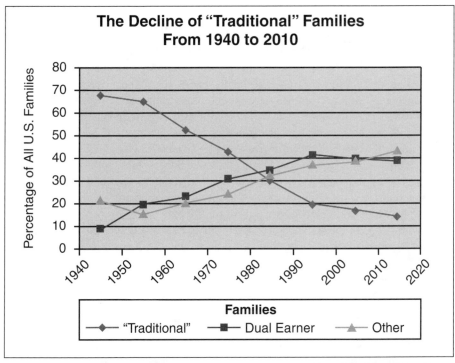

Figure 1. The decline of "traditional" families from 1940 to 2010. "Traditional" families = husband breadwinner/wife homemaker; dual-earner families = husband and wife workers; other families = single-parent families, couples with only wife worker, and other related people living together. From *Gender and families* (p. 163), by S. Coltrane, 1998, Thousand Oaks Press, CA: Pine Forge Press. Copyright 1998 by Pine Forge Press. Reprinted with permission.

increase in both of these areas during that same time period. Patterns show that grand-parents will continue to provide substantial amounts of care, and the use of family day care homes will continue to be important in the future (U.S. Bureau of the Census, 1996).

The demand for lower-wage jobs is projected to increase because of continued global restructuring and growth, particularly in the service sector. Women are expected to constitute the majority of the work force in the next decade. It is predicted that occu-pations with the most openings will be service, administrative support, and professional specialty (Acker, 1992). By the year 2005, women will constitute nearly half the total labor force (Kutscher, 1991). In fields where women are already significantly repre-sented, their representation in higher-paying jobs most likely will increase (Silvestri & Lukasiewicz, 1991). If income inequality in the overall population continues in its cur-rent direction, pressure will increase on both partners to become and stay employed. Dual-income families will be able to stay in the middle class, whereas families with only one income will have to fight to stay out of poverty.

As higher education professionals, we should be prepared for the influence of these factors on enrollment in higher education and consequently on our apartment communities.

Enrollment Trends and Characteristics

Cicero once said, "I shall always consider the best guesser the best prophet." His-torically the business of forecasting student trends in higher education has been a best guess, to say the least. For example, during the late 1960s, some prophets of doom pre-dicted campuses without students once the job of educating the last of the 79 million baby boomers (1946-1964) ended. While there was a modest decline in enrollment, a new mix of students emerged that include increasing numbers of adult learners, fe-males, minorities, and advanced-degree-seeking students. Factors affecting enrollment in higher education not only include such student demographics, but also are impacted significantly by federal and state policies and regulations, general global economic trends, and new technologies. In addition, institutional characteristics and geographical location may have an influence on trends in enrollment.

Knowledge of these student trends as well as student attitudes provides a founda-tion for organizational planning and decision making. Decreasing occupancy means lower revenues to cover operating costs and support department goals. Anticipating and understanding the characteristics of our residents allows us to intentionally develop liv-ing environments that promote education and personal development. At the University of Arizona, the residence life department expresses this idea in its mission statement. The fundamental purpose is to support the academic mission of the institution by offer-ing an environment that is:

> safe and secure . . . provides clean, comfortable, and memorable living spaces . . . and provides an abundance of purposeful, intentional and in-volving opportunities for residents to grow and develop. . . . In addition to providing the traditional student-centered support network, Apartment Housing services an additional client—the family. (The University of Ari-zona, 1995)

Domestic Enrollment

Despite earlier predictions, the late 1970s and early 1980s were a period of growth for higher education, fueled primarily by a significant increase in nontraditional (25 years old and older) and female students. Between 1970 and 1980, enrollment grew from approximately 5.5 million students to around 9 million. By 1990, it reached 14 million, and increased to about 14.8 million by 1994. According to projections, between 1988 to 2008, the 18- to 24-year-old student population is expected to increase nearly 20%. During this same period, enrollment by nontraditional students is estimated to increase slightly more than 18 % (National Center for Educational Statistics [NCES], 1998; see Figure 2). This continuing enrollment trend by nontraditional students reflects the general age profile of the United States.

Another pattern worth noting has been the increasing and sustained enrollment in higher education by females. Women traditionally represented a minority of students enrolled at colleges and universities. In about 1986, women overtook majority enrollment and this figure continues to increase. In 1988 women represented 54% of students enrolled in colleges and universities in the United States. According to projections, enrollment by women is expected to increase to 57% (NCES, 1998; see Figure 3).

In the NCES (1998) report, an increase of more than 2 million students from 1994 to 2004 is predicted (see Figure 4). One way to understand these figures is to determine the characteristics of future students by first looking at the current population. A recent report on the diversity among undergraduates from the American Council on

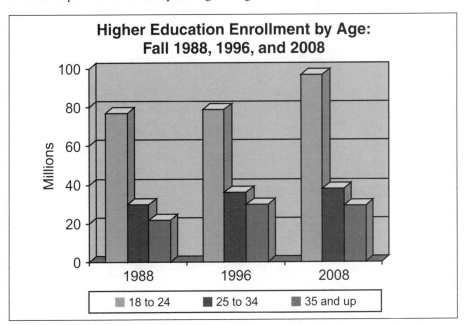

Figure 2. Higher education enrollment by age: Fall 1988, 1996, and 2008. The data are from the *Supplement to the Education Directory* (p. 15), by the National Center for Educational Statistics, 1998, Washington, DC: U.S. Department of Education. Copyright 1998 by U.S. Department of Education. Adapted with permission.

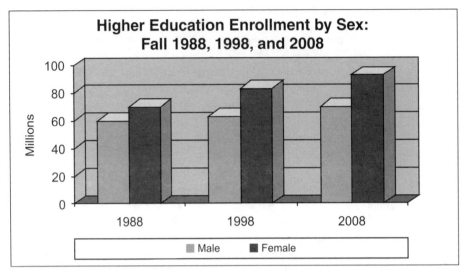

Figure 3. Higher education enrollment by sex: Fall 1988, 1998, and 2008. The data are from the *Supplement to the Education Directory* (p. 17), by the National Center for Educational Statistics, 1998, Washington, DC: U.S. Department of Education. Copyright 1998 by U.S. Department of Education. Adapted with permission.

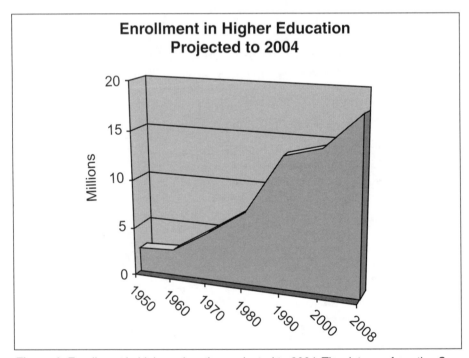

Figure 4. Enrollment in higher education projected to 2004. The data are from the *Supplement to the Education Directory* (p. 26), by the National Center for Educational Statistics, 1998, Washington, DC: U.S. Department of Education. Copyright 1998 by U.S. Department of Education. Adapted with permission.

Education (1994) indicated that in 1992 the student population consisted of 53% female, 21% nonwhite, 24% nontraditional (25 years of age and older), 5% students with disabilities, and 2% international students. (According to the Institute of International Education [IIE] (1998), the latter figure is around 10% when graduate students are included; see Figure 5). These trends have been increasing incrementally without any indication of decline.

One of the factors that has influenced enrollment figures is the age of the general population. The Kiplinger Washington Letter (1993) reported that the most significant increase in the general population that may impact enrollment in higher education for the next 25 years will occur in the age ranges of 25 to 44 years of age and 45 to 64 years of age (see Figure 6).

The traditional-age population will remain steady until 2020, when it will begin to increase. One final statistic that is worthwhile to include is that the percentage of degrees in all categories earned by women has significantly increased (see Figure 7). In fact, in both earned Bachelors' and Masters' degrees, women have now become the majority.

International Enrollment

According to IIE (1998), during the 1993-1994 academic year there were 1.1 million international students (including U.S. citizens) attending colleges and universi-

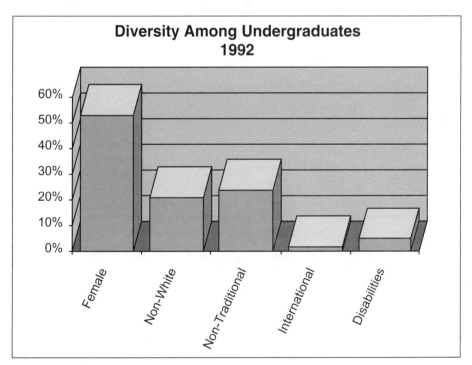

Figure 5. Diversity among undergraduates in 1992. The data are from the American Council on Education, 1994, *Research Brief, 5*(1), p. 38. Copyright 1994 by U.S. Department of Education. Adapted with permission.

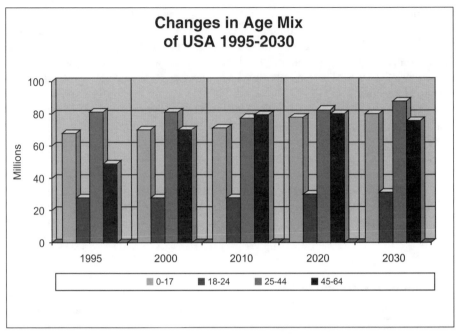

Figure 6. Change in U.S. age demographics from 1995 to 2030. The data are from "Kiplinger Washington Letter," by *Kiplinger Washington Letter, 70*(7), p. 1. Copyright 1993 by the Author. Adapted with permission.

ties around the world. The regional distribution is shown in Table 1.

While the historical trend suggests generally increasing numbers of international students, determining the specific source and final destination of these students is somewhat more problematic. First, any change in the international political climate may affect students' educational plans. Second, economic factors, such as those currently taking place in Mexico, may negatively impact a student's ability to continue his or her education. In addition to any broad international developments that may affect enrollments, the IIE (1998) has also identified seven "vectors" that contribute to the

Table 1

Regional Distribution of International Students (1993-1994)

Africa	201,000
Asia	519,000
Europe	245,000
Latin America	82,000
North America	45,000
Oceania	8,846

Source: Institute of International Education (1998)

choice of a host country. These include (not in any priority order): linguistic ability, historical relations, economic ties, geographical proximity, cultural affinity, political harmony, and the strength of the host country's educational structure.

It would also be worthwhile to note that 67% of international student provide their own funding and 70% of international graduate students are married. Taken together, it becomes increasingly clear that international students place a high value on keeping the family together and will carry that additional financial burden. In this analysis, it may be worthwhile to consider specific institutional factors that might influence international enrollment such as the mission, policies on recruitment, and availability of funding sources.

Who will be our students of the future? Based on these statistics, this growing student population will consist of increasingly older and diverse groups. In addition, women will most likely continue to maintain at least their current levels of enrollment. All of the following scenarios are likely: Many students will begin their academic careers later in life, return to school and either complete their education or receive training for a new career, and/or return to school due to unanticipated changes in technology. Based on this analysis, it is also likely that students will either have families of their own or will no longer fit the traditional residence hall student profile.

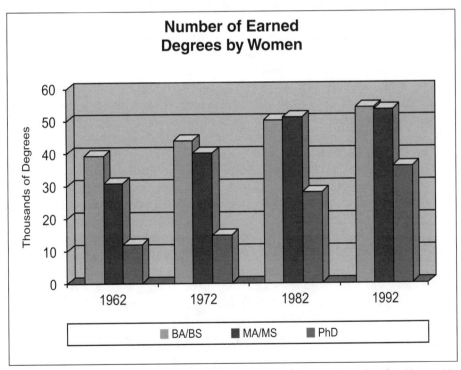

Figure 7. Number of earned degrees by women. The data are from the *Supplement to the Education Directory* (pp. 61-63), by the National Center for Educational Statistics, 1998, Washington, DC: U.S. Department of Education. Copyright 1998 by the U.S. Department of Education. Adapted with permission.

Programming Trends

The wellness model promotes the need for individuals to make responsible choices. It also emphasizes that individuals are jointly responsible to themselves and to the larger community. It has been popular on university campuses and continues to have value. Some new trends are emerging, however, that may be even more applicable in the setting of the educational institution. As we develop programming, we should consider the opportunities we have to promote interaction and understanding between the adult students who are likely to be living in our apartment communities and the faculty and staff at our institutions. The trend toward placing emphasis on the out-of-class residential experience has sparked a number of changes. Leaders in higher education are working together to join the living experience with the academic mission of the institution in a more structured way. This movement has validated the staff and their programming efforts and the desire of housing staff to promote an interactive connections between faculty and residents out of the classroom (Zeller, 1994, 1995).

As the projected trend is for college students to be older, we will need to adapt and redesign some of the traditional student services to meet the needs of the entire adult age range. For example, administrators can promote an effective learning environment for adult students by: (a) developing administrative structures that help adult students overcome some of the common difficulties facing them in returning to the college environment (demands on time, unfamiliarity with administrative procedures, anxiety from long absence from the classroom, basic study skills), and (b) facilitating faculty efforts to become more effective teachers of adults by teaching them to learn more about adult students and helping them to develop more appropriate classroom approaches to this population (Miller, 1987; Rejto, 1997). As we develop programming, we should consider the opportunities we have to promote interaction and understanding between the adult students living in our communities and the faculty and staff at our institutions. Such programming will promote an institutional appreciation for the broad diversity of backgrounds and rich experiences of residents in apartment communities.

According to Mable (as cited in Zeller, 1987), student affairs professionals are in a position to focus with new energy on student development with academic affairs. Zeller (1987) noted that residence life professionals will be able to meet this challenge by developing well-planned goals and then working hard to achieve them. He asserted that by meeting this challenge, as educators within our institutions, the position of residence life staff will be enhanced and staff will ultimately be able to provide a more comprehensive educational experience to students. According to Zeller (1987), one of the first things to accomplish is the development of common goals and objectives for academic services and student services. This should result in unifying the institution in its educational purpose.

Housing administrators also will have an opportunity to promote effective orientation for adult students. According to Baker (1992), an orientation program for adult students should stress services such as child care; psychological and learning services; and marriage, family, and personal counseling. An orientation program should also include spouses and families. The types of recreational, athletic, social, and cultural activities provided for these students should be planned to meet the interests of a wide range of age groups, particularly because of the trend toward an increased number of older residents.

Professional and paraprofessional staff (including resident assistants, assistant directors, community advisors, or programmers) are highly effective models and change agents for students. Students observe their work and the need for professional judgment in confrontation, crisis intervention, and/or personal counseling (Mosier, 1984). Training staff to be competent in a community of such diversity as apartment housing is a tremendous challenge. According to Miriam Rosado at he University of Michigan, "We as administrators have an obligation to create more opportunities for resident staff to examine their own values and stereotypes and determine how these affect their individual interactions with people who are culturally different. Rather than assuming that the ethnic values of our diverse resident staffs will disappear through assimilation, we must recognize that these community leaders are shaped by their own social and cultural experiences" (Patterson, 1998, p. 22). As the trend continues toward more structured training programs for resident staff in apartment communities, it will be important to determine what laws, specific issues, and community standards staff will be required to address in order for appropriate training to be developed. Multicultural differences and expectations specific to the apartment community at a given institution will vary and will also be an important part of staff training (Patterson, 1998).

Additional factors will carry implications for international families who will attend our institutions. The United States is much less likely to fund child-centered programs such as child care centers and universal health insurance than other modern industrial democracies. The assumption that individual families are the only ones responsible for their children puts tremendous pressure on families to work out their own arrangements for child and health care. This pressure is even greater on international students and their families and the adjustments they need to make when they study in the United States. The types of services we can provide to support child and health care needs are likely to benefit all families (Coltrane, 1998). "The role of apartment administrators is to provide options for child care, whether that be traditional center care, parent cooperatives, play groups, community programs, resident to resident child care, or resource and referral services" (Shere, 1996, p. 14). This role will be important to recognize as apartment staff respond to the trends toward the enrollment of an increased number of older students (many with children) projected for our institutions.

Baker (1992) suggested that particular attention be given to having access to at least one counselor with experience and certification in marriage and family counseling. The counselor should also be able to offer assistance in communication techniques, marital preparation and enrichment, and parenting. Baker (1992) also suggested that particular attention be given to those marriages in which only one spouse is engaged in study.

Baker's (1992) recommendations were directed at the institutional level, but providing family social services within apartment communities is another rapidly growing trend. In addition to being available to support healthy community activities, establishing a professional staff person in this position within the apartment community can enhance a number of other support services. Therapy, parenting classes, relationship skills, conflict mediation, and follow-up on domestic disturbances are some of the services being provided. A social services coordinator can also promote the involvement of volunteers from other institutional and community organizations to provide programs for residents and act as a referring agent to other types of services within the institution or the larger community. The trend toward adding such a staff person is one that is likely to greatly improve the quality of life in the apartment community and add to the satisfaction and the success of the student in addition to providing support to the student's family (Palan, 1996).

Although the invitation to privatize management of these services has met with some resistance, it will be likely to continue in the future (Hoffman & Meddaugh, 1996). Institutions cannot always afford to provide the types of services described above because of the competition for existing resources. The private housing provider who is in the business of delivering high quality, low-cost student housing to multiple locations can and should be able to devote resources that meet the needs of their "campus" clients. Privatization of residence life services can have the same objective as the institution, that is, to further student education. This trend is one to watch as effective partnerships can be developed between student services and housing.

Facility Trends

Facilities management indirectly and directly affects a majority of the housing budget (Grimm, 1998). Utilities, repairs, new equipment, damage, or vandalism, whether considered direct or indirect, all affect the budget. As on-site evaluations occur, Grimm (1998) stated that the purpose of an assessment would be to identify deficiencies of various systems or components within the facilities. Stoner, Grimm, and Hanchar (1996) defined a deficiency as "a necessary system or component in the facility which is unsafe, no longer works, does not conform to current code, no longer performs the designated function, or requires more resources to maintain that would be required to replace" (p. 14). As administrators struggle to identify funding sources to take care of deterioration, and then develop plans to move from deferred maintenance to preventative maintenance, it will be important to consider these factors and assess the functions and systems of our facilities on a routine basis. It will be particularly important to be prepared to meet the demand for electronic delivery systems and information technology and to anticipate future needs as new technologies are developed. Institutions must agree on their understanding of the learning environment's effect on the physical environment. Results of the 1997 survey of higher education facilities conditions showed that where determined campus leadership placed deferred maintenance as a priority on their agenda, action followed (Grimm, 1998).

As institutions plan renovation or new construction projects, it will be valuable to consider some of the demographic trends predicted for the future. Asking who will be living in the apartments will certainly lead to better decisions about the physical features and quality of life to be offered in the facilities. For example, the current trend toward providing community centers, computer labs, and child care facilities within the apartment community indicate how housing operations are responding to providing facilities that meet residents' needs.

Privatization will continue to be a trend as an attractive option because of the high cost of construction or renovation and the limited funding available for facility improvements. Many institutions are already involved in some sort of privatization (laundry services, cable TV, uniforms, maintenance and custodial services, etc.). The current use of privatized services and those to be used in the future are likely to change in order to give students the best quality of education and service at the best price.

Professional Development

Zeller (1987) suggested that housing professionals have to make a more concerted effort to promote what is currently being done by staff with regard to cocurricular education and developing a sense of community to presidents and other institutional leaders. Based on anticipated trends in higher education in recent studies by the National Institute of Education's Study Group on the Conditions of Excellence in American Higher Education and a group commissioned by the Carnegie Foundation for the Advancement of Teaching, Zeller (1987) made some specific recommendations for residence life professionals:

1.   Assess current mission statements and goals to be sure that programs and services are aligned with the academic mission of the institution.

2.   Develop programs that offer a variety of high-quality and intensive educational and skill development opportunities and state the expected learning outcomes of those programs openly and proactively.

3.   Address the need to be able to measure student growth as an outcome of programming efforts.

4.   Provide opportunities for applicable and practical skill development experiences within the residence life program.

5.   Communicate the impact of programs and services in educational and developmental terms and encourage the active involvement of presidents, academic administrators, faculty, and students.

6.   Encourage all students to become involved in residential living by making them aware of available opportunities and by actively soliciting their participation.

7.   Develop residential opportunities that allow for student-faculty interaction outside of the classroom.

Another trend that some housing professionals are considering is the Certified Property Management (CPM) program. This certification program consists of a number of specific courses that eventually lead to certification as a property manager. Because the CPM program is particularly appropriate in an apartment setting, certification of more housing professionals is a likely trend. Other housing professionals are pursuing options in real estate training, child-care certification, and maintenance certification.

The professional standards of the Association of College and University Housing Officers-International (1999) are a measuring stick for many housing professionals. Those basic guidelines will continue to shape what we do and how we do it. Housing professionals stay in housing because they are motivated to do so by the sense of reward in working with students, the opportunities they have to impact students, and the creative atmosphere offered by the college environment. They frequently thrive on change. Higher education administrators can promote job satisfaction among housing professionals by allowing them to expand their responsibilities as the institution expands its services (with proper fiscal adjustment), by promoting the development of personal and career goals, and by evaluating how housing professionals feel about the environment they work in and the positions they hold (Sayer, 1996).

Conclusion

"The integration of a strong mutual effort by students and college and university staff to provide for the complexity of human needs is producing a powerful and positive impact on students" (Mosier, 1984, p. 25). According to Mosier, this is possible because the intentional, democratic, planned approach to community development is very representative of many residence life programs.

Housing staffs are in a particularly influential place as institutions develop a vision for the future because of the ideals and experience of the great historical interaction of the qualities that are enhanced in a common residence, such as ethics, community, citizenship, instruction, co-curricular programming, and peer learning (Ryan, 1995). Enrollment trends, changes in family arrangements, and employment trends presented in this chapter will influence community policies and regulations, particularly those that define who can live in apartments on campus. The trends also are likely to influence the types of community and institutional services and support we provide, when they are provided, what staffing we might need, and how to make the best use of our facilities. As the residents living in our apartment communities change, we will need to be ready to change our practices to meet their needs and recognize their successes.

Apartments professionals will continue to talk to others about their work. Although there has been a growing interest in the amount of information about apartment communities, a great need still exists in the areas of documentation, research, and publishing specifically as they relate to apartments issues. "As we head into the 21st century, individuals and their families are confronted with a more diverse array of possible life experiences than has ever existed before" (Cooney, 1993, p. 52). Apartments staff will need to continue to be on the cutting edge of a changing community and must continue to be "willing to constantly evaluate assumptions and procedures to make sure they still fit and serve" their residents (Lutzka & Finney, 1996, p. 7).

References

Acker, J. (1992). The future of women and work. *Sociological Perspectives, 35*, 53-68.

American Council on Education. (1994). *Research brief, 5*(1), 38.

Association of College and University Housing Professionals-International. (1999). *ACUHO-I professional standards*. Columbus, OH: Author.

Baker, H. K. (1992). Service needs of traditional age and adult graduate students. *NASPA Journal, 30*(1), 20-29.

Coltrane, S. (1998). *Gender and families.* Thousand Oaks, CA: Pine Forge Press.

Cooney, T. M. (1993). Recent demographic change: Implications for families planning for the future. In B. Settles, R. Hanks, & M. Sussman (Eds.), *American families and the future: Analysis of possible destinies* (pp. 37-55). New York: Haworth.

Grimm, J. (1998). The deferred maintenance problem: Start with an assessment. *Talking Stick, 15*(6), 6-8.

Hoffman, R., & Meddaugh, G. (1996). Breaking with tradition. *Talking Stick, 13*(6), 6-7.

International Institute of Education (1998). *Open doors.* New York: Author.

Kiplinger Washington Letter (1993, February 12). *Kiplinger Washington Letter, 70*(7), 1.

Kutscher, R. E. (1991). New BLS projections. *Monthly Labor Review, 114,* 3-16.

Lutzka, J., & Finney, J. (1996). Student apartments—Who are we? *Talking Stick, 13*(6), 7.

Miller, K. A. (1987). *Administrative roles in helping faculty adapt to adult learners.* Paper presented at the Annual Meeting of the Speech Communication Association, Boston.

Mosier, R. E. (1984). A response to Dr. Stamatakos' "College residence halls: In search of educational leadership." *Journal of College and University Student Housing, 14*(2), 24-29.

National Center for Educational Statistics. (1998). *Projections of Education Statistics to 2008,* pp. 11-48, 53-64. Washington, DC: U.S. Department of Education.

Palan, K. (1996). Family social services improve family housing community. *Talking Stick, 13*(6), 16.

Patterson, L. (1998). Family housing/apartments staff training is the same as hall staff training. *Talking Stick, 15*(6), 21-22.

Rejto, P. (1997). *Non-traditional student needs assessment, Fall, 1997.* University of Arizona, Tucson Arizona Student Unions, Office of Student Programs.

Ryan, M. (1995). The collegiate way. *Talking Stick, 12*(7), 8-16.

Sayer, E. (1996). The motivational factors affecting job satisfaction of housing professionals. *Talking Stick, 13*(7), 28-30.

Schmidt, J. M. (1992). The future of family housing. In V. Gore (Ed.), *ACUHO-I Family Housing Monograph* (pp. 83-87). Columbus, OH: Association of College and University Housing Officers-International.

Shere, L. (1996). Child care as part of the university apartment mission. *Talking Stick, 13*(6), 14.

Silvestri, G., & Lukasiewicz, J. (1991). Occupational employment projections. *Monthly Labor Review, 114*, 64-94.

Stoner, K. L., Grimm, J. C., & Hanchar, J. (1996). Facilities for the future: Where to begin. *Talking Stick, 13*(6), 12-14.

U.S. Bureau of the Census. (1995). Population profile of the United States. *Population Reports* (Series P-23, No. 189). Washington, DC: Government Printing Office.

U.S. Bureau of the Census. (1996). Who's minding our preschoolers? *Current Population Reports: Household Economic Studies,* (Series P-70, No.53). Washington, DC: Government Printing Office.

The University of Arizona. (1995). *Residence life mission statement.* Tucson, AZ: Author.

Zeller, W. J. (1987). The National Institute of Education and Carnegie Foundation reports: A residence life perspective. *Journal of College and University Student Housing, 17*(2), 8-12.

Zeller, W. J. (1994). Residential learning communities: creating connections between students, faculty and student affairs departments. *Journal of College and University Student Housing, 24*(2), 37-43.

Zeller, W. J. (1995). Join in the learning imperative. *Talking Stick, 12*(7), 15.